D0843139

British Trotskyism

Theory and Practice

British Trotskyism

Theory and Practice

JOHN CALLAGHAN

Basil Blackwell

© J.T. Callaghan, 1984

First published in 1984 by
Basil Blackwell Publishers Ltd.,
108 Cowley Road, Oxford OX4 1JF.

Basil Blackwell Inc.,
432 Park Avenue South, Suite 1505,
New York, NY 10016, USA.

British Library Cataloguing in Publication Data
Callaghan, John, *19— -*
British Trotskyism
1. Communism – Great Britain – History – 20th
Century
I. Title
335.43'3'0941   HX243

ISBN 0–85520–742–6

Typeset by
Banbury Typesetters Ltd., Banbury
Printed and bound in Great Britain by
The Camelot Press Ltd, Southampton

Contents

List of abbreviations   vii

Introduction   1

1   Trotsky's Rationale for the Fourth International   7
        Leninism and Democracy   16
        Conclusions   22

2   The Revolutionary Communist Party 1944-9   27
        Origins   27
        Economic Perspectives   31
        Tactics and Internal Life   34
        International Perspectives   42
        Conclusions   50

3   The Split in the Fourth International   53
        Conclusions   64

4   The Ascendancy of Healyite Orthodoxy   67
        The Club   67
        The 1956 Crisis of Stalinism   69
        From SLL to WRP   76
        The SLL-WRP Internal Regime   81
        Conclusions   85

5   The International Socialists   90
        Origins   90
        The Theory of State Capitalism   91

The Permanent Arms Economy   94
The Versatility of Theory   96
The Nature of the Organization   99
Components of the Rank-and-File Strategy   108
The Objective Conditions   110
The Trade Union Bureaucracy   113
Abandonment of Rank and Filism   115
Conclusions   118

6   The New Left and the Politics of the International Marxist
Group   122
The Re-unification of the Fourth International   122
Origins of the International Marxist Group   126
The New Rise in World Revolution   130
Northern Ireland   137
Leninism and Feminism   143
The IMG Organization   154
To the Socialist League   157
Conclusions   161

7   The Militant Tendency   163
Entrism   163
Traditions   166
Policies   169
An Organization within an Organization   175
The Organizational Status of Militant   178
The Labour Party Young Socialists   186
Conclusions   188
Appendix: Militant's Analysis of the Economic Crisis   191

Conclusion   198

Appendix 1: Trotskyist Groups Prior to the RCP   207

Appendix 2: Trotskyism in Britain   208

Appendix 3: Major International Divisions in Trotskyism   209

Notes and References   210

Bibliography   242

Index   253

List of Abbreviations

AIL	Anti-Internment League
ANL	Anti-Nazi League
CND	Campaign for Nuclear Disarmament
COMINFORM	Communist Information Bureau
COMINTERN	Communist International
CPGB	Communist Party of Great Britain
FI	Fourth International
ICFI	International Committee of the Fourth International
IMG	International Marxist Group
ILP	Independent Labour Group
IS	International Socialists
ISC	Irish Solidarity Campaign
ISFI	International Secretariat of the Fourth International
LPYS	Labour Party Young Socialists
RCG	Revolutionary Communist Group
RCP	Revolutionary Communist Party
RSL	Revolutionary Socialist League
SLL	Socialist Labour League
SWP	Socialist Workers Party
TOM	Troops Out Movement
USFI	United Secretariat of the Fourth International
VSC	Vietnamese Solidarity Campaign
WIL	Workers International League
WRP	Workers Revolutionary Party
YCL	Young Communist League

Introduction

The Trotskyist tradition arose out of the struggle within the Communist Party of the Soviet Union after the death of Lenin. Trotsky's fight for a democratic internal regime in the CPSU was progressively extended by him and his supporters to include all problems of revolutionary tactics and strategy.[1] The term 'Trotskyism' was used by opponents to insinuate a political deviation or alien force within Bolshevism and the international Communist movement: all factions contesting for leadership of world communism sought Lenin's mantle and the legitimacy it conferred. Likewise all sought to anathematize opponents as betrayers of this Leninist legacy.

Trotsky saw himself as an embattled — often lone — defender of the traditions of Marx and Lenin: 'The ideas I am defending . . . are not really my ideas but those of Marx, Engels and Lenin. I have made it my task to protect these ideas from complete discredit by the Soviet bureaucracy and to analyse the newest developments by the methods of Marx.'[2] While this is still disputed by most representatives of the Communist Parties,[3] this study will be concerned to examine Trotskyism, which sees itself as the sole legitimate offspring of Bolshevism, as it has functioned in Britain during the post-war period.

Chapter 1 of my examination of Trotskyism will consider the intellectual legacy of this current in relation to the Bolshevik tradition and Trotsky's own rationale for the establishment of the Fourth International. This discussion is not primarily concerned with the traditional, and by now, sterile, dispute between Communists and Trotskyists over who should take credit as the true heirs of Lenin. I am far more concerned to identify the points of concordance between Leninism and Trotskyism in order to facilitate an understanding of far left preoccupations in Britain since the war.

It is the same point of focus which explains my periodization. British Trotskyism began in 1932,[4] yet I have chosen to ignore the pre-war period[5] and give only cursory attention to its wartime history. This is partly because of the minuscule nature of the organizations concerned in the pre-war period. The Fourth International itself was not founded until 1938. But more important is that Trotsky's timing was determined by expectations of a generalized revolutionary offensive following the war. Since these prognoses inform every line of the key document of the foundation conference of the Fourth International (FI) — the 'transitional programme' — which Trotskyists still regard as a guide to tactics, the post-war period has been the truly testing time for this movement and the best context in which it could reveal its strengths and weaknesses. Furthermore, Trotsky's revolutionary optimism of the late 1930s is resonant of the heroic period of Bolshevism and the early Comintern. To the extent that this metaphysic informs the basic assumptions, the language — even the tactical and organizational considerations of the movement — then to this extent a study of the British far left will reveal much about the nature of Bolshevism. We think it can be shown that Trotsky's rationale for the Fourth International gave renewed, perhaps even added, emphasis to the key Bolshevik assumptions of the period 1914-24 and that the thinking of contemporary far left groups is still guided by this problematic.

In a sense this is only adding detail to Isaac Deutscher's dictum that . . . to the end Trotsky's strength and weakness alike were rooted in classical Marxism,[6] as long as we use the term 'classical' Marxism to refer to the positions adopted in the very productive period of Marxist intellectual history, 1900-24.[7]. But it is a very different procedure from that adopted by the authors of several recent studies of contemporary Trotskyism in Britain.[8]. For these books make no attempt to analyse the intellectual traditions behind the programmatic and tactical aspects of Trotskyism which they report. Indeed the whole matter is reduced to the nihilistic obsessions of so many far left Stavrogins.[9] Despite this nescience, these books are evidence of the upsurge of interest about the far left of late.

Most immediately, of course, this has been brought about by

events within the Labour Party. The move to the left within that organization since 1971 has once again drawn attention to Trotskyist entrism (which I examine in chapter 7) in relation to the Militant Tendency. However, I need to mention the tactics of entrism throughout this study: its more recent notoriety is the result of alarm, in certain quarters, at the more general drift to the left within the Labour Party from which Militant may have benefited, but cannot be said to have caused. It is certainly true that the far left has experienced a genuine if modest renaissance in Britain since 1968. Indeed a recent Fabian tract, which speaks of the 'key ideology of Trotskyism', *á propos* the Labour Party, attributes its growth within social democracy to the growth of a significant Marxist sub-culture in Britain during the years since 1968.[10] I examine key elements of this in chapter 6 which is concerned with the relationship of the Trotskyists to mass campaigns such as CND and the Anti-Nazi League.

My intention in each of these chapters, as throughout this study, is to examine the practical workings of Trotskyism and how these are guided by the key theoretical assumptions which this tradition inherited from the heroic phase of Bolshevism.[11] My approach is to set the political practice of the far left in the history of the period and pursue a chronological study of the principal organizations. As a history this work is exceedingly selective, but not, I hope, arbitrary. The chief guide to my choice of material on which to focus attention is the question of democracy. There are several justifications for this.

In the first place one of the main claims and chief attractions of Trotskyism is that on the question of democracy it is vastly superior to the principal alternative Marxist traditions such as Stalinism and Maoism. Trotsky's fight, as noted, began as a fight for democracy within the CPSU. Throughout the 1930s Trotsky laboured indefatigably against the persecution distortions and murders of the Soviet bureaucracy. In all this his moral superiority may have been as important to his followers as his intellectual and political superiority over Stalin. The Trotskyists made internal democracy a *necessary* feature of revolutionary organizations. Trotsky himself made a political advance on Lenin by explicitly recognizing the necessity for pluralism in the immediate post-revolutionary state.[12] There is little reason to doubt Trotsky's belief in Marx's conception of socialism as the result of proletarian self-emancipation and as a higher form of democracy than that of the liberal-democratic state.

Yet, for all this, Trotskyists are widely regarded as enemies of democracy[13] or, at best, luke-warm adherents of it. Trotskyist organizations are commonly viewed as authoritarian formations run by tiny cliques of 'professional' revolutionaries.[14] Relations between Trotskyist groups are generally acrimonious and they allegedly seek to manipulate the members and supporters of other organizations such as CND. Erstwhile supporters of Trotskyist groups have even described the persona of a typical member in terms reminiscent of Eric Hoffer's 'true believer':[15] an austere, puritanical fanatic emerges from both accounts.

Several inter-related aspects of this paradoxical relationship of Trotskyism to democracy will be examined throughout this study. These are:

(1) the internal regimes of far left organizations;
(2) the character of their relationships to groups and organizations within which they work such as the Labour Party, CND and the Anti-Nazi League;
(3) the character of their relations with each other;
(4) their conception of bourgeois democracy and tactical attitudes towards it.

These questions touch on most facets of Trotskyist theory and practice. The centrality of democracy in the Marxist version of the socialist project[16] and its appearance as a focal point in the emergence of Trotskyism itself — all of this alone would justify my choice of central theme. However there is also the question of how appropriate the Bolshevik strategic model is in countries such as Britain, where liberal democracy appears to be well established and well supported. It would make little sense discussing the political practice of the far left without taking-up the larger issue of how this relates to the institutions and political culture of liberal democracy. The thesis advanced here will attempt to show that the classical Marxist tradition, of which Trotskyism is a principal organized legatee, was not only unable to theorize the liberal-democractic state, but advanced a theory of imperialism and the imperialist epoch that prejudiced Marxist discussion against taking this issue seriously. The Bolshevik experience reinforced these tendencies and added some new dimensions — notably the militarism of Comintern and the alleged universalism of the Bolshevik scenario — which helped to create a powerful metaphysical pathos among Communists that incorporates an imagery and associations inimical to internal democracy and political pluralism. This, rather than just the organizational precepts of Leninism, is at the root of authoritarian tendencies among Trotskyists.

These problems of a theoretical and tactical sort are strikingly

obvious on the far left for other reasons. In the first place the grossly
uneven nature of the contest between Stalinism and Trotskyism
inclined the latter to a conservatism in matters of Marxist theory
precisely because the preservation of the key ideology (Leninism)
was all that the puny forces of the Trotskyist movement were
capable of: major practical interventions were beyond it in the 1930s.
In consequence the movement was vulnerable to a liturgical style of
resolving political disputes from its inception and prone to adopt an
uncritical stance towards Bolshevism. Secondly, the continued
marginality of the Trotskyists after the Second World War
encouraged political introversion, schism, and an exaggerated stress
on possession of the 'correct' programme. This too encouraged
conservatism in theory and practice for, as Anderson has observed:
'In general, the progress of Marxist theory could not vault over the
material conditions of its own production — the social practice of the
real proletariat of the time.'[17] The conditions of this marginality —
economic boom and cold war — aided the growth of a closed circle
psychology among Trotskyists and the degeneration of far left
organizations into mere sects.

Whereas the response of mainstream 'Western Marxism' to these
conditions was a retreat into a rather abstract philosophical or
literary-critical discourse,[18] the revolutionary temper of Trotskyism
prevented such an escape. Indeed a belief in the actuality of the
revolution remained its distinguishing characteristic for all its
becalmed practical state. This is well illustrated by a debate which
Felix Morrow opened during the war. While the leadership of the FI
insisted on adherence to all of Trotsky's pre-war prognoses, Morrow
observed the enlarged power and status of Stalinism and warned that
'decades of struggle' rather than catastrophic revolutions awaited the
Trotskyists.[19] He was critical of the FI's adherence to the Bolshevik
model of revolution as the immediate future of its national sections
and envisaged instead that the Trotskyists would long remain one
among many working-class tendencies within the reformist parties.
The FI's vision, on the other hand, was one of insurrections and/or
police states in Europe supported by American arms. In particular, it
is noteworthy that the FI could not envisage the reconstruction of
democracy or even its survival where it already existed in Europe.
Equally significant, the immediate deduction from this diagnosis was
that the tiny sections of the FI must pass straight away to the
construction of mass revolutionary parties. It is also of moment that
Felix Morrow was expelled from the American Socialist Workers
Party in 1946 for disagreeing with Trotsky's *ex cathedra* predictions.

In chapter 1, I try to explain why this vignette could appear so often within British Trotskyism by examining key elements of the theoretical legacy it inherited from Bolshevism. Chapter 2 examines the history of the Revolutionary Communist Party, 1944-9, which is in many ways a larger, more prolonged version of the Morrow affair. The RCP is also significant in the course of *British* Trotskyism, however, because the polemics which preoccupied (and finally destroyed it) together with its leading personnel remained dominant on the far left for most of the post-war period. In chapter 3 the debate about Trotskyist orthodoxy, begun in chapter 2, is considered at the level of the International itself and the resulting split in the FI. I next examine the nature of the current led by Gerry Healy which dominated the far left between 1947 and 1968. In chapters 5, 6 and 7 I trace the course of British Trotskyism through the salient developments which affected the International Socialists, the International Marxist Group, and the Militant Tendency. For these organizations my emphasis is on developments after 1968 and the new period opened up, symbolically, in that year.

1

Trotsky's Rationale for the Fourth International

It is impossible to understand the politics and idiom of the Trotskyist left unless one begins with the assumptions and analyses on which they are based. The most important of these is the conception of the present epoch as one of 'wars, civil wars, and revolutions'. The Trotskyists inherited this characterization from the Third International which claimed that: 'The present epoch is the epoch of the disintegration and collapse of the entire capitalist world system, which will drag the whole of European civilisation down with it if capitalism with its insoluble contradictions is not destroyed'.[1] The Comintern's *Theses On Tactics* in 1921 clearly stated the objective basis for revolutionary socialism as follows: 'The revolutionary character of the present epoch consists precisely in this, that the modest conditions of life for the working masses are incompatible with the existence of capitalist society and that therefore the fight for even the most modest demands grows into the fight for communism'.[2] This analysis, as Avenas observes, '. . . was the objective basis for the foundation of the Third International. It was not simply a conjunctural analysis . . . but the fundamental tendency of the epoch beginning with the October revolution.[3] For the entire Comintern leadership the 'imperialist war' of 1914–18 signalled that the nation state had become a barrier to the further development of the productive forces.

Social relations under capitalism had become a fetter to material progress. But the Bolshevik revolution had demonstrated that in this epoch the proletariat had the objective opportunity to overthrow the capitalist system, and the existence of a new workers' state would, for as long as it lasted, alter the balance of forces on an international scale in favour of the socialist revolution in other countries.

This did not mean that capitalism was necessarily doomed, since it was argued by Lenin, among others, that it could always find a purely economic way out of its crises.[4] But if the world socialist revolution was indefinitely delayed, the alternative, in Lukacs' words, would be '. . . a long period of crises, civil wars, and imperialist wars on an increasing scale to the "mutual destruction of the opposing classes" and to a new barbarism.'[5] The choice — between barbarism and socialism — was of long-term character in that the analysis of Comintern did not suppose that socialist revolution was on the immediate agenda in every advanced capitalist country. On the contrary, it was acknowledged that the emergence of crises and revolutionary situations was spasmodic and uneven. It was the increasing frequency and intensity of such crises which gave the epoch its specific character and which provided the objective basis for a political practice which assumed the 'actuality of the revolution'.

Trotsky adhered to all of these substantive elements of the Comintern analysis until his death. If there was anything specific to his contribution it was that he took the logic of this position to a novel conclusion. For the theory of permanent revolution explained that in this epoch there were no longer any insurmountable barriers to the proletarian revolution even in backward countries.[6] However, certain of Trotsky's formulations concerning the nature of the present epoch suggest that it involves an absolute decline in capitalist productive forces. As Mandel points out, these errors do not represent Trotsky's considered position, which suggested that even in the epoch of capitalist decay revolution is not permanently possible in each capitalist country.[8] But the tenor of Trotsky's later formulations on this question suggest the contrary. That these later, and perhaps more salient, analyses influenced Trotsky's followers in the immediate post-war situation is attested by the fact that Mandel himself was arguing in the middle forties that capitalist booms were 'no longer possible' in its epoch of decay.[9].

The actual conditions of economic depression — civil wars, the rise of fascism and impending world war — in which Trotsky wrote during the thirties probably contributed to the catastrophic images and language that he then employed. Exaggerations in analysis could be similarly located. The problem that they created was that Trotsky's followers in the post-war years seem to have inherited the whole package and persisted in such errors even when conditions had changed radically. Recent critics of Trotsky make the same mistake as his uncritical followers in the 1940s in supposing that 'Trotskyism' involves errors of contingent prognosis as a *necessary feature* of his methodology.[10] This is not to deny that a certain fatalism can be detected in some of Trotsky's later prognoses,[11] but there is no evidence of a negative methodological determinism (of the type Hodgson detects) in Trotsky's analyses of France, Spain, China and Britain. These are remarkably concrete conjunctural analyses which do not rely on an intuitive or *a priori* assessment of the epoch. His analysis of the development of the class struggle was in each of these cases an attempt to assess the actual political developments in each specific country rather than a broad characterization of the period.

This can be demonstrated by considering Trotsky's rationale for setting up the Fourth International. Between 1923 and 1933 Trotsky's 'left opposition' regarded itself as a faction of Comintern striving to reform that organization. In that period Trotsky did not believe that the organizational regime created by Stalin was permanent. Even in 1930 when the Trotskyists created the International Communist League any idea of forming rival Communist parties remained foreign to them despite the virtual impossibility of working to win over the Stalinist parties. The slogan was still 'all eyes to the Communist Party. We must explain to it. We must convince it'.[12] Trotsky argued that 'it would be a criminal act on the part of the opposition Communists to take, like Urbahns & Co, to the road of creating a new Communist Party, before making serious efforts to change the course of the old party'. (p.239) All this was changed when the KPD, the Comintern's most powerful section, succumbed to the Nazis without a fight in 1933.

Trotsky's most valuable literary activity in the years immediately preceding the German *débâcle* was his analysis of fascism which was concerned to expose the dangers of the Comintern's pseudo-analysis. However, it was completely ignored by the audience it was addressed to. When Hitler swept the KPD aside, Trotsky saw in the success of the Nazis — the Comintern's '4th of August' — a betrayal comparable in scale to that of social democracy on the outbreak of the 1914 war.

Trotsky immediately proposed the creation of a new German Communist Party, having concluded that the KPD's political bankruptcy had been made manifest. The ECCI presidium, on the other hand, ruled that the KPD's tactics had been 'completely correct'. Trotsky allowed another seven months to elapse before

passing his verdict on Comintern. In October 1933 he argued that:
'Only when it became clear that no open indignation was aroused in
the ranks of the Communist International after the latter had
surrendered without a fight the most important of its positions did it
become clear that no hopes remained for the regeneration of this
organisation.'[13] The perspective of reform was now dead: 'Apart
from all else, the success of the Nazis indicates the Comintern's
incapacity to learn, to mend its ways, to reform itself.'[14]

Trotsky also reasoned that 'now that the strongest party of the
Comintern has left the stage, there is no means, no channel, and no
lever left by which to act upon the clique that rules the Comintern'.
(p.18) The logic of this new situation caused Trotsky to revise his
analysis of the Soviet bureaucracy. In 1936 he concluded that a
'political revolution' was now required if the USSR was to achieve
socialism. Trotsky assumed that the success of the Nazis would have
momentous repercussions, that unlike China in the 1920s, Stalin's
policies in Germany would be revealed throughout the world for
their true worth. The mass labour movements would now listen to
the Trotskyists as they had never before.

Because reform of the Comintern had become a hopeless prospect
the political necessity was to build a new International. To those, like
Isaac Deutscher, who recognised the bankruptcy of Comintern, but
who believed that the defensive condition of the European working
class advised against creating a new International, Trotsky had this to
say:

From time to time they even declare that they are really not against the
Fourth International as such but that they did find it *not timely*. This
objection, however, is devoid of all content. What is involved is not a
mathematical but a political problem, where the time factor is secondary.[15]

This clearly establishes the political priority of Trotsky's decision.
Yet, given this, Trotsky also believed that objective conditions were
propitious for the new International despite the massive defeats
experienced by the working class. He recognized the psychological
barriers which would obstruct a smooth transfer of political
allegiances and envisaged a protracted struggle to overcome these
problems.[17] He did not underestimate the Comintern's capacity to
obstruct this process. Indeed, Trotsky called it '. . . the chief
obstacle on the road to the international revolution'.[17] Yet Trotsky
could also foresee events which would undermine both capitalism
and the leaderships of the mass working-class organizations. World

war and fascist reaction, in particular, would call forth powerful remedies or, failing this, would issue in a new barbarism.[18]

Trotsky's attitude on the question of the correct tactics for defeating fascism underwent considerable change after 1933.[19] He came to see fascism as the inevitable destiny of the Western democracies unless socialist revolutions pre-empted it. His reasoning became mechanistic in that he argued that fascism represented 'the political regime that crowns the regime of economic decay' just as liberal democracy had served the regimes of expanding competitive capitalism.[20] Thus the Comintern policy which sought unity with democrats was doomed to failure, for 'when the whole train is plunging into the abyss the distinction between decaying democracy and murderous fascism disappears in the face of the collapse of the entire system.'[21] Apart from all else, Trotsky's position seriously underestimated the popular feeling for unity, following the success of the Nazis in 1933, which the popular front policy was in part designed to channel. Just as this was occurring, the Trotskyists were establishing *separate* organizations and arguing the futility of defending democratic gains as the main strategy for defeating fascism. Their isolation could not have been more complete.

But their situation was based on the conviction that the objective conditions were 'rotten ripe' for socialism and that only the political bankruptcy of the Comintern prevented its realization. Thus 'the world political situation as a whole is chiefly characterised by a historical crisis of the leadership of the proletariat'. The central task of the Trotskyists, therefore, '. . . consists in freeing the proletariat from the old leadership, whose conservatism is in complete contradiction to the catastrophic eruptions of disintegrating capitalism and represents the chief obstacle to historical progress'.[22] Necessarily, the Trotskyists would aim their fire at the Stalinist parties because, as Trotsky said in 1934: 'For a revolutionary Marxist, the struggle against reformism is now almost fully replaced by the struggle against centrism.'[23]

The centrists — those who wavered between reform and revolution, at least in rhetoric — were in the ascendancy because straightforward reformism was being killed off by the collapse of capitalism, and Stalinism ('bureaucratic centrism') had destroyed the revolutionary purpose of the Comintern. This aspect of Trotsky's political legacy may help to explain the untiring monologue which his followers directed at the Communist parties. To appreciate their preoccupation with Stalinism it is necessary to recount Trotsky's analysis of the Soviet Union, as it developed in the 1930s.

Trostky had warned of the danger of capitalist restoration in the Soviet Union and, until 1933, had used the analogy of 'Thermidor' to describe it. (The day on which Robespierre fell [27 July, 1794] was called 9th of Thermidor on the French revolutionary calendar: it symbolizes the end of the revolution's radical phase and began the process which led to the personal ascendancy of Napoleon Bonaparte.) After 1933 he revised his position, arguing now that Thermidor was an accomplished fact represented by the state and party bureaucracy 'crowned by the Bonapartist clique of Stalin'. However this did not mean that capitalism had been restored in the Soviet Union. The degeneration of the Russian revolution — caused in the main by the isolation and material backwardness of the Bolshevik state — gave rise to the growth of bureaucracy. This process was accelerated by the militarisation of life during the civil war and the resurgence of the petty bourgeoisie during NEP. But Trotsky also saw that politial factors, such as the banning of party factions in 1921, also played a part. 'The degeneration of the party became both cause and consequence of the bureaucratisation of the state.'[24] In so doing Trotsky became specifically committed to a political pluralism of parties in the post-revolutionary state.[25]

The personal role of Stalin is, in Trotsky's account, dwarfed by these other factors. In fact Trotsky implicitly acknowledged his own part in the process of degeneration by recognizing the consequences which the banning of opposition parties and factions had for the revolution, even though he always maintained that these were temporary expedients forced on the Bolsheviks by the circumstances they had faced.[26]

However, he rejected the old idea that the Soviet Union was state capitalist. The bureaucracy, according to Trotsky, had no independent position in the process of production and distribution and therefore no independent property roots. It was to be understood as a parasitic outgrowth and its disproportionate appropriation of the material income implied only that it enjoyed privileges of consumption rather than a special set of property relations.

Stalin's zigzags in domestic and foreign policies testified to the balance of rival class forces in the USSR which kept the Bonapartist groups around Stalin adapting politically to suit whichever class temporarily gained the ascendancy. The bureaucratic 'caste', argued Trotsky, was politically conservative and determined the reactionary character of Stalin's policies. Stalin's 'defence' of socialism thus employed methods which unwittingly prepared for its overthrow.

For Trotsky, socialism in the USSR could progress only if the bureaucratic and conservative layers were removed: '. . . inasmuch as the question of overthrowing the parasitic oligarchy still remains linked with that of preserving the nationalised (state) property, we call the future revolution *political*'.[27]

To achieve this political revolution it was necessary, in Trotsky's view, to construct a revolutionary party in the USSR. But its success would depend a great deal on the advances made by revolutionaries in the rest of Europe. So both tasks were ultimately dependent on the construction and development of the Fourth International.

Trotsky never allowed his opposition to the Soviet bureacracy to excuse his followers from their duty as revolutionaries to defend the Soviet Union against 'capitalist warmongers'. During the war this would take the form of agitation among the working class to take the side of the Soviet Union. Under normal conditions the Trotskyists argued that the gains of October could only be preserved in the USSR if revolution took place in other European countries. Trotsky was convinced that Stalin's policy of seeking allies among the capitalist states against the Nazis would lead to inevitable defeat in war for the USSR irrespective of the fortunes of Stalin's alliance policy: such was the determination of capitalism to crush the surviving gains of the Bolsheviks. For Trotsky the coming war was like any other capitalist conflict. It had nothing to do with the defence of democracy but revolved essentially, around questions of markets and colonies. For him 'the victory of any one of the imperialist camps would spell slavery, wretchedness, misery, the decline of human culture'.[28]

By 1938 he had realised that it was too late to prevent the outbreak of war by revolutionary action: but he believed that the war itself would greatly accelerate the revolutionary process.

Even if at the beginning of a new war the true revolutionaries should again find themselves in a small minority, we cannot doubt for a single moment that this time the shift of the masses to the road of revolution will occur much faster, more decisively and relentlessly than during the first imperialist war.[29]

Failure in this project would lead to '. . . a super-fascism . . . necessary so as to preserve the dictatorship of the trusts',[30] but it is evident that Trotsky envisaged the growth of the Fourth International as being closely linked to the post-war capitalist crisis he anticipated.

Certainly the pre-war steps taken to launch the Fourth International were less than dramatic. In the summer of 1933 the Independent Labour Party convoked a conference (the London conference) which representatives of the International Communist League attended. These urged the delegates to support the struggle to build a rival international organization to that of the Comintern. Only four of the 14 groups attending supported this call; these were the SAP of Germany, the OSP of Holland, the RSP of Holland and the International Left Opposition. Trotsky failed to arouse the support of the Maslow-Fischer German emigré group or of the Treit Group of France. And even the fusion of the two Dutch groups — achieved soon after the conference — proved arid when their Leader, Sneevliet, broke with Trotsky and withdrew the group from the Trotskyist movement. The SAP leaders also broke with Trotsky. But Trotsky's biggest obstacle was the emotive feeling for workers' unity, which followed in the wake of the German debacle, rather than the dissent of small groups. In 1935 he denounced as 'stupid gossip' rumours that he intended immediately to launch the Fourth International. This shows his awareness of the numerical and political impotence of his followers in that year. Yet three years later the Fourth International was launched, though these factors had not significantly changed in the interim.

In a sense the Fourth International was stillborn due to unfavourable circumstances. Trotsky himself explained the rise of Stalinism as partly a consequence of the working-class defeats of the inter-war years: there was nothing in 1938 to suppose that the situation had changed[31] — except, of course, the perspective to which Trotsky constantly returned of a post-war revolutionary crisis of greater intensity than that of 1918. Trotsky's timing was probably influenced by the fact that the coming war would let loose centrifugal forces which, in the absence of a central international organization, would create disarray in the ranks of his followers.

His major contribution to the conference which founded the Fourth International in September 1938, *The Transitional Programme for Socialist Revolution*, clearly demonstrates Trotsky's belief in the imminence of socialist revolutions in which his followers would play the leading political role. Deutscher correctly describes it as '. . . not so much a statement of principles as an instruction on tactics, designed for a party up to its ears in trade union struggles and day-to-day politics in striving to gain practical leadership immediately'.[32] Organizationally too, the FI was structured in the belief that it would soon command the allegiance of millions.[33]

It seems clear, therefore, that Trotsky's decision to begin the process of constructing a new International was based on his analysis of the political meaning of the Nazi success of 1933. The precise timing of its foundation, in 1938, appears to have been based on his estimation of the likely political repercussions the world war would create. Given these considerations, the numerical and organizational weakness of Trotsky's followers was regarded as a secondary, temporary problem.

Trotsky was aware that 'he who swims against the current is not connected with the masses'. The left opposition had had ten years' experience of such political isolation between 1923 and 1933 when it endeavoured to reform the Comintern. During this period the failed revolutions in Germany, China and Poland had strengthened the theory and practice of 'socialism in one country'. Yet nobody would seriously argue that this fact of political isolation made the Trotskyists wrong to oppose Stalinism.

Similarly it cannot be reasonably argued that the creation of the Fourth International was a mistake because the conditions were unpropitious for its growth. In a sense it was the logical outcome of Trotsky's original decision to oppose international Stalinism, once the latter proved incapable of reforming itself. It must be seen as part of Trotsky's declared ambition to save the soul of revolutionary Marxism from complete discredit and to preserve the line of continuity stretching back to the founders of historical materialism.

Trotsky correctly predicted the liquidation of the Comintern by Stalin.[34] Where Trotsky erred was in analysing the Second World War through the prism of the first imperialist war. This catastrophic perspective is at the root of his other mistaken prognoses (such as his vision of the rapid demise of social democracy and Stalinism; the inevitable military defeat of the Soviet Union in the absence of socialist revolutions; and the generalization of fascist regimes throughout the capitalist world if these systems were not overthrown and replaced by socialism). Serious though these mistakes are, the creation of the Fourth International can be justified on the grounds of preserving the Marxist programme in the epoch of capitalist decay.

At any rate this is how the Trotskyists themselves defended their International. Pierre Frank emphasizes its role as the organization 'which defended the fundamental political and organizational policies of Leninism',[35] and stresses the importance of the Fourth International's struggle in the domain of ideas. An investigation of the FI's key theoretical positions is required if we are to understand properly the strategic and tactical preoccupations of the British far left. Moreover we may discover explanations for the undemocratic practices of some of these groups. Certainly it is easy to find contemporary Marxists who attribute the far left's authoritarianism to its avowed Leninism.[36]

LENINISM AND DEMOCRACY

As already noted, Trotskyism arose as a struggle against a degeneration of the Bolshevik revolution. But Trotsky rejected the common explanation of this as an inevitable development stemming from the organizational practices of Bolshevism. Indeed the Trotskyist tradition has always claimed that Leninist principles of organization are absolutely essential if a revolutionary party is successfully to lead a socialist revolution.[37] Yet as will be shown below, organizations subscribing to Trotsky's views nevertheless in practice reproduce the authoritarianism associated with Stalinism.[38] This seems peculiar, even perverse, given the origins of Trotskyism and the fact that even now '. . . if there is one thing that uniquely characterises modern Trotskyism it is an obsession with bureaucracy'.[39]

I will argue that the source of this authoritarianism is to be located in a certain combination of factors. These are: the acceptance by the far left, of the Leninist conception of the imperialist epoch together with certain organizational and political practices that are predicated upon it, in the context of a long period in which political conditions were inimical to the advance of revolutionary politics. The principles of democratic centralism are not in themselves the main cause of authoritarian inner-party regimes, in my view.[40] But these deformations can be partly attributed to purely organizational or personal practices.

While Michels implied that betrayal of the mass is an inevitable concomitant of centralism, Leninists diagnose this problem quite differently — concluding, in fact, that betrayal results from structural weaknesses in social democratic organizations and that these can be overcome by a highly selective recruitment policy. This is designed to produce a vigilant, active and sophisticated membership. Lenin's democratic centralism, according to its advocates, exists to guarantee that the decisions of this membership are actually implemented by the leadership. The result, it is vaunted, is a highly disciplined, efficient machine which is, at the same time, highly democratic internally. By these accounts, the elitist Leninism of 'What is to be done?' was a temporary aberration which Lenin subsequently repudiated himself.[41]

The very active membership that is required by a Leninist organisation must be extremely difficult to sustain when the group — tiny and isolated — labours in a hostile ideological environment. But this point is further underlined when it is considered that the group derives its *raison d'être* from an assumption of the 'actuality of the revolution'.[42] Clearly the problems of maintaining a stable, highly active cadre are increased when decades of political and economic (capitalist) stability have to be endured: how, then, can the membership be reconciled to a style of poltitics which is geared to the 'actuality of the revolution'? Not only will early disillusion lead to a volatile membership as significant numbers leave the party fairly soon after joining — thus ensuring that at any given time the political sophistication of the rank and file is poor, but those who remain — the small proportion of long-standing members — will, as *de facto* custodians of the group's ideology, perforce adopt a conservative attitude to that ideology. They will have neither the resources nor the experience to develop theory if the group is marginal to mainstream political movement or, as Trotsky put it, 'swimming against the current'. But more important it is precisely when the would-be Leninist vanguard is rendered impotent by objective developments beyond its control (for example the post-war boom and the cold war) that the group will stress *long-term* justifications for its existence. It is to these that I now turn, because it is my contention that the undemocratic practices I will have occasion to describe below, stem in *some* measure from *theoretical* assumptions central to the Leninist tradition. Through the mechanisms afforded by the cult of Lenin and the metaphysical pathos generated by the heroic phase of Bolshevism certain errors and ambiguities of theory and language have been accepted uncritically by the followers of Trotsky. What I am attempting to do is to explain something of the temper and idiom of contemporary Trotskyism by seeking out the implications and mood of certain central theses of Leninism that are maintained by the far left to this day.

The starting point for this is the theory of imperialism contained in Lenin's 'popular outline' of 1914.[43] This summary of the main arguments of Hobson, Hilferding and Bukharin faithfully reproduces the conventional wisdom (among Marxists) of the day concerning the 'moribund', 'over-ripe' and 'stagnating' nature of capitalism in the heartlands of the system. The world war, it was argued, expressed the desperate nature of the capitalist crisis —

which was now a permanent feature of the system. As we have seen, for Lenin August 1914 signalled the beginning of an epoch which would be characterized by wars, civil wars and revolutions: such conflagrations were the very essence of imperialism which *must* divide and re-divide the world.

I will not analyse the erroneous economic assumptions behind these arguments.[44] For my purposes it is more important to examine the political conclusions that emerged from Lenin's analyses; he was, after all, engaged in a search for the appropriate strategy and tactics of 'world revolution', and, in particular seeking to counter the propaganda of the Second International and the likes of Kautsky. Of especial interest to us is the tendency of Marxists to regard 'bourgeois' democracy as a mere sham: this gained currency in the period after 1914. Marx himself had, of course, said very little on the subject. Nonetheless his brief remarks are somewhat more rounded and less mechanistic than those of Lenin, Hilferding and Bukharin. The latter groups of theorists believed that with the emergence and dominance of finance capital (which they greatly exaggerated) the economic preconditions for classical liberalism had been replaced by a monolithicity within the ruling class. Since, they reasoned, the relative autonomy of the bourgeois state had been founded on the inner divisions of the bourgeois class, the hegemony of finance capital, established at the turn of the century, must lead to the identity of big capital and the state. Lenin assumed that monopoly capitalism signified the demise of competition and economic growth. Thus: 'The political superstructure of this new economy of monopoly capitalism (imperialism is monopoly capitalism) is the change from democracy to political reaction. Democracy corresponds to free competition. Political reaction corresponds to monopoly.'[45] Here it can be seen that Lenin attempts to derive political forms from economic stages in a simplistic manner and somewhat mechanistically deduces general laws from a reading of the 1914–18 conjuncture. But this basic analysis, for all its faults, was central to Comintern perspectives during the period involving Trotsky (and beyond), as Claudin has shown.[46]

Trotsky's adherence to Lenin's theory of imperialism is as certain as his lapses into the same kind of class reductionism and mechanistic logic as that of Lenin cited above. Thus we have already noted Trotsky's characterization of fascism as the natural counterpart to decaying capitalism and liberal democracy as the regime best suited to the needs of competitive capitalism. That this was not merely intended as a characterization of German or Italian capitalism but of capitalism *per se* is attested by Trotsky's insistence that the distinction between '. . . decaying democracy and murderous fascism disappears in the face of the collapse of the entire system'.[47] While it is true that Trotsky's catastrophism becomes particularly pronounced during the actual crises of the 1930s and came to serve as a rationale for the Fourth International, it is important to recognize it as part of a longer tradition stretching back through Comintern.[48] This catastrophism was a concomitant of Lenin's theory of the imperialist epoch as one of wars, civil wars, and revolutions. The Leninist belief in the actuality of the revolution was predicated upon it. This world view supported a theory of inter-imperialist rivalries (the objective basis for socialist internationalism) and from this an explanation of the emergence of revolutionary socialist consciousness. It also provided a theory of the 'labour aristocracy', by which reformism was held to have an objective basis in the material corruption of part of the working class, by virtue of colonial super-profits, which enabled the capitalists to buy off a layer of skilled proletarians. Considering the controversy which surrounds the concept of labour aristocracy, and the ambiguities of its varied usage, it is a testimony to the theoretical conservatism of Trotskyism and to its cult of Lenin, that it makes very frequent use of the phrase and always as if it is entirely unproblematic. We will simply note that by attributing political conservatism among wage earners to the higher standard of living enjoyed by a minority layer within the proletariat, Lenin implies that poverty is the source of class struggle and revolutionary consciousness, and that the bulk of the workers are only held back from revolution by a corrupt minority. Neither proposition accords with the facts.

It seems clear that armed only with this dubious understanding of the roots of reformism and convinced of the demise of democracy as an inevitable result of monopolistic stagnation, the militants of the Comintern confidently based themselves on catastrophist perspectives. The organizational structures of Comintern, the 21 conditions, and the militaristic metaphor and imagery which litter Communist debate and tactics, all attest to the literal way in which the theses of imperialist decay were understood. These cannot be explained simply in terms of the revolutionary conjuncture 1917–21, for the apocalyptic tone of Bolshevik pronouncements did not abate even after the third congress of Comintern acknowledged the ebb of the revolutionary wave. Furthermore, revolutionary optimism continued to be based on a fairly crude economism. According to this analysis, the objective basis for revolutionary politics was the inability of capitalism to concede material reforms and thereby support reformist 'illusions' within the working class.[49] The united front tactic itself fully reflects this faith in the moribund state of reformism by proposing joint work with social democrats while making it clear that the Communists' intent was to destroy them. Comintern not only spoke of the need to 'brand . . . the bourgeoisie [and] also its helpers, the reformists of every shade, systematically and pitilessly'. Trotsky accurately reflected its mood when he observed that 'this struggle is such that at any moment it may replace . . . the weapon of criticism by the criticism of the weapon'.[50] Obviously, only an organization in desperate straits could be expected to accept an alliance on these terms.

Clearly, this Comintern economic orthodoxy has very definite political implications. In the first place, reformism was held to be rooted in the more or less perilous and 'extraneous' factor of colonial super-profits: there was nothing about capitalism which enabled structural factors of the system to promote reformism, according to this analysis. Secondly, the Comintern believed reformism to be historically bankrupt, owing to the alleged incapacity of the capitalist system to grant further material reforms to the workers' movement. Such an analysis reinforced the Communists' claim that they occupied a unique role as *the* workers' party: on the level of theory the Comintern had already arrogated to itself the part of strategist and tactician for the *whole* working-class movement. Thus in words echoing the *Communist Manifesto*, the *Manifesto of the Communist International* declared the tasks of Communists to be:

. . . to generalise the revolutionary experience of the working class, to purge the movement of the corroding admixture of opportunism and social patriotism, to unify the efforts of all genuinely revolutionary parties of the world and thereby facilitate and hasten the victory of the Communist revolution throughout the world.[51]

The comprehensive role assigned to Comintern by Trotsky (who wrote the *Manifesto*) faithfully reflects the Communist conviction that the International would not only play a vanguard role in the coming socialist revolutions, but do so without the aid, (and probably in spite of the obstructions), of other avowedly proletarian parties. The united front policy did not alter this conviction. Even as the new tactic was introduced, the Comintern took further measures to reinforce the rigidities of organization, centralism and discipline already extant. This augmented the dependence of the national sections on Moscow at precisely the time when they required wider discretion in the framing of policies and tactics suited to local conditions. Such measures emphasized the self-sufficient mentality of the Communist movement and the completely subordinate role it assigned to its 'partners' in united front work.

The Communists assumed that '. . . the epoch of imperialism . . . [is] . . . a long series of civil wars'.[52] Extreme political polarizations were thus involved in this process in which '. . . parliament has become a weapon of falsehood, deception and violence, a place of enervating chatter . . . parliamentary reforms lose all practical significance for the working class'.[53] For Trotsky bourgeois democracy was merely a 'hypocritical form of the domination of the financial oligarchy' while for Lenin 'the most democratic bourgeois republic is no more than a machine for the suppression of the working class . . . by a handful of capitalists'.

Clearly, by their involvement in this deception, the reformist parties proved themselves misleaders of the working class and antipodal to the revolutionaries who, according to Comintern could see that 'what capitalism is passing through today is nothing other than its death throes. The collapse of capitalism is inevitable.'[54] This emphasis on the Communists as the only true, precognitive proletarian party was bolstered, ironically, with the defeats of the Spartacists and the Bavarian and Hungarian Soviets. None of these events apparently led to a re-examination of assumptions, concerning the preparedness of the European workers' movement for socialist revolution. But they did lead to a greater emphasis, among Communists, on the need for a Bolshevik-type vanguard party and correspondingly greater scepticism concerning the quasi-spontaneous impulsion of the masses towards the seizure of power. Failures such as that of the Spartacists augmented the prestige of Bolshevism.

The Communist attitude towards all elements of 'bourgeois' democracy was undoubtedly hardened by the armed intervention of these liberal-democratic states against the USSR. Likewise the hostility of social democrats towards the Bolshevik experiment and the role of a section of German social democracy in the violent repression of the Spartacist uprising — such events encouraged the Bolsheviks in the dim view they took of 'bourgeois' democracy. It should also be remembered that in 1918 there were only ten countries with universal adult suffrage and this number fell in the inter-war period. The thesis of the decay of bourgeois democracy and its replacement by capitalist authoritarianism thus had some basis in fact. But Lenin also played down the significance of democratic gains where they had been achieved by workers.[55] Especially after the dissolution of the constituent assembly, the Bolsheviks were inclined to counterpose the forms and content of council democracy to those of liberal democracy, such that conciliar forms of popular rule — from having played no significant part in Marxist thought before 1905 — were after 1917 increasingly regarded as the exclusive, superior alternative to all bourgeois democratic institutions. Necessarily, given these suppositions, the allegiance of workers to many of the institutions of liberal democracy within the advanced capitalist states was apt to be ignored by Communists or dismissed as a false consciousness. Like other such illusions, the imminent economic catastrophe of capitalism was expected to dissolve it.

In Trotsky's later writings, certain of these habits of thought became more pronounced to form central elements of his immediate theoretical legacy to the Fourth International. The conviction that the economic collapse of capitalism was at hand was expressed by Trotsky in the most unqualified terms.[56] Further, by denying that any useful distinction existed between liberal democracy and fascism (on the grounds that the surge towards war and economic collapse was leading all the warring parties to the same fate) Trotsky reinforced and encouraged the viewpoint, established in the early years of Comintern, which regarded liberal democracy as a mere sham.

We will see that, despite the almost total refutation of Trotsky's *ex cathedra* predictions, the Fourth International clung to these erroneous perspectives. Indeed, in chapter 2 I show that for most Trotskyists a faith in the imminent collapse of capitalism was regarded as a necessary component of the Marxist programme. Those able to foresee a temporary period of capitalist expansion were expelled as heretics in the late 1940s. By the early 1950s, as I recount in chapter 3, the perspectives of *economic* collapse were modified to encompass the prospect — now held as inevitable — of world war-revolution. Not until the mid sixties was the FI leadership prepared to consider an alternative perspective.[57] However, the events of May 1968 seem to have led the far left straight back to its traditional preoccupations of vanguardism and catastrophism.

CONCLUSIONS

I have argued that, while it is possible to find more cautious assessments in the writings of both Lenin and Trotsky, the essence of Comintern in its early years was a preparations for wars, civil wars and revolutions. At the most general level this was supported by Lenin's theory of imperialism which purported to explain the *moribund* nature of capitalism and from this deduced the demise of parliamentary democracy and reformism. Undoubtedly the militants who subscribed to these perspectives were inclined to regard the world Communist Party as *the* vanguard of the working class, uniquely destined and qualified to lead the coming socialist revolutions. But it would be inaccurate to attribute the moments of arrogance and sectarianism in Communist history solely to a mere theory, however important I may argue it was.

I am more concerned to regard these catastrophist perspectives as the product of a combination of factors — the world war, the Bolshevik revolution and the post-war crises being among them — rather than the result of ideological convictions alone. The Communist acceptance of catastrophism is tied up with the mood or temper which predominated in Comintern. This ethos came to be regarded as an essential feature of Bolshevism and involved widespread acceptance among the militants of all that they associated with the imagery conjured by the Leninist triumph in Russia. Trotskyism — which emerged to defend this legacy — has by its theoretical conservatism preserved this idiom intact. This does not merely apply to the Leninist theory of the imperialist epoch with its tendency to make little of the institutions of 'bourgeois democracy'; nor do I refer simply to the mental habit of regarding reformism as a corruption based on imperialism and in process of withering away. I suggest that the precedence given to the preservation of classical doctrines by Trotskyism *also* ensures that this tradition is the repository of the unconscious mental habits and political style of Bolshevism.

For, as Liebman has pointed out, it was the fate of Lenin that the cult of his name led to the elevation of all aspects of his politics, including the erroneous and counter-productive.[58] Thus the vice of excessive invective, which Lenin occasionally indulged in, was *subsequently* made into a virtuous model for imitation by Leninists after Lenin's death. The conditions under which Trotyskyism was born led Trotsky to contend for Leninist legitimacy against Stalin — and in so doing, Trotsky also adopted an uncritical attitude to Leninism. Later the puny forces of world Trotskyism — faced with an enormous disparity between their resources and the political tasks they had taken on — were induced to give exaggerated emphasis to the importance of programme and political leadership. In this way the Comintern's early belief in the singular claims of Marxists to proletarian leadership was given an added twist by the Trotskyists for whom 'the world political situation as a whole is chiefly characterised by a historical crisis of the leadership of the proletariat'. While at first this statement expressed the profoundly held conviction that capitalism was 'objectively' 'rotten-ripe' for socialist revolution, yet surviving by virtue of the social democratic and Stalinist betrayers, it soon came to express the obsession with internal disputes of Trotskyists unable to make an external impact. The latter could not, in other words, resist the temptation of repeated splits and internecine disputes conducted in the name of creating *the* vanguard, i.e. as if problems of strategy and tactics were simply problems of programme or even of its 'correct' interpretation.

A corollary of this is the habit which recurs throughout the history of the far left of regarding opposing tendencies *within* the Trotskyist tradition as expressions of 'bourgeois' or 'petty bourgeois' class interests. Just as the preoccupation with the 'correct' Marxist programme could often become an idealist faith in the political efficacy of ideas, so dissent was as often interpreted as the intrusion of alien (bourgeois) ideas, of unconscious betrayal. In this, the Trotskyists could cite the precedent created by Trotsky during his intervention against Shachtman and Burnham in the American SWP.[59] The liturgical style of 'resolving' differences of opinion by quotations from the classic texts (a style inimical to inner-party democracy due to its encouragement of a high priest mentality among the 'theorists') was drawn from the same quarter, it having been Trotsky's misfortune to resort necessarily to this technique when dealing with Stalinist falsifications. But there were also other practices, well established within the early Comintern, which led in the direction of stifling proper political discussion.

The process of merely anathematizing doctrinal opponents has a long history in the Communist movement and derives its current legitimacy from Lenin and the denunciatory tone of Comintern documents. When combined with the practice of reducing internal factional differences to the influences of 'outside' class interests, the habit of employing violent polemic has acted against the emergence of inner-party democracy in far left groups. Likewise the militaristic discipline of Comintern, its language of warfare and centralized command structures stress an instrumentalist conception of the vanguard which survives both as a political idiom and as a model of inter-party organization in some of today's far left groups.[60] It is these aspects of the Trotskyist-Bolshevist legacy that help to account for the tolerance of authoritarianism in far left groups: the membership is disposed to regard such 'toughness' as a feature of Bolshevism. If this is found congenial, it is because of the inordinate role assigned to *the* revolutionary party in the making of socialism which the Trotskyist tradition has emphasized. For those who subscribe to this conception of 'vanguardism', violations against inner-party democracy may be seen as 'objectively' necessary or in some other sense useful to the cause.

These dispositions may also be supported by the unconscious habit of talking in terms of a single proletarian party which, according to Geras '. . . has been endemic in Marxism since its inception'.[61] Despite Trotsky's very real pluralist commitment, he shared with Lenin, Luxemburg and Marx the propensity to think and write about *the* revolutionary party. This may have unintentionally encouraged the rather arrogant belief that one party *can* represent the 'historic interests' of the working class as a whole without critical opposition. Furthermore this mentality also disputes the need for independent organization of the labour movement to represent the *specific* demands of diverse groups, factions and causes within this mass. On the contrary, the single vanguard party is imagined to embody all the demands of all of these splinters; to possess the requisite knowledge for all these currents: and to perceive all the measures required for their defence. Lest this be thought exaggerated, let me anticipate the discussion of British Trotskyism by quoting one of its principal figures who said 'we are monopolists in the field of politics. To make a successful revolution in Britain, the working class will require to do it through one party and one programme . . . that is why we are out to destroy all competitive parties.'[62]

It is because the Trotskyist organizations of my study are mainly composed of recent recruits that these organizations are unable to sustain more than the most meagre political culture. The political education of this rank and file consists in the main of learning and defending 'the line' of the organization. Beyond this, only a few pamphlets by Lenin and Trotsky will have been read before the erstwhile recruit has completed his or her life in the organization. This is the context in which those aspects of the far left's legacy discussed above will have their impact. In other words, it is precisely because such a high proportion of far left militants are new members, that factors of political idiom and imagery are very signifiant elements of the Trotskyist legacy. Whereas the carefully qualified analyses of Trotsky may be unread or forgotten, the dramas of Bolshevism and the early Comintern, the polemic and emphatic generalizations of Lenin and Trotsky are taken in. Even the relatively stable leadership echelons of the Trotskyist groups would seem to be inspired by the aspects of Comintern doctrine that I have stressed.

I will show later that my interpretation of the salient theoretical heritage of Trotskyism accords with that of the Trotskyists themselves. The 'stony one-sidedness' that animated so much of Comintern practice continues to animate contemporary Trotskyism and the theories which lie behind it are regarded as definitive. In the next chapter I examine this orthodoxy at work in the 1940s and consider the frustrated attempts to modify it by the Revolutionary Communist Party.

2

The Revolutionary Communist Party
1944-9

ORIGINS

The RCP was created in January-February 1944 from the fusion of the Revolutionary Socialist League (RSL) and the Workers International League (WIL). Since 1939 the RSL has been recognized as the official section of the Fourth International. It was itself the production of a fusion which the WIL rejected as unprincipled and artificial. The FI had a similarly low opinion of the WIL which the foundation conference of 1938 placed in the category of 'national groupings . . . reactionary in essence'.[1]

However, during the war, the WIL overtook the official British section in both organizational and numerical strength. The RSL was the victim of intense internal disputes promoted by three groups (which fact seemed to vindicate the WIL's verdict on the 1939 fusion). While the RSL was totally submerged within the Labour Party, the WIL emphasized open politics, though it maintained fractions of its supporters within the Young Communist League, the Independent Labour Party and even inside the Anarchist Federation and the Non Conscription League. The RSL's commitment to entrism contributed to its decline. In the conditions of the wartime electoral truce, the Labour Party — already depleted numerically by military conscription — became something of an empty shell, at least until 1943. According to Howell 'Labour membership declined by almost half between 1939 and 1943 and then began to rise, while in many city seats the party's presence was no more than titular'.[2] By

1942 the WIL claimed a membershp of 250 of predominantly working-class composition. It absorbed a number of smaller revolutionary groups, including Sid Bidwell's Revolutionary Workers League, but as its newspaper *Socialist Appeal* attests, its chief orientation was to the CPGB membership and to trade union militants — especially the miners.[3]

The militant exuberance of the WIL, which projected itself as the British section of the FI in the pages of *Socialist Appeal,* is evinced by a pamphlet it produced entitled *Preparing for Power*.[4] But in its wild revolutionary optimism the WIL was no different than the official sections of world Trotskyism.[5] In part this undoubtedly reflects the real shift of public opinion to the left. According to Paul Addison '. . . the evidence suggests that by the summer of 1942 a major upheaval in public opinion had taken place. Indeed opinion may have been further to the left in 1942 than it was to be in 1945'. When it entered negotiations for fusion with the RSL, at a specially convened conference in January 1944, both groups contributed to the atmosphere of great revolutionary expectations which envisaged their combined force of 400 militants being imminently transformed into an organization which would lead the British working class. The conference announced that 'The unification . . . takes place in the period of the dissolution of the Comintern and when the open degeneration of its national sections into agencies of the ruling class is shattering the unity of the Stalinist ranks. In ever increasing numbers these militants are finding their way into the ranks of the Fourth International.'

The confidence of British Trotskyists was partly connected with the transformation, since 1941, of the CPGB into a conservative force in industry. Despite the CPGB's 'ardent support for the Coalition after Russia's entry into the war' and 'its appeals for higher productivity and no strikes' it was able to benefit from wartime radicalism. Membership rose from around 12,000 in June 1941 to almost 60,000 by the end of 1942. This was based on the great prestige of the Red Army and the general Soviet war effort with which the CPGB was associated. The Trotskyists gained nothing from this and, as we shall see, little from their involvement in strikes. But the mere fact that the CPGB was against strikes and for greater productivity (under the banner of national unity) enabled the Trotskyists to champion basic trade union demands alone. This earned the latter a special notoriety and gave them the feeling of some influence among rank-and-file trade unionists.

In fact their position was very weak, and even the CPGB over-estimated it.[6] The fusion of the RSL and WIL was chiefly promoted by the International Secretariat of the FI (ISFI) and against the wishes of many members of the RSL. Even the name of the new organization was hotly contended. The joint negotiating committee ruled that 'any attempt to name the fused organization a "Party" must be rejected as adventuristic in view of the extreme weakness of its numbers which renders it impossible for it to act as a party in the present circumstances'.

The fused organization was to keep the name Revolutionary Socialist League. But by February 1944, Jock Haston — a leader of the WIL — persuaded a majority to accept the name Revolutionary Communist Party. This was in line with the WIL's predilection for independent and 'open' party work rather than entrism. The elected leadership of the RCP — mainly ex-WIL members — committed the new organization to this approach supplemented by fractional entrism within the ILP and Labour Party. The group's official newspaper would continue to be *Socialist Appeal* while the entrists would canvass an organ called *Militant*.

But by far the most important consideration was the RCP's perspective of imminent capitalist crisis and revolutionary situations in Britain and Europe. This catastrophism was inherited from Trotsky, though at the time it was not confined to Trotskyists. As Addison observes '. . . many of the judgements of the time have an apocalyptic ring'. Orwell, for example, said that '. . . if we can hold out for a few months, in a year's time we shall see red militias billeted in the Ritz . . .'[7] In any case, 'the war had awakened a more radical impulse than anything Britain had known for generations'.[8] Furthermore, though they were the main beneficiaries of it, the leaders of the traditional, mass labour organizations were not the main instigators of this radicalism:

In the political articulation of the experience of war, the left-wing activists played a considerable part. In barracks and mess decks, in factories and air-raid shelters, in organized, and even more in unorganized, discussions and debates, the anti-Fascists of Popular Front days now found an audience receptive as never before to the message of socialist change.[9]

David Coates remarks that 'the Labour Party leadership in 1945 was taken by surprise both by the achievement and by the size of its electoral victory over its partners in the wartime coalition'.[10] This is, perhaps, not surprising since under the conditions of the wartime electoral truce 'the Labour Party organization was declining . . . in membership, propaganda, meetings, CLP activity [and] social activities'.[11] The RCP, on the other hand, predicted a massive Labour victory and *Socialist Appeal* had campaigned for an end to the electoral truce since 1940 under the slogan 'Labour To Power'.

Yet, if Paul Addison is correct, the radicalism of 1945 — at least for the 'leftish intelligentsia' — was inspired by Wells rather than Lenin and Mass Observation characterized the mood of the population as 'non-political', 'pro-Russian', and a sentiment for 'something better' which was also against 'vested interests and privilege'.[12]

There is not much in this that the Trotskyists could exploit in a situation which was far more favourable to the CPGB (if it was favourable to any 'extremist' organization). But in fact the marginalization of the political extremes was a process supported by the 'institutional collaboration' of the TUC which consented in 1940 to a ban on strikes which lasted until 1951.[13] Regulation 1A(a) — invoked by Bevin from April 1944 — was designed to deal with agitators who would defy this agreement and four RCP leaders were the first to be prosecuted, and imprisoned, under it.[14]

By February 1944, however, events in Italy and the Balkans gave reasons to believe that Trotsky's prognoses would be confirmed and the FI observed that these struggles were tending spontaneously to adopt the Soviet form, despite the absence of revolutionary leaderships in the countries concerned. All the European sections, including the British, were consequently instructed to apply the workers' front tactic which consisted of establishing a network of factory nuclei. Even in Greece, Italy and France, where radicalism was more thoroughgoing than in Britain, the FI was too weak to apply this tactic. In Britain there was no prospect of its application.

The RCP was, however, anticipating an accelerated decline of the British economy which would provide the objective basis for agitation in favour of the transition to the Soviets. Its conference of August 1945 envisaged the bloody collapse of British imperialism in India. The consequent loss of 'economic tribute', it was argued, would entail a greater rate of exploitation of British workers in order for the bourgeoisie to maintain its position. The RCP believed that mass redundancies, the elimination of the 'labour aristocracy' and the repression of trade unions, would emerge as the chief measures of this ruling-class offensive. But this would create conditions which would be 'the most revolutionary in the whole of British history'.[15]

The 1945 general election was viewed in this perspective.

Whereas, according to Foot, Labour succeeded '. . . against all odds and orthodox prophecies',[16] the RCP erred at the opposite extreme in its unorthodox analysis. This analysis predicted a Labour government '. . . carried to power by the greatest wave of radicalization witnessed in the history of the British workers'. The RCP expected that the Labour government would face tremendous pressure from its rank and file 'to carry out revolutionary measures' and, unable to do so, the party would be split from top to bottom.

Yet the RCP had been able to test the mood of the electorate during the Neath by-election in 1944 when Jock Haston polled 1,781 votes. Despite the fact that during the campaign *Socialist Appeal* reached a peak circulation of 20,000, there is no obvious reason why the RCP should ascribe revolutionary pretensions to the British electorate. When *Socialist Appeal* exclaimed '1,781 vote revolutionary communism' it was engaging in wishful thinking rather than a revolutionary analysis of the situation. The perspective of economic crisis — by assuming a mechanically determinist relationship between unemployment and revolutionary class consciousness — was the only argument in the RCP's arsenal to sustain the prognoses of socialist revolution in Britain. The fact that the war years were, perhaps paradoxically, the crucible in which was '. . . inaugurated an era of consensus' in British politics testifies to the real nature of the leftward swing in 1945.

ECONOMIC PERSPECTIVES

Though they predicted a Labour landslide the RCP leaders did not commit their organization to entrism though analagous circumstances had first prompted Trotsky to recommend it in 1934. But this debate will be considered later. In fact the leadership's determination to build an open party came to be regarded as heretical as did its 1945 perspectives which entertained '. . . the possibility of a temporary post-war boom lasting for one or two years'. Yet apart from this *caveat* the leadership's economic perspectives were as 'orthodox' as those of the ISFI. Thus, it stated:

We are now on the threshold of the greatest crisis yet witnessed in the history of British capitalism . . . indeed, the period of the world crisis from 1929 onwards, with its unemployment queues of over three million, will appear a rosy picture in comparison with what the working class faces in the next period.

Clearly the RCP's argument envisaged only a slight delay — of one or two years — before the catastrophe befell British capitalism. Yet this was enough to provoke the intense disapproval of the ISFI together with a 'minority' within the RCP. Moreover the political character of this disapproval was more appropriate for polemics against the FI's enemies than for use against the leaders of one of its national sections.

The ISFI's main resolution at the world congress of 1946, acknowleged '. . . the undeniable weakness of the revolutionary working class' but asserted that capitalism's productive forces 'remain on a level approaching stagnation and collapse'. It predicted '. . . an oncoming crisis more profound and extensive than the 1929–33 one'.[17] The only self-criticism this document allowed for the perspectives of 1944 (which talked of the imminence of Soviets throughout Europe) was confined to 'the rhythm of the process' which, it conceded, was slower than expected. Though 'the new and powerful revival' of the Communist parties was noted, the ISFI's perspectives still envisaged the imminent creation of alternative revolutionary parties representing the FI.

The RCP, however, was prepared to go further in correcting its perspectives document of the preceding year. It realized that the ISFI was refusing to acknowledge observable trends and developments. The RCP delegates to the 1946 world congress moved an important amendment to the main perspective document presented by the International leadership. This amendment argued that Europe's economic recovery 'will be on the basis of US loans' and that though the latter had emerged from the war as the world's foremost power, this did not entail a straightforward undermining of the British economy. Indeed the RCP argued that the USA 'must also make concessions' in order to preserve its position. Britain's economic recovery would also be assisted, they said, by 'measures of industrial rationalization through nationalization'.

The RCP observed that the wartime destruction of capital and the exhaustion of inventories provided the basis for a post-war re-stocking boom. The June 1946 plenum of the international executive committee of the FI (IEC) disagreed and added to its differences with the RCP 'majority' by announcing that entrism, based on '. . . the undeniable radicalization of the masses in England . . . flowing through the channel of the Labour Party', was the right tactic in Britain. The IEC further argued that the unique structure of the Labour Party '. . . based . . . upon the structure of the working class movement as such, on the trade unions', gave a special significance to the entrist tactic in Britain. The RCP majority disagreed, claiming that there was no organized left-wing in the Labour Party, and so the debate about economic perspectives became connected with a debate about tactics.

By January 1947, the ISFI felt moved to write directly to the RCP central committee, arguing that there was no prospect for an economic boom. On the contrary, '. . . the present situation sets new objectives for entry: the setting into motion of *the entire awakened British working class* along the path of revolutionary action, this time within the framework of the Labour Party itself'.

In their reply, the RCP majority observed that the economic recovery of Britain had already surpassed the limits envisaged by their 1946 perspectives document. 'How long could this last?', they asked. 'Certainly for not longer than a few years at most' was their estimate. Furthermore *'the orientation and strategy of the RCP is firmly based on the long-term perspective of crisis and decline . .* ' [my emphasis]. The RCP argued that this did not justify entrism, however, because the Labour Party was dormant in the constituencies: 'There has been no major influx of members, no increase in the activity of Wards in traditional areas of militancy like Scotland (Glasgow). Just the opposite. The youth are absent too. The Leagues of Youth do not exist.' Under such circumstances, argued the RCP, the best way to pressurize the Labour Party was to work in the trade unions: this tactic, they argued, was also justified by the unique structure of the Labour Party. In any case, the perspective of setting 'the entire working class in motion', they pointed out, was unreal even for an organization twenty times the size of the RCP.

The unreality of the ISFI's arguments, however, became greater as the debate became increasingly dogmatic. Its favoured prodigy within the RCP, Gerry Healy — who led the disaffected minority — argued that the perspective of economic revival '. . . calls for complete revision of our programmatic estimation of capitalism. It means that capitalism in Britain is becoming more virile — something which is obvious nonsense. What the Political Bureau [of the RCP] have to do involves much more than the formal correction of a mistake — they must revise the Marxist analysis of imperialist decline'.[18] This view, which regards the Leninist conception of the imperialist epoch as synonymous with the stagnation of the capitalist world economy, was also put forward by the leadership of the FI. Thus, in September 1947, Ernest Mandel intervened in the RCP internal debate on behalf of the International to argue that an economic boom in Britain was now 'impossible' because '. . . in the period of capitalist decadence British industry *can no longer* overgrow the stage of revival and attain one of real boom'.[19]

On this occasion, Tony Cliff replied for the RCP majority in an article which simply observed that by all the key economic indicators there was *in fact* an upturn in the UK economy. (Tony Cliff [Ygael Gluckstein] came to Britain from Palestine and joined the RCP. He developed a theory of state capitalism in connection with the USSR and became a leader of the Socialist Review Group, forerunner of today's Socialist Workers Party.) But Cliff's argument was ignored by the ISFI which, in November 1947, endorsed its earlier positions in a document entitled *The World Situation and the Tasks of the Fourth International*. This foresaw 'a period of economic and political difficulties, convulsions and crises in one country after another, which inevitably set in motion great struggles of the proletarian masses'. Indeed the document argued that the prospects for the survival of capitalism had worsened since 1946 and that the situation threatened 'to become catastrophic especially in France and Italy *as well as in Britain*'. [my emphasis]

Enough has been said here to indicate that the Fourth International's catastrophism was seen by its protagonists as a principled, programmatic stance. Thus those within its ranks who promoted any other perspective were very soon cast in the mould of heretics. The methods employed against the RCP majority support this conclusion, as we shall see, as does the vehemence of the verbal attacks heaped upon them. In order to pursue this argument further, it is necessary to consider the internal life of the RCP and examine the faction fight which consumed so much of the organization's energy before finally destroying it.

TACTICS AND INTERNAL LIFE

We have seen that the ex-WIL leaders of the RCP did not favour entrism, though the tactic was practised by other Trotskyists in Britain and was advocated by Trotsky in 1934. The RCP debate on this issue was opened by Healy in 1945[20] who argued that the coming radicalization of the British working class would first express itself via an influx of militants into the Labour Party. The RCP leadership argued that this was simply not happening; that political activity in the CLPs was very low. They pointed out that the RCP's Labour Party fraction was having very limited success and that the RCP won more new recruits from the CPGB than from the Labour Party.

With the Labour Party's landslide victory at the polls in 1945 Healy returned to this theme, arguing that its electoral victory was '. . . the result of a mass radicalization of the workers and broad sections of the middle class determined on a break with monopoly capitalism and the outmoded defenders of capitalist politics'. According to Healy, the Tories '. . . do not conceive of any more electoral victories, which means the beginning, on their part, of a move towards extra-parliamentary measures'.[21] Though both sides in the dispute initially based themselves on the perspective of the imminent radicalization of the working class, as the debate went on some significant differences emerged.

Healy's 'minority' took the ISFI 'line' that economic recovery was impossible, while the RCP majority were more inclined to take cognizance of actual developments. The greater realism of the majority came through in its estimation of the value of entrism — all the evidence pointed against this tactic. The minority's aversion to empirical evidence was transformed by Healy into a philosophical difference. When Jock Haston innocently remarked on the need for 'empirical adaptation', Healy argued at great length that this represented '. . . renunciation of the methodology of Marxism' and the 'political bankruptcy' of the majority.[22] The whole arraignment was based on Healy's corruption of 'empirical' into 'empiricism', yet the majority were compelled to circulate another lengthy article in order to refute Healy's allegation.

Such arguments could do little to educate the membership of the RCP yet internal disputes in political organizations are sterile unless this is achieved. However, the evidence suggests that the real object of the Healy 'minority' was completely to oust the RCP leadership, rather than simply change the latter's tactical line. On issues as diverse as the nature of the Soviet Union, British perspectives, organizational matters and economic questions, the minority always contrived to oppose the leadership. The voting figures from the RCP's conference of 1946 showed that the minority acted as a faction for at least a year before it declared itself such.

The minority saw itself as the defender of 'orthodoxy'. This orthodoxy was interpreted as a detailed defence of Trotsky's pre-war prognostications — especially those which concerned the economic collapse of capitalism. They shared this position with the ISFI which declared that

The Majority leadership of the RCP is an unprincipled factional clique which monopolises and misuses the party apparatus for factional purposes:

deprives the Minority of representation on the Political Bureau; creates an atmosphere of crisis and ideological terror in the ranks and hounds worker critics with expulsions and threats.[23]

There is no evidence for any of these charges except that concerning the lack of minority representation on the PB. But the RCP justified their exclusion on the grounds that the Political Bureau was concerned to enforce decisions taken and there was no room for dissenters on the executive. However, the minority were proportionally represented on the Central Committee and at Annual Conference — the two policy-making bodies. Far from it being the majority that was undemocratic, the evidence suggests an authoritarian minority. While it must be said that both sides were ludicrously short on logical argumentation, and that 'the various economic perspectives had no necessary correlation with strategy on the question of the Labour Party', the issues were resolved by the authoritarian action of the minority backed by the ISFI. Prior to the RCP Conference of 1947, the minority declared itself 'a faction of all those in favour of entry, on the basis of the programme of the Fourth International for the purpose of gaining the greatest possible support by the next congress'. But it also argued that

in the event of the faction not gaining a majority, then, confident in the correctness of the entrist tactic, we shall request the IEC to so organize the British Section so as to allow the supporters of entry to work within the Labour Party under their own control, subject to the supervision of the International Secretariat.[24]

The minority remained only one-seventh of the RCP membership up until 1948 when, with the support of the ISFI, the RCP was effectively split into two separate organizations to facilitate Healy's rise to the leadership of its entrist group. Thus an edict from the ISFI achieved that which internal discussions had failed to bring about — the conversion of the open party into an entrist group. But before passing comment on these developments, I will examine how the leadership line of the RCP operated in practice.

The RCP was politically orientated to the Communist Party in 1944. The emergence of the PCI and PCF as mass organizations for a time persuaded the RCP that a similar metamorphosis was possible for the CPGB. However, by 1945 this had been over-ruled by the CPGB's continuing zeal for 'national unity' and the 'one world' ideology then propounded by Stalin. When the wartime alliance (which had been the precondition for the CPGB's support of industrial peace) collapsed and the Cominform was set up in 1947, the CPGB adopted a left rhetoric, but there was still no sign of it 'seriously challenging the Labour Party for the leadership of the masses', as the RCP had predicted.

Even so the RCP continued to address the CP rank and file through the pages of its press. Partly this was based on the RCP's poor regard for the ILP and the Labour Party. The rightward shift of the former — always regarded as a centrist organization by Trotskyists — made entrism inapplicable and Haston made a similar evaluation of the Labour Party. There was no significant upsurge of rank-and-file militancy within it during 1945. Indeed the leadership of the RCP claimed that apathy was the main characteristic of the working class during the 1945 general election. The CP, they argued, organized bigger public meetings and had a bigger proportion of active members than the Labour Party. Furthermore, the CP was beginning to regard Trotskyists as 'ultra lefts' rather than 'fascists' and this, Haston argued, was a 'capital gain'. The main factor, however, in supporting the RCP leadership's argument was the fact that 'the figures for party recruitment show that it is from this field — members and sympathisers of the CP — that by far the largest single grouping of workers from other political organizations has been recruited'. To cultivate this most fertile field of recruitment, the RCP produced regular features in *Socialist Appeal* specifically aimed at the CP membership; theoretical articles in *Workers International News* regularly considered the nature of Stalinism; and the RCP membership was exhorted to challenge local CP members to debate. But what was unusual in the RCP's approach to this work was the belief that a 'national faction' or 'left centre current' was emerging within the CPGB during 1945 and 1946.

While it is true that disaffected elements existed in the CPGB in the middle forties, these were hankering for a return to the 'true Leninism' of the thirties (which was very far removed from, and very hostile to, Trotskyism). Furthermore the CPGB was precisely a Stalinist party which would tolerate no organized internal opposition.[25] In any case from 1947 — with the left turn of Cominform and the statization of capital in Eastern Europe — the morale of the CP was boosted and its internal problems once more deferred. Yet the RCP continued to win more new recruits from the CP than from any other organization. Though it resumed fraction work inside the ILP in 1946, only one recruit came from this source in the first six months of such entrist activity, prompting the RCP's withdrawal from the organization in September of the same year.

The Labour Party milieu proved to be equally uncongenial. The RCP's activists in this quarter reported, in September 1946, that 66 of them operating in 46 wards of the Labour Party could name only *36 potential* recruits to the RCP.[26] They argued that attendances at ward meetings were low and that political items rarely appeared on the agendas — even resolutions of solidarity with local strikers were unusual. Sales of *Socialist Appeal* and *Militant* reflected this indifference to political issues, it was argued. Whereas the 66-strong fraction could manage to sell only 118 copies of *Socialist Appeal* between them in the Labour Party, the average sales per member of the RCP was 36 copies; indeed, even the lowest recorded invidual sale was eight, yet this surpassed the average for those RCP members operating within the Labour Party.[27]

During the first half of 1946, the RCP recruited only six people from the Labour Party. The following year the organization lost more members than it gained by the entrist fraction; the number of entrists had fallen to 60, 12 of whom had been added from the parent body. The almost inert state of the Labour League of Youth — in which RCP-ers were agitating for a higher maximum age for membership — compounded the problem in an area in which Trotskyists subsequently made significant advances.

The leadership of the RCP regarded these facts as a vindication of their commitment to building an 'open party', but still had to explain the organization's failure to achieve numerical growth. Instead of reaching the targeted membership figure of 1,000 in 1946, the group's actual strength was around 300-50. The leadership blamed the economic revival and the electorate's faith in the new Labour government for this. The strategy outlined for 1947 involved 'an awakening tempo in the industrial field' in which the RCP hoped to gain via rising working-class militancy'.

There were several factors which obstructed the RCP from making the political advances in the trade unions which they now acknowledged to be impossible in the rival political organizations. In the first place the RCP was short of the necessary numerical 'muscle' to give practical strength to their policies. Even when the organization took an important initiative — as in championing the squatters' movement — the greater weight of the CPGB eventually prevailed. Despite the RCP's working-class composition, the CPGB had a much stronger base in industry.

The war years were exceptional. Then the RCP was the unrivalled champion of the shop floor in those factories where it had members.

Its Militant Workers Federation was more than a paper organization for as long as the CPGB refrained from industrial militancy. But it was the revival, in 1947, of the CP militancy — rather than Bevin's 'Regulation 1A(a)' — which reduced the MWF to impotence. This is why the RCP could not repeat its successful interventions such as in the Newcastle apprentice boys' strike of 1944. The perception of industrial strength which this had given, combined with token representation in mining, shipyards, engineering and aircraft, was dispelled with the onset of the economic boom. In 1946 the MWF could not record one useful initiative and in 1947 the RCP folded it up.

Yet trade union activity remained the only practical hope — given the RCP's failure to impress the members of other political bodies — and it accordingly received greater emphasis than other issues in the group's press. Its propaganda stressed the antagonism of the trade union bureaucracy and the union rank and file. Even after the failure of the MWF, the RCP sought to give organizational expression to this via rank-and-file bodies. It took over the Building Workers' Campaign Committee which the CPGB abandoned in 1946. This was initially confined to Glasgow and London, though the RCP attempted to transform it into a national organization. In June 1946, the BWCC launched its own national bulletin. However the high hopes this raised were disappointed in the following 19 months. Though seven issues of the bulletin were printed (with a circulation of less than one thousand), the BWCC failed to take root and even the London and Glasgow sections crumbled, thus explaining the CP's original attitude towards them.

This episode merely serves to demonstrate a recurring dilemma for far left organizations: in constructing such 'bridges to the masses' (which are intended to break the group's isolation) the organizations run the risk of exhausting their efforts in fruitless exercises which merely compound their frustration and underline their impotence. The limited extent of the RCP's trade union base was an obvious handicap in such projects as the BWCC.

Seventy nine per cent of the membership belonged to trade unions but 35 per cent of the 350 members belonged to the 'basic unions' (defined by the leadership as comprising engineering shipyards, docks, construction). Since just under one third of the membership were resident in London (which district also accounted for 75 per cent of the RCP's recruitment successes) the RCP was unheard of in some parts of the country. The group's representation in the trade unions was just as uneven.[28]

TABLE 2.1

Convenors	8	
Local trade union branch officials	57	(AEU 14)
District committee representatives	9	(AEU 3)
Shop stewards	36	(AEU 13)
Delegates to trade councils	60	
Area committee members	3	(AEU 2)

As table 2.1 shows, the RCP had more of a presence in the Amalgamated Engineering Union than in any other trade union. But this was where the CPGB was traditionally strongest and, consequently, where the RCP faced the stiffest competition for their influence over militants. In the whole of 1947 the RCP failed to win a single member because of its direct involvement in strikes — despite the emphasis on this side of its agitations. The 'awakening tempo' of industrial conflict, predicted by the leadership in 1946, failed to materialize.

The RCP's stagnation helped to create, by 1947, the context in which the ISFI was able to split the organization on the grounds that entrism would yield better results than open party activities. The only defence of the Haston leadership, which still commanded the great majority of members, was to tighten up the group's organizational efficiency and complain of 'the closed circle psychology' which, Haston alleged, affected the membership. This, he said, '. . . scared off potential recruits and lost members by demanding fully-fledged Bolshevik status' from everyone.

From 1946 membership and sales of *Socialist Appeal* declined, causing the group to reduce the number of full-timers it employed. The RCP's demise was accelerated when the minority faction became responsible only to the ISFI after the 1947 conference. By December 1948 the remaining part of the RCP issued a 'Statement on Perspectives' which acknowledged the impossibility of surviving as an open party. Objective circumstances, they argued, militated against this course and entrism in the Labour Party was the only alternative. However, the RCP majority reiterated its conviction that the Labour Party itself was an arena of low political activism which did not justify the ISFI's perspectives and those of the minority. What was now envisaged by the majority was a long period of patient, systematic entrism in which the RCP would retrench.

The ISFI saw in this statement 'an expression of liquidationist tendencies' by which 'the whole programme of the FI is threatened'.

The Secretary of the Fourth International, Michel Pablo, had already accused Haston, Grant and other leaders of the RCP of collusion with renegades and heretics and of secret adherence to the 'unorthodox' theory of state capitalism.[29] In 1947 they had been identified as intending '. . . to ovethrow the Trotskyist line of the International', but this line of argument reveals more of the mentality of the ISFI than it does of the motives of the RCP leadership. Of course the truth or falsity of a theory or policy cannot be settled by reference to its propounder's motives. However such 'unmasking' of ideological opponents was often substituted for scientific argument in the Marxist tradition and seems to be particularly entrenched within the FI leadership at this time.

As we have seen, the critiques made by the RCP of the ISFI's policy statements were mild in the extreme and, furthermore, closer and more accurate approximations to real developments than those of the International leadership. The ISFI was blind to this because of its defence or 'orthodoxy' which can only be understood as a dogmatic refusal to reject Trotsky's pre-war prognoses in the light of actual developments.   This was the burden of Haston's argument when he stated his reasons for leaving the FI in June 1950. He had

. . . arrived at the conviction that in its present form and on the present road there is no future for the organization as at present constituted . . . the contemporary analysis of political events which placed our movement in the vanguard of the working class when the Old Man (Trotsky) was alive has been replaced by an abysmal failure to analyse the great changes following World War 2.

Haston specifically details the following as instances of the ISFI's political bankruptcy:

. . . the incredible thesis of the 'ceiling above which production could not possibly be pushed' and the whole discussion of boom or slump . . .

. . . the fact that India had achieved political freedom and the right to determine its own form of government under the leadership of the Indian bourgeoisie . . . denounced as a denial of the theory of the permanent revolution . . .

five years after the event . . . the beginning of a grudging admission . . . plain to every petty bourgeois politician that capitalism had been overthrown in Eastern Europe.

In China, the FI . . . failed to recognize a revolution when it was in the process of taking place.

In regarding the RCP's legitimate criticisms as threats to Trotskyist orthodoxy, the ISFI not only revealed its own dogmatism but also encouraged this same mentality in the minority faction led by Gerry Healy. This grouping, as we shall see, subsequently established itself as the principal far left grouping in British politics until the late 1960s. Throughout this period it has become increasingly dogmatic and sectarian. The damage it has done to the credibility of Trotskyism is difficult to estimate; but it is beyond doubt that the ISFI (from which it split in 1953) bears much of the responsibility. I shall argue in the next chapters 3 and 4 that 'Healyism' was sufficiently formed by 1947 to warrant correction, but that this was not forthcoming, because until 1953 it complemented the ISFI's own unreconstructed 'Trotskyism'. For the moment, however, we will consider the debates and analyses of the FI on international issues between 1944 and 1950 where these questions are raised incidentally.

INTERNATIONAL PERSPECTIVES

Though it was quite marginal to the main political events of the 1940s, the Fourth International formally recognized its responsibility to come to terms with them in theory. On the international plane the FI's analyses follow the pattern described above in relation to its perspectives for Britain; that is, in 1944 it based itself on Trotsky's more specific prognoses and only reluctantly, and belatedly, revised or rejected them as events proved them wrong. The RCP too began with optimistic and confident forecasts of revolutionary events in which the FI would play the leading role:

For the first time since 1923, this fight between Stalinism and Trotskyism will occur on an entirely different basis, on the basis of a revolutionary wave much more powerful than the one which took place at the end of the first world war, in spite of the weakness of the revolutionary parties and the disintegration of the strongest organisation of counter-revolutionary terror ever known in history.

By August 1945 the RCP claimed that 'The workers of Europe are breaking bourgeois parliamentary politics and social democratic reformism, and are turning to revolutionary politics and communism, though unfortunately at this stage to the Stalinist parties, its caricatured and distorted form'.[30]

So between 1944 and 1945 the RCP leadership came to modify its expectations in recognition of the powerful upsurge of mass support for the Communist parties of France, Italy and Greece. While formally adhering to Trotsky's dictum that the Communist parties were 'counter-revolutionary, through and through', the ISFI, by 1947, could envisage these parties resorting to civil war and articulating 'a real class policy'.[31] This, it was envisaged, would result in the event of a third world war which — being a conflict betwen imperialism and the first workers' state — would soon be transformed into an internationally waged class conflict.

This novel speculation was given its most developed form in the early 1950s by Michel Pablo, the FI's Secretary. For now it is sufficient to note that this 'war-revolution' thesis sat side by side with more orthodox positions. Thus in 1946 the ISFI ruled that 'in the trial of strength which at present characterises the relationship between Imperialism and the USSR only the intervention of the proletarian revolution can prevent the imminent fatal outcome for the latter.[32]

The contradiction between this and the belief in the revolutionary potential of the Communist parties is stark when we recall that, for Trotsky, the revolutions which would save the USSR from reaction would be totally independent of the Stalinists. The ISFI undoubtedly subscribed to Trotsky's views on this matter. Thus in an exchange with Natalia Sedova the (American) SWP argued that

if we leave aside the prospect of workers revolution or such a state of unrest and insurgence as that which followed the first world war . . .then there is no room to doubt that an economic, and, if necessary, a military offensive of the allies against the Soviet Union is predetermined as soon as accounts are finally settled with the Nazis and the Japanese; perhaps even before.[33]

This argument of the SWP in 1945 was reiterated by the ISFI in April 1946: 'the contradictions of the international economic and political situation, and above all the antagonism between the US and the USSR will goad imperialism into once more attempting to bring, within a briefer interval than in the past, the issue to a head via the outbreak of a new world conflict'.[34]

The RCP, on the other hand, had taken a more cautious line as early as their 1945 conference. The main leadership resolution stated that '. . . only on the basis of a complete defeat for the European working class, the total destruction of its organizations and the introduction of a Yankee black reaction could it be possible to regroup the forces of European capitalism for an anti–Russian assault.'

The RCP majority unsuccessfully attempted to amend the FI's international perspectives along these lines at the world conference in 1946.[35] The propensity of the ISFI, at this time, was to stress the negative features of the Soviet Union and its international position. Whereas the RCP acknowledged that '. . . the emergence of Russia from World War II as the second world power was unforeseen by the movement', the ISFI pronounced that Soviet productivity of labour manifested a tendency to decline. Indeed the original draft of the ISFI thesis on Russia declared that

Failing a mass movement capable of coming actively to its support, the USSR incurs the risk of being destroyed in the near future *even without direct military intervention* but simply through the combined economic, political and diplomatic *pressure* and the military *threats* of American and British Imperialism. [My emphasis][36]

Though this was omitted from the final draft, the RCP, with some justice, argued that it expressed the spirit of the ISFI's analysis of 1946. The RCP leadership, on the contrary, predicted 'the speedy reconstruction of the Russian economy'. Such statements earned the RCP the rebuke of 'friendly criticism' towards Stalinism from the ISFI. Yet, as we have remarked, it was the 'Stalinophobic' ISFI which, in 1947, allowed for the Stalinist parties adopting a 'real class policy'.

The contradictory and confused character of the ISFI's analyses of the Soviet Union was determined by several interrelated factors. In the first place the ISFI seems to have adhered to a rather simplistic interpretation of Trotsky's dictum that, in foreign affairs, the Soviet Union is 'counter–revolutionary through and through'. The FI's leadership was equally adamant in following Trotsky's prognosis of the inevitable collapse of the Soviet Union in the absence of European socialist revolutions. Yet, unlike Trotsky, the ISFI had actually witnessed the spread of Soviet power in Eastern Europe and the emergence of the Italian, French and Greek Communist parties as mass organizations. Instead of straightforwardly acknowledging the facts of the new situation, the ISFI combined dogmatic defence of Trotsky's pre–war predictions with Pablo's innovative and speculative generalization concerning the possibility of the CP's becoming genuine revolutionary parties 'under pressure of the masses'. To a certain extent these contradictory positions were simultaneously maintained in the 1940s because the FI failed to formulate a coherent analysis of the Soviet social formation. Its failure in this quarter contributed to its incomprehension concerning the transformation of Eastern Europe from capitalist to non-capitalist status in 1947.

Though Trotsky's analysis of the Soviet Union was more sophisticated than those alternative theories which its 'Friends' and enemies alike put forward, it was deficient in one important respect: its broad sociological categories underlined the absence of any economic analysis. Yet, ultimately, any characterization of the Soviet social formation from a Marxist perspective would have to rest on such a foundation.

The RCP leadership grappled with this problem at the organization's conference in 1946 and brought upon themselves charges of 'revisionism' from the minority. While Haston insisted that the Soviet Union was a 'degenerated workers' state' the arguments he adduced to substantiate this formula belong to theorists of Soviet state capitalism. The RCP leaders argued that 'the state in Russia occupies the same position in relation to the economy as the capitalist to the single enterprise'. They further maintained that commodity production in the Soviet Union has the same character as in the capitalist economies. When asked by the minority, 'Is production for profit the prevailing mode of production in the Soviet Union?' a majority spokesman replied unequivocally in the affirmative.[37]

Significantly the minority did not proffer a systematic alternative analysis, though Lawrence drew attention to the Soviet economic plans which, bureaucratically mismanaged, nevertheless provided the framework for the production of use-values and precluded production for profit and the operation of the law of value.[38] The majority leadership undoubtedly believed that its analysis was orthodox and was quite unconscious of the fact that it had more or less described the workings of a state capitalist economy. The minority were no clearer in that they were unable to demonstrate the contradictions in Haston's argument. Ted Grant — the RCP's leading theoretician — alluded to three tendencies within the organization on this issue: 'the orthodox, the Shachtmanite and left Stalinist'. Of these, 'the orthodox' position was held to belong to the majority and 'the left Stalinist' to the minority. Though of obvious polemical intent, Grant's remarks emphasize the theoretical confusion within the RCP.

This, rather than dishonesty, explains the majority's analysis. In a subsequent debate on this issue Haston argued that to deny the workings of the law of value in the USSR is an innovation and not Trotskyist. To understand these mistakes — which were in part based on the absence of an authoritative account (that is, one written by Trotsky) — it is also necessary to note actual developments within the Soviet Union at this time. The recent introduction of inheritance laws and the system of state bonds, combined with evident stability of the regime may have tempted a 'pessimism' about the Soviet social formation within the ranks of the FI. Certainly there is an overriding emphasis on the negative features of the regime — those, that is, pointing in the direction of a restoration of capitalism. We have already noted this 'Stalinophobia' in the ISFI's theses and how in certain respects the RCP distanced itself from it. But it is also present in Haston's writings and may help to account for his contradictory analysis of the Soviet Union (that is, an economy which is, in all important respects, exhibiting capitalist characteristics but which is called a 'degenerated *workers' state*').

Certainly the RCP majority claimed that 'the capitalist characteristics of this state assume tremendous and growing proportions'. Similarly the ISFI argued in 1947 that the Soviet Union is '. . . a workers' state degenerated to the point where all progressive manifestations of the October conquest are more and more neutralised by the disastrous effects of the Stalinist dictatorship'. The RCP leaders essentially concurred with this description in portraying the USSR as a system in which the 'wage slaves' were 'brutally exploited' by a bureaucracy which devoured a 'growing proportion of the social product'. It is not, therefore, surprising that Grant and Haston briefly flirted with the theory of state capitalism.

Within the RCP, Tony Cliff was the chief exponent of this idea and in August 1949 each member of the organization received a typed copy of his *Russia: A Marxist Analysis* in which the theory is propounded. One convert to this view, writing in July 1974, asserted that 'inside our own party . . . it would be true to say that this position is gaining strength'.[39] However, neither Haston nor Grant ever committed themselves to the theory on paper.[40] In fact Grant took responsibility for rebutting Cliff's views.

In his reply to Cliff, Grant observes that the former nowhere spells out the political consequences which proceed from his state capitalist theory. In particular Cliff's theses are held to be at fault in omitting to make clear whether state capitalism is progressive or reactionary in relation to Western capitalism. Grant also maintained that the theory has consequences for the Leninist conception of the epoch as one of imperialist decay. For if Cliff's account is correct, state capitalism — not socialism — will replace the traditional capitalist economies.[41] Grant further maintains that the state capitalist theory assumes that which it sets out to prove by using concepts fashioned by Marx to analyse capitalism and foisting them upon material (most of it statistical) drawn from Soviet experience in an artificial way.

However Grant did little to counteract Cliff's conclusions. Whereas Cliff argues that the law of value shapes the Soviet economy by virtue of the latter's place in the world economy which is dominated by *capitalist* priorities, Grant wishes to prove that the law of value operates *within* the USSR.[42] Likewise when Grant denies that systematic exploitation began in the USSR after 1928, he does so in order to argue that it *also* operated *before* 1928. Grant concurs with Cliff in identifying the profit motive as the motor force of the Soviet economy and only adds that the economic plan 'abates' the power of the market. In all these respects Grant, probably unwittingly, strengthened the state capitalist case by showing that capitalist priorities were as dominant in the USSR as in the economies dominated by private property. To this extent the development of the SWP — the organization which currently subscribes to the state capitalist theory — can be traced back to a failure of the ISFI and RCP effectively to refute the ideas of its founder, Tony Cliff, in the 1940s.

The FI in the 1940s was apt to give the appearance of an organization whose *raison d'être* required that it emphasize the counter-revolutionary role of the Soviet state even at the cost of obscuring reality. Nowhere is this more evident than in the theses and debates which deal with Eastern Europe. Along with the Chinese revolution this was one of the most important issues of the period, especially for socialists.

During the early days of Soviet occupation of Eastern Europe the FI was clear in characterizing the occupied countries as capitalist. The RCP conference of 1945 also understood that the preservation of capitalism in the 'glacis' (Eastern Europe) was in some way connected with the deals struck by the 'big three' at Teheran and Yalta. In this way 'the Red Army is used as a weapon of counter-revolution in the hands of the Bonapartist bureaucracy.[43] For the RCP this involved the 'plunder' and 'enslavement' of the peoples of Eastern Europe, which facts served to highlight the profoundly non-socialist features of the USSR. As early as July 1946, however, the RCP called upon the ISFI to establish a position on the nature of the Eastern Europe states which would take account of changes introduced by the Soviet Union. By the end of 1947, the ISFI ruled that the glacis was 'moving into a total integration' with the Soviet economy and that this 'necessitates . . . structural assimilation to the latter and the abolition of capitalism'. The ISFI believed that the abolition of frontiers was *crucial* to this process of assimilation but that the process itself was only a tendency doomed, ultimately, to frustration. For

while capable of imposing on the bourgeoisie, through diplomatic and military pressure, certain measures contrary to its interests (the 'Molotov Plan') the bureaucracy will, in the long run, prove to be incapable of successfully carrying out a reliable structural assimilation which demands the destruction of capitalism. *This can only be achieved on a large scale by the proletarian revolution.*[44] [my emphasis]

To leave the sections in no doubt the ISFI pointed out that 'to deny the capitalist nature of these countries . . . means seriously to consider the historic possibility of a destruction of capitalism by "terror from above" without the revolutionary intervention of the masses'.[45]

Thus the criterion 'revolutionary intervention of the masses' was invoked by the ISFI as the determinant of the character of those social formations. This is surprising since Trotsky had argued, during the Soviet-Finnish war, that *failure* to transform property relations in occupied Finland would have raised doubts about the existence of progressive elements in the Soviet Union.[46] Though he profoundly disapproved of Stalin's aggression Trotsky *expected,* in other words, the sovietization of Finland. The FI, on the other hand, argued that 'the reactionary features of the Russian occupation by far outweigh its progressive features' despite the fact that statization of property was proceeding apace when these lines were written in 1947.

The second world congress of April 1948 belatedly acknowledged these developments but interpreted them as follows: '[The] mixed corporations, Soviet-owned stock companies, preferential trade treaties, etc. [are] forms of capitalist exploitation . . . The nationalized sector itself continues to retain a capitalist structure'.[47]

All these states — including Yugoslavia — were said to be nothing other than 'extreme forms of Bonapartism'. The inability of the ISFI to comprehend the process of transformation persisted. By 1949 it argued that the entire experience was ephemeral. Thus:

The appearance of transitional regimes of the buffer zones type . . . merely gives expression to the interlude character of the historic period proceeding from 1943 up to the present: an interlude between the low point of the world-wide decline of the proletarian revolution and the new world revolutionary upsurge which has only been seen in its rough outlines up to the present; an interlude between the Second World War and the final clash between imperialism and the USSR. Only within the framework of this limited interlude do the buffer zones and all the phenomena associated with it appear in their true light as provisional and temporary.[48]

In fact by invoking 'the new world revolutionary upsurge' the ISFI was merely evading an analysis of Eastern Europe. The RCP, on the contrary, attempted to amend the *Draft Theses on The Fourth International and Stalinism* to take cognizance of the actual transformation of Eastern Europe in 1947.[49] But this failed to budge the ISFI. Only the Stalin-Tito split, which became publicly known in the summer of 1948, caused the ISFI to revise its analysis — and then only in relation to Yugoslavia.

Even in 1949 the ISFI continued to regard Tito as a typical Stalinist and referred to '. . . the undeniable existence of a police regime in Yugoslavia'. But within six months of this statement the secretary of the FI was hoping that '. . . if the Tito regime does not compromise with imperialism but on the contrary develops *a more consistently revolutionary line* . . . we may yet witness the debacle of Stalinism in the years to come on a vast scale'.[50]

The job for revolutionaries, according to Pablo, was to 'assist in its (Titoism's) favourable evolution'. This completely overlooked Tito's fearsome record as an anti-Trotskyist which, as Ted Grant observed for the RCP, had even been denounced by the Cominform. Undeterred by this the ISFI directed an open letter to the Central Committee of the YCP and the FI's theoretical journal published an article in which the concept of permanent revolution was raised into an objective process above questions of revolutionary strategy and leadership so that the YCP could be accommodated to it.[51] Tito's opposition to Stalin became proof of Tito's adherence to revolutionary politics and this became proof of how Stalinism could become revolutionary 'under pressure of the masses'. Furthermore Titoism 'could very well become the springboard from which the Fourth International will launch out to win the masses'.[52]

The RCP developed a completely different, more sober analysis, of Titoism. Grant argued[53] that Titoism was an expression of Yugoslav cultural and national independence which had been able to come to the fore because the Yugoslav revolution had taken place independently of the USSR and was therefore more able to resist

Soviet encroachments. But this should not, argued Grant, prevent the FI from recognizing the YCP as a bureaucratic machine totally intolerant of organized opposition. On another occasion the majority leadership of the RCP argued that 'our exposure of the bureaucratic manner of the expulsion of the YCP (from Cominform) must not mean that we enter the camp of Tito . . . who . . . remains Stalinist in method and training'. They argued that the ISFI open letter to Tito was of an opportunist nature and all the more so considering the ISFI's rejection of an RCP amendment which wanted acknowledgement of the non-capitalist nature of Eastern Europe at the second world congress.

Only in 1951 did the ISFI accept the designation 'deformed workers' state' for each of the Eastern European countries. While it is true that some, like Hansen and Cochran of the American SWP, had reached this position earlier they had done so empirically — merely by observing the similarities between the Soviet and Eastern European states. The basis for the FI's tardiness in this matter seems to have been the belief that a Soviet bureaucracy capable of transforming the relations of production in the 'buffer zone' constituted a different political entity from that characterized by Trotsky as being 'counter-revolutionary through and through'. Ironically, Trotsky anticipated this objection and had already provided a resolution of the apparent contradiction.[54].

CONCLUSIONS

Despite the obvious shortcomings in its analyses, the RCP leadership showed signs of attempting a genuine understanding of the main economic and political problems which it faced in the 1940s. However, it was prevented from pursuing this path by its own minority which, aided and abetted by the ISFI, invoked a spurious Trotskyist orthodoxy in order to remove the Haston leadership. The eventual splitting of the RCP — by the ISFI — soon led to the demoralization and departure of many supporters of the old majority. Others — Haston included — opted for an entrism conceived as a necessary retrenchment to enable the small forces of British Trotskyism to withstand the long years of isolation and hostility which they foresaw as a consequence of the developing cold war and economic boom. This perspective, according to the ISFI, threatened the whole programme of the Fourth International.[55] In this way the international leadership reiterated its conviction in the imminence of economic catastrophe which it apparently construed as an essential tenet of Trotskyism.

By their insistence on regarding departures from this faith as departures from orthodoxy, by further claiming that such deviations represented the influence of alien class forces, and by their promotion in Britain of Healy — a particularly enthusiastic champion of this approach — in these ways the ISFI created an atmosphere congenial to Healy's subsequent authoritarian hegemony and theoretical sterility. With the accession of the RCP minority, the promise of a more critical, relatively dynamic Marxism was crushed by the late 1940s. Not until the late 1960s did it show signs of re-emerging.

Whereas the RCP was groping towards recognition of the new economic reality of post-war Britain, the FI as a whole held fast to a crude breakdown theory in which economic collapse was seen as a sufficient precondition for a tremendous explosion of revolutionary consciousness. By this mechanism the FI imagined itself propelled out of obscurity and into the vanguard of the world revolution. The RCP, on the other hand, recognized the novelty of American economic hegemony and adumbrated the part played by nationalizations in establishing economic stability in Britain. While the FI adhered to Trotsky's early speculation which expected wars between the rival capitalisms of America and Britain, the RCP recognized the enlightened self-interest represented by Marshall Aid and its role in stabilizing the capitalist world economy. The RCP was likewise prepared to face the facts concerning the survival of the USSR, the sovietization of Eastern Europe and the emergence of mass Communist parties in Western Europe. It also recognized the significance of Indian independence and the Chinese revolution. It is possible that had the FI, for example, faced the former question the Trotskyists would have been among the first Marxists to revise Lenin's theory of imperialism and modify or reject the many practical stances which emerge from it. In the event they have been among the last to do this.

However this is mere speculation. What is clear is that the RCP episode of British Trotskyism was chiefly characterized by a major tactical and strategic disorientation. Not only were Trotsky's pre-war calculations found wanting, and new political problems hard to resolve by orthodox formulae (such as a characterization of the so-called 'glacis' that would be consonant with Trotsky's depiction of a 'degenerated workers' state'), but, more fundamentally, the orthodoxy to which the Trotskyists adhered pertained to *party* political behaviour and had little of relevance to say to a becalmed sect. Moveover the bulk of the Bolshevik-Comintern theoretical legacy assumed the imminence of dramatic revolutionary events, as did Trotsky's. By 1949 at the very latest, Britain could clearly be seen to have stabilized. For those who wished to preserve the Trotskyist legacy without alteration, as for those, equally, who recognized its shortcomings, entrism was the common solution. Entering the Labour Party was tantamount to accepting that Trotsky was wrong and that Trotskyists were marginal to working-class politics in Britain. But the Trotskyists showed no recognition of this. Indeed as the next chapter relates, the gap between received theory and actual developments merely resulted in cognitive dissonance and related attempts to find short cuts to political prominence, of which entrism is merely the most common example.

3

The Split in the Fourth International

The foundation of the Fourth International was predicated upon the political bankruptcy and collapse of Stalinism in an epoch of the decay and disintegration of capitalism. And yet out of the Second World War there issued a number of developments which indicated the spread and consolidation of Stalinism. In France and Italy the Communist parties were transformed into mass organizations and emerged as heroes of the resistance and the liberation. In Eastern Europe the Red Army occupation became, from 1947, the basis of statization of business property. In Yugoslavia and China genuine revolutions were accomplished by Communist parties loyal to Stalinism (if not to Stalin). At the same time the political influence of the Fourth International remained negligible while the capitalist countries of Western Europe survived both fascism and the post-war crises to begin a long period of stable social and economic development.

We have seen that the FI resisted acknowledgement of these facts throughout the 1940s and encouraged fidelity to a bogus orthodoxy — especially in sections, such as the British RCP, which were groping towards a fresh analysis of the post-war situation. I will show now that this orthodoxy was replaced in the early 1950s by a rather desperate political opportunism when it was forced to take cognizance of the developments mentioned above. But the British section of the FI (now led by Healy) determinedly resisted all and any innovations in policy and perspectives and actually broke with the FI in 1953.

The ostensible source of this schism, then, is on the theoretical plane. In February 1951 Michel Pablo began the process in an article entitled, 'Where are we going?' published in the FI's theoretical journal *Quatrième Internationale*. The theses propounded by the FI's Secretary were not, however, brought into the preparatory discussions for the Third World Congress which was held later that same year. Yet Pablo's analysis of Stalinism and the world situation since 1947 became the subject of bitter contention within all sections of the FI. It is necessary, therefore, to review its main arguments.

Pablo begins with the claim that his article is a further exposition of ideas contained in the document *Theses on International Perspectives* which was adopted by the second world congress. He characterizes the world situation in terms of an antagonistic division between the capitalist and non-capitalist blocs. The first of these, says Pablo, exhibits '. . . basic, chronic disequilibrium'.[1] This capitalist sector is further undermined by the break up of the colonial sector of imperialism and the termination of the economic unity of capitalist Europe since the foundation of the Soviet buffer zone. Against this side of the world equation Pablo asserts the growing political and economic power of the Soviet Union. In so doing Pablo inverts the FI's previous stress on the crippling weakness of the Soviet economy and the USSR's vulnerability on the international political plane. This imbalance, he argues cannot be set right by restoring the equilibrium of capitalism because there is 'no possibility' for this 'without restoring a world market embracing the lost territories'.[2] But, for Pablo, the growing colonial revolution rules out this consideration in serious calculations. Furthermore, the Korean war illustrates the disadvantages of imperialism at '. . . the level of social relations and class relations . . . internationally'.

The only way the capitalist world can end this period of unstable equilibrium, continues Pablo, is by precipitating a war. 'Consequently', says Pablo '. . . discussion among Marxists cannot take place over the question of whether war is inevitable or not, so long as the capitalist regime remains standing, but is limited to questions of how soon, the conditions for the outbreak of war, as well as over the nature and consequences of war'.

Indeed, Pablo argues that panic and rearmament may force the USA to '. . . prefer war with all its risks to a new retreat on the Korean model . . .' within two or three years. However this war, in Pablo's model of a world divided simply into capitalist and non-capitalist sectors, will from the beginning become an international civil war, especially in Europe and Africa: 'These continents would rapidly pass over under the control of the Soviet bureaucracy, of the Communist Parties, or of the revolutionary masses'. So that 'war under these conditions, with the existing relationship of forces on the international area, would essentially be Revolution'. According to Pablo:

These two conceptions of *Revolution* and of *War,* far from being in opposition or being differentiated as two significantly different stages of development, *are approaching each other more closely and becoming so inter-linked as to be almost indistinguishable under certain circumstances and at certain times.* In their stead it is the conception of Revolution-War, of War-Revolution, which is emerging and upon which *the perspectives and orientation of revolutionary Marxists in our epoch should rest.*

According to Pablo, the leadership of the masses during the unfolding of war-revolution will be provided by the Communist parties in most countries. This is because

the Yugoslav affair as well as the moral and victory of the Chinese revolution, also the unfolding colonial revolutions (Korea, Vietnam, Burma, Malaya, the Philippines) have demonstrated that the Communist parties retain the possibility *jn certain* circumstances, of roughly outlining a revolutionary orientation, that is to say of finding themselves compelled to engage in a struggle for power.

In Pablo's view, the Communist parties are forced to respond in a revolutionary way to mass pressure when the circumstances dictate it. Trotskyists, especially those in the Third World, must aid this process, says Pablo, by playing the part of a 'left opposition' to the Communist parties, giving them critical support. Pablo insists that they must not regard a victory for the local Communist Party as synonymous 'with a pure and simple victory of the Soviet bureaucracy'. According to Pablo, the fate of Stalinism itself will be settled by war-revolution but '. . . this transformation will probably take an entire historical period of several centuries and will in the meantime be filled with forms and regimes transitional between capitalism and socialism and necessarily deviating from "pure" forms and norms'.

Initial reaction to these theses varied considerably within the FI. The political committee of the American SWP objected only to the notion of centuries of deformed workers' states.[3] The 'majority' of the French section, however, submitted a comprehensive critique which claimed to detect 'abandonment of a class strategy' and the 'liquidation' of the FI in Pablo's analysis.[4] This latter charge arose because Pablo proposed a new tactic: 'entrism *sui generis*' or deep entry by the Trotskyists within the Communist parties where these had the support of significant sections of the proletariat as in Italy and France. The majority of the central committee of the French section were suspended from the FI some months after the third world congress when they refused to lead the Partie Communiste Internationale (PCI) into the PCF. This authoritarian action of the ISFI was supported by the American SWP.[5] Cannon, the leader of the SWP, argued that independent party work was neither primary, nor even the most essential political commitment of the FI. Entrism *sui generis* was, therefore, the correct tactic because, says Cannon '. . . the French Stalinist workers, by the logic of the irreversible international trend of things, must be impelled more and more on a radical course'. Far from being revisionist, Pablo's position, according to Cannon, was 'completely Trotskyist'.[6]

In June 1951 Pablo further expounded his views concerning the duration of deformed workers' states.[7] The idea that states of the type in Eastern Europe would last for centuries, he explains, was intended to suggest that the construction of socialism would consume a whole historical period, it was not intended to imply a pessimistic view on the expected longevity of Stalinism. Ernest Mandel also entered the debate in 1951 in order to focus on other features of Pablo's political perspectives.[8] He too identified the Third World War as an imminent prospect and, therefore, an urgent political problem. Mandel concurred with Pablo's estimation of the new international balance of political forces since 1943. He observes, too, that all the essential reflections in Pablo's initial statement were present in the theses of the second world congress. But Mandel sought also to emphasize the negative aspects of Stalinism. The Yugoslav and Chinese revolutions, together with developments in East Asia, accentuate the crisis of Stalinism via polycentrism. For Mandel the crisis of Stalinism is now generalized and chronic: '. . . it is because the new revolutionary wave contains in embryo the destruction of the Stalinist parties as such that we ought to be much closer today to the Communist workers'.[9] Mandel, like Pablo, was certain that a powerful upsurge of the masses could push the Communist parties to the left 'up to the conquest of power'. But Mandel draws back from attributing a revolutionary role to the CPs and does not even mention entrism *sui generis*.[10] What, then, did the third world congress actually agree on?

The 'Theses on orientation and perspectives'[11] committed the

Fourth International to the following political position:

(1) Imperialism is preparing for a world war. From the start this war will be transformed into a civil war.

(2) The Communist parties are not reformist; they bear a contradictory character based on (a) allegiance to Moscow and (b) a genuine mass base to which they are potentially responsive. The Fourth International must 'penetrate' this mass base.

(3) Where there are no small Stalinist or reformist parties the FI will strive to become the revolutionary leadership directly.

(4) Where reformist influence is massive, as in Great Britain, the Fourth International will 'integrate itself in these organisations' to 'develop a conscious left-wing in their ranks'.

(5) Where the majority of class conscious workers support the Communist Party '. . . our organizations, necessarily independent, should orient towards more systematic work among the ranks of these parties and the masses they influence'.

(6) In Europe the FI's supporters, where possible, should enter the Communist parties.

(7) Entrism *sui generis* should also be adopted in Asia where the CPs lead the revolutionary elements in the masses.

Despite a certain ambiguity between points (5) and (6) — (is the 'independent' commitment compatible with entrism?) — the position adopted by the third world congress does not differ from that outlined in Pablo's initial argument. The refusal of the PCI to bury itself within the PCF earned its leadership suspension from the FI, suggesting that the latter had a very clear and fixed understanding on the question of entrism *sui generis*. And the tenth plenum of the IEC in February 1952 instructed all the national sections (save those where Stalinist or reformist parties did not dominate the labour movement) to adopt this tactic. Pablo made the position very clear in an essay called 'The building of the revolutionary party'.[12]

In this he argues that independent party work is appropriate only in a limited number of countries (Latin America, Ceylon, USA, India, the Middle East and the African Colonies). In Bolivia and Ceylon, he advises, 'power is within reach'. But in countries such as Britain entrism in the mass reformist party is now referred to by Pablo as the correct *strategy*. This is because 'we are entering them (reformist parties) in order to remain there for a long time banking on the great possibility, which exists, of seeing those parties, placed under new conditions, develop centrist tendencies which will lead a whole stage of radicalisation of the masses, and of the objective revolutionary processes in their respective countries'. Thus the slogan for Britain must be 'Labour to power on a socialist platform'.

Where CPs are mass organizations, entrism must account for their authoritarian internal regimes. This necessitates, argues Pablo, independent organizations alongside the entrist group. Since, under pressure of the Third World War, enormous centrist currents can be expected to emerge from within the CPs, the situation doubly requires parallel open organizations to complement the work of the entrists.

The entire internal and external work of the Trotskyist organisations will thus have as its aim to speed up the radicalisation of the Stalinist workers and their development of a revolutionary leadership emerging basically from within their own movement through the experience of the struggles to come and the tasks which these struggles will impose on the mass of Stalinist militants.

Though Pablo envisaged that entrism *sui generis* would require the simultaneous existence of an open party he also foresaw, somewhat mysteriously, the need to give up the sale of *Unite* and *Verité* (organs of the Italian and French Trotskyists respectively). Such reasoning was cited against Pablo by opponents who saw it as evidence of the Secretary's duplicity and cunning: to propose liquidation of the Trotskyist press — was this not the first step towards liquidation of the whole Trotskyist movement?

Certainly, *interpretations* of the theses of the third world congress varied within the International. Political tendencies emerged within the SWP and the British section which claimed that the leaderships of these organizations were effectively ignoring decisions taken at the congress on the new tactical line. The leadership of the American SWP became convinced that the dissidents within its ranks were 'instigated in Paris'[13] (i.e. by Pablo). Yet J. P. Cannon also stood by his earlier endorsement of Pablo's theses; he simply rejected the latter's 'special interpretation' of them. 'In my opinion', said Cannon, 'it is not a matter of withdrawing support from a general line, but of explaining what we understand by it.'[14] According to the SWP leadership, this special interpretation was one which encouraged a soft approach to Stalinism now that the CPs were considered capable of genuine revolutionary action and leading a 'healthy' socialist revolution. In the first instance, however, the SWP could find no evidence for their allegations apart from the statements of the so-called Cochran-Clarke fraction within the American section. There was no proof that Pablo was promoting them. As for the British section, its leadership advanced no independent arguments on this issue at all and contented itself in following the course taken by J.P. Cannon.

The ISFI's statements on the uprising in East Berlin in 1953 hardened the suspicions of those, like Cannon and Healy, who, according to some contemporary Trotskyists, were already searching for sinister explanations for their domestic problems.[15] Articles by Pablo, Cochran, Clarke (USA) and Lawrence (Britain) which seemed to stress the mildness of the Soviet represssion of the East German workers were taken as proof of the ISFI's capitulation to Stalinism. In the American section, J.P. Cannon and his followers forced the Cochran-Clarke faction to leave the SWP in September 1953. Pablo's culpability for the conflict within the SWP and the Healy group (where J. Lawrence challenged Healy's grip over the organization) was inferred because he refused to endorse Cannon's fight against the SWP's dissident faction.[16]

Though the documentary material can offer no evidence either to prove or refute the allegation that Pablo acted as an international organizing centre for his 'agents' in the national sections of the FI, it is possible to settle the matter of his supposed adaptation to Stalinism. In 1953 he published an article called 'The rise and decline of Stalinism'[17] just a few months after the appearance of Isaac Deutscher's *Russia After Stalin* with which it had a great deal in common.[18]

Pablo, like Deutscher, was 'optimistic' regarding the extent of the disintegration of Stalinism both within and outside the Soviet Union. In 'The rise and decline of Stalinism', Pablo locates the demise of Stalinism, in three interconnected areas. First the Malenkov reforms were cited as evidence of internal thaw following Stalin's death. Second, the external consequences of these reforms on the European Communist parties were said to constitute 'a relaxation of the brake' which Kremlin control had previously represented and which had prevented the CPs from a more responsive orientation to their particular national movements. Third, Pablo argued that the European Communist parties were being penetrated by 'ideas opposed to the interests of the Soviet bureaucracy'.[19] Pablo set these changes within the context of the fundamental change in the balance of world forces which, he earlier claimed, had taken place since 1943. For him it was the totality of these political changes which had induced de-Stalinization. For instance, these objective changes had undermined the Stalinist policy of peaceful co-existence which had purported to take advantages in the field of foreign policy from divisions between the capitalist countries. This had been made obsolescent by the rise of the colonial revolution which had stimulated 'a world imperialist united front against the revolution' based on the post-war hegemony of the USA.[20] The disruption of the Soviet *modus vivendi* with the West was significant, argued Pablo, because 'the disruption of the basic equilibriums of Stalinist Bonapartism undermines the very foundations of the bureaucratic dictatorship in the Soviet Union'. For Pablo the deepening and maturation of this disruption within the Soviet Union was assured by the growing pace of the colonial revolution which made Stalinist conservatism untenable.[21] To this radicalization of East–West relations, Pablo added the objective processes at work within the USSR (the reconstitution and growth of the Soviet proletariat, the development of the productive forces and the advent of mass education) which would also undermine Stalinism.

Pablo argued that none of this made the FI superfluous or even called for changes in its programme. He perceived that the Malenkov reforms attempted, merely '. . . to establish the dictatorship on a *broader* basis, to associate broader sections of the bureaucracy more directly with the exercise of power by guaranteeing them against arbitary purges'. For Pablo, the Malenkov reforms attempted to reduce internal contradictions by buying off the workers with higher levels of consumption and material prosperity. If anything this made '. . . the task of a new political revolution in the Soviet Union . . . more burning than ever'. Moreover, Pablo argued, this was being made more, rather than less possible because 'the conditions are being created for the reconstruction and the upsurge of the Bolshevik-Leninist party in the Soviet Union'.

Pablo was equally sanguine about the opportunities, created by these developments, for the accelerated demise of the Western Communist parties in countries, like Britain, where the CP was already small. Here it was possible 'completely to eliminate Stalinist influence'.[22] But

in countries where the Communist parties are a majority in the working class, they can, in certain exceptional conditions (advanced disintegration of the possessing classes) and under pressure of very powerful revolutionary uprisings in the masses, be led to project a revolutionary orientation counter to the Kremlin's directives, without abandoning the political and theoretical baggage inherited from Stalinism'

This would, however be '. . . a gradual process, a disintegration, molecular for an entire period, of the Stalinist ideas inside these parties, as well as of the bureaucratic relations which extend from the Kremlin down to the ranks of these parties'.

Before the ideas contained in 'The rise and decline of Stalinism' were approved by the fourth world congress (1954), the SWP and the Healy Group in Britain had already declared war on them by forming the International *Committee* of the FI (ICFI) in November 1953. With the French 'majority' and the Swiss and New Zealand sections, Cannon and Healy refused to engage in the discussions preceding the world congress or to adhere to the positions of the third world congress, which they had helped to create. Instead they declared themselves opposed to the 'Pablo clique' and firmly stated, that in so doing, they expressed the views of the vast majority of organized Trotskyists.[23] The ISFI formally requested of Healy that he should '. . . abstain from any organisational measures in opposition to the comrades in [his] section who defend, as they ought, as [he] ought to do [himself] first of all, the line and discipline of the International'.[24] In the event Healy's 'impulsive and authoritarian temperament'[25] led him to take organizational measures.[26] The attitude of the ICFI was summed up by Cannon who said: 'Its stated objectives are not the "reform" of a movement which needs no reformation but rather the re-affirmation of the accepted programme and the removal of a usurping secretarial apparatus by administrative action'.[27]

The decision, made by the SWP, to fight for the removal of Michel Pablo, was avowedly based on its rejection of the latter's theoretical revisionism. Yet we have shown that Pablo's ideas were accepted by the SWP and the Healy group at the third world congress. Further, the SWP leaders evinced no sympathy, let alone support, for the French majority when it took an early stand against 'Pabloism'. J.P. Cannon then maintained that Pablo was 'completely Trotskyist'. Even when Healy and Cannon began to have second thoughts, these were privately expressed and took the form of objections to idiosyncratic interpretations of Pablo's theses. Indeed as opposition hardened, the splitters were increasingly inclined to read between the lines and suspect tendentious motives or discover cryptic suggestions in the theses of the ISFI. All of this suggests that the splitters were fishing for 'theoretical' justifications for the split.

Pablo was accused of having exaggerated the scope of the Malenkov concessions and 'The rise and decline of Stalinism' was also found guilty of recommending entrism in the Communist parties of Eastern Europe. This, it was alleged, ran counter to the orthodox position of arguing that a political revolution was necessary in such countries, for it meant that Trotskyists would become members of organizations which hold state power and which constitute '. . . the direct and principal oppressor of the working masses'.[28] Apart from this one, serious, objection to Pablo's argument, the SWP were more concerned with

. . . the recent writings of comrades Pablo and Clarke [which] go beyond the stated positions on 'The rise and deline of Stalinism' . . . but the point to be emphasized is that the resolution contains or at least indicates the political premises for their more extreme conclusions. These premises are not clearly and fully expressed in all respects. But they are there.[29]

Here, the SWP refers to the writings by Pablo and Clarke in the theoretical journal *Fourth International* — writings which represented only their own speculative opinions and not those of the ISFI. Clarke argued that the self-reform of the Stalinist bureaucracy was possible, while Pablo merely addressed the same problem in the form of a question.[30] But merely by posing the question Pablo, as far as the SWP was concerned, implied a revisionist answer.

Clearly the individual musings of Pablo and Clarke could not justify an organizational split in the FI. Even if, as claimed by the SWP, these private opinions were in some way the logical outcome of certain interpretations of ISFI official theses, these were not grounds for a split unless there was reason to suppose that the matter could not be resolved by discussions within the FI. It is here that Pablo's record of settling ideological, and even tactical, disputes within the national sections by administrative measures is relevant to the 1953 dispute.

Though both Cannon and Healy supported Pablo's interventions in the British RCP and French PCI, they were likely to view a similar move against themselves with foreboding. That they suspected that this would happen is shown by their correspondence. Healy, for example, argued that Pablo '. . . proceeds with all the old Cominternist vices. His methods sickened me to the point that it almost made me physically unwell . . . they want an International of spineless creatures . . .'[31]

Healy came to this conclusion because, he alleged, Pablo attempted to bribe him into a political break with J.P. Cannon.[32] Since the SWP was prevented by the Voorhis Act from direct participation in the International, they relied on Sam Gordon (their representative in Britain) for information regarding its internal affairs. Gordon and Healy collaborated closely during the early 1950s and, in an atmosphere of suspicion and factionalism, anecdotes and gossip, transmitted by them to the SWP, were likely to confirm the latter's doubts about Pablo. These doubts sprang, in the first instance, from Pablo's apparently benevolent attitude towards the Cochran-Clarke faction which challenged the SWP leadership. It is this which explains the Cannon leadership's contradictory position: having supported the Third World Congress theses they objected to 'special' interpretations once the faction within the SWP came to champion them.

Thus Cannon simultaneously compared Pablo's methods with those of the Comintern[33] and proposed (on such an assumption) a most naïve strategy with which to combat him at the fourth world congress. This was, namely '. . . to formulate the documents for the Fourth World Congress in such a way that there can be no possible misunderstanding as to what they really mean'.[34]

Between this statement (of September 1953) and November 1953 the SWP arrived at the decision to boycott the Fourth World Congress because '. . . they will not permit a democratic Congress'. It was only at this point, when the decision to form the ICFI had been made, that the SWP, for the first time, openly stated its political differences with the ISFI. In its 'Open Letter', the SWP objected to the following features of Pabloism:

(1) the existence of '. . . an uncontrolled, secret, personal faction in the administration of the Fourth International which has abandoned the basic programme of Trotskyism';
(2) the idea that revolutions inevitably give rise to deformed workers' states; and that these last for centuries;
(3) the ridicule of the struggle to build independent revolutionary socialist parties;
(4) the belief that the Stalinist bureaucracy will reform itself under pressure of the masses;
(5) and the 'Statement' of the International Secretariat of the FI on the Berlin uprising which demonstrates its authors' Stalinist sympathies.

The authors of the Open Letter quote from the ISFI Statement to demonstrate this latter argument thus:

. . . the Soviet leaders and those of the various 'People's Democracies' and the Communist Parties could no longer falsify or ignore the profound meaning of these events. They have been obliged to continue along the road of still more ample and genuine concessions to avoid risking alienating themselves forever from support by the masses and from provoking still stronger explosions in the immediate future and, if possible, to effect a transition 'in a cold fashion' from the present situation to a situation more favourable for the masses.[36]

For the SWP the above indicated that the ISFI was taking a line more sympathetic to the leaders of the USSR than to the Berlin workers. It regarded this Statement as symptomatic of strong revisionist tendencies in Pablo's politics. Indeed the SWP argued that '. . . the lines of cleavage between Pablo's revisionism and orthodox Trotskyism are so deep that no compromise is possible either politically or organizationally'.[37] The SWP's intransigence as revealed in this statement typified the approach of both sides to this doctrinal dispute and made a split in the FI inevitable. The habit of regarding difference of interpretation or of emphasis as representative (epiphenomena) of different class approaches seems to have been widespread within the FI. This belief or practice obtruded again when tempers had cooled and the principal parties to the dispute were ready for reconciliation. As the next chapter reveals, the British Trotskyists — junior partners of the SWP in the 1953 clash — had become the most dogmatic champions of this class reductionism by the 1960s. However, it remains for me to discuss the wider implications of the Pablo episode.

CONCLUSIONS

Pablo's war-revolution theses were not, in themselves very remarkable. In chapter 2 we noted their first appearance — and general acclamation — at the second world congress. With the death of Stalin, Pablo was converted to the 'optimism' which characterized Isaac Deutscher's contemporaneous analyses of Soviet domestic politics. He then sought to fuse the war-revolution theses with the 'thaw' in international Stalinism. Some of these ideas — as the majority of the French section were quick to point out — *could* be interpreted in such a way as to violate central shibboleths of Trotskyism. Thus the vision of 'centuries of deformed workers' states' could negate the Trotskyist project of building new revolutionary parties to conduct a political revolution in the countries of the Eastern bloc. Entrism *sui generis* could have 'liquidationist' implications for the FI.

As we have seen, the leadership of the French PCI was summarily suspended for its objections to Pabloism while the eventual splitters pronounced the latter 'completely Trotskyist'. This reminds us that Cannon (SWP) and Healy (The Club) were prepared to sanction the authoritarianism of the ISFI in removing the democratically elected majorities of national sections with which they happened to disagree. Indeed the technique used against the PCI replicated that pioneered against the British RCP: the minority faction was recognized as the official section.[38] Familiarity with this authoritarianism of the ISFI may explain the conversion of Healy and Cannon to an anti-Pablo stance *once they themselves were faced with factions claiming fidelity to the Pablo line.* This is, at any rate, the theory advanced by many within the far left today.[39] This explanation has the merit of showing why the violent doctrinal dispute which ostensibly caused the split was apparently forgotten when the FI eventually re-unified; i.e. the real cause — suspicion of Pablo's organizational manoeuvrings — had been removed with the departure of Pablo himself. An explanation which stresses the primacy of narrow organizational considerations also accounts for the *rapid* conversion of the SWP from regarding Pabloism as benign ('completely Trotskyist') to depicting his theses as totally revisionist ('abandoning the basic programme of Trotskyism'). In this view Cannon et al were converted to an 'anti' position because the Cochran-Clarke faction of the SWP was perceived to be a puppet manipulated by Pablo for the latter's self-aggrandisement.

It is difficult to settle this matter by reference to the relevant documents though the circumstantial evidence cited suggests the precedence of organizational factors in causing the split. Especially in the case of the British section — which made no contribution to the dispute at the doctrinal level — Healy's fear of losing personal ascendancy is in my view likely to account for the anti-Pablo campaign. The ideas advanced by Pablo are of more interest to me as another attempt by the FI to discover an 'objective process' or mechanism which would do for the organization what Trotsky's pre-war predictions had failed to do: namely to catapult the FI into a position of proletarian leadership. It seems that the FI leadership required visions of impending catastrophe both to satisfy its quest for a *raison d'être* and remain faithful to key elements of the Bolshevist-Trotskyist legacy.

The dispute recounted here is also significant in respect of another matter. The ferocious concentration displayed on questions of conflicting textual interpretations reflects an introversion which is perhaps the result of the FI's marginal role in real politics. Perhaps the internecine disputes of the early 1950s are simply *ersatz* revolutionary politics or a compensation for the impotency of Trotskyists to affect the course of events. Certainly there is detected a growing tendency to turn to matters of theoretical and programmatic hair-splitting in search of a solution for the practical problems of political isolation. This may also contribute to the greater intensity and frequency of authoritarian actions within the Trotskyist camp.

4

The Ascendancy of Healyite Orthodoxy

THE CLUB

The RCP was destroyed by its failure to achieve any serious and developing implantation in the working class. But this demise was accelerated by the sterile and largely misconceived factional struggles within it. These were able to consume the energies of its membership and ultimately demoralize its leadership because they were fuelled by the ISFI which patronized and elevated the minority led by Gerry Healy. The success of the latter tendency was based on its advocacy of entrism and this inaugurated a lengthy period in which British Trotskyists worked within the Labour Party.

Initially this tactic was justified by reference to an anticipated upsurge in class consciousness which, its promoters argued, would find organized expression within the Labour Party. From December 1948 the entrists, self-styled 'the Club', published *Socialist Outlook* which addressed itself to the Labour left via attacks on the party's right wing. (The minority faction had allowed the RCP's entrist journal *Militant* to run down. The last issue of *Socialist Appeal* was in July 1949.) The difficulties involved in maintaining a Marxist approach while doing this, however, are reflected in the deteriorating politics of the Club's newspaper. While *Socialist Outlook* managed to obtain the patronage of social democrats such as Bessie Braddock, it did so only by adapting to the Labour milieu.[1] The old RCP majority had predicted this development as an inevitable danger of entrism, though they too opted for this tactic in

1949 as the lesser of the evils confronting the organization.[2]

Healy demanded, however, a majority on the executive bodies of the Club on the grounds that his minority faction had been proved correct in demanding entrism since the mid-1940s. Although this hegemony was supposed to be a temporary arrangement pending the establishment of a fully democratic regime at the Club's 1950 congress, Healy's leadership proved to be incompatible with any internal dissent. *Before the congress was convened* the executive committee of the Club began a series of expulsions.[3] Among those who left of their own accord were adherents of Tony Cliff's state capitalist theory of the USSR. Partly in consequence of entrism and partly because the Club took the orthodox position of supporting North Korea (a 'deformed workers' state') in its war against South Korea, *Socialist Outlook* suspended the usual Trotskyist propaganda against Stalinism. Under these circumstances, the theory of state capitalism, 'which had hardly caused a ripple' in 1947, gained adherents.[4] The ideological confusion of the Healy leadership is attested by the fact that in 1950 it was also publicizing the revolutionary socialist credentials of Tito. Yet it was precisely at this time that Tito revealed the true nature of his anti-Stalinism by voting for neutrality in the United Nations' debates on the Korean war. Though they held the same position, the one — Tito — was hailed as a revolutionary socialist while the other — Cliff — was regarded as a renegade.[5]

From 1950 adherence to the orthodox analysis of the Soviet Union became a *sine qua non* of membership of the Club. Healy explained the emergence of the Socialist Review Group as a capitulation by those who could not withstand the pressures of the cold war as these developed during the Korean conflict. In fact, of course, Cliff's theory pre-dates this though the cold war, combined with conditions of full employment and growing material prosperity, did permit Western governments to mobilize the population against communism — especially as this was firmly equated with Stalinism. These adverse conditions go some way in explaining the low profile approach of the Club itself. For as Haston and Grant had argued, retrenchment via entrism was the only realistic perspective as an alternative to sectarian isolation.

But the Club viewed matters differently. Having failed to locate the rising class consciousness anticipated since 1945, Healy and the ISFI from 1950 identified 'Bevanism' as the first sign of a new and powerful 'centrism' which they could exploit politically. In order to gain access to this new Labour left, the Club moderated *Socialist*

Outlook and even joined in selling *Tribune*. Healy even talked of the possibility of enacting socialism from Parliament.[6] All of this testified to the impressive support for Bevan within the Labour Party constituencies'[7] and the tendency of the Club to drift with this movement.

Had the Club been more inclined to examine this phenomenon critically, however, it would have discovered that beneath the surface the Bevanites were organizationally the weakest of Labour lefts and that Bevan's own individualism and parliamentarianism was partly responsible for this.[8] The Bevanites were particularly inclined to reduce the struggle for socialism to a question of party leadership and this strategy obviated the need for mobilizing the party's rank and file and launching extra-parliamentary political initiatives.[9] They were even timid of invoking the sovereignty of annual conference because that body was dominated by right-wing trade union leaders.[10] Yet they did not manage to mobilize rank and file support in the trade union movement either.[11] Ideologically the Bevanites were equally weak, according to Paul Foot, who says that 'advocacy of public ownership was a sufficient qualification for joining (them)'.[12]

Thus to the extent, (which was great) that the Club looked to the forces coalescing around Bevan as a congenial political milieu in which to promote a Marxist alternative, the chances of advance were slim indeed. The Club's progress was negligible against any of the usual criteria of political development and on the ideological front there is reason to believe its development was retrogressive. This might account for aspects of Healy's particular response to Pabloism in the International. We have already seen that the Club made no analytical contribution in the dispute of 1953 yet Healy followed the SWP's lead with alacrity. This, and the subsequent defection of John Lawrence, editor of *Socialist Outlook,* (*Socialist Outlook* was proscribed by the Labour Party in 1954) — to the Communist Party may be explained as symptoms of the Club's stagnation. Healy's violent reaction to Pabloite liquidationism is ironic in view of the extent to which the Club had already liquidated itself in the Labour Party. But it may also reflect a fear that the ground had been unwittingly prepared for entrism *sui generis* in the Communist Party.

THE 1956 CRISIS OF STALINISM

In fact the Healy organization was saved from shipwreck by the invasion of Hungary in 1956 and the crisis this provoked in the CPGB. The Trotskyist tradition then as now was relatively sophisticated and alert in its analyses of official communism and, to a certain extent, anticipated the form in which centripetal tendencies in Eastern Europe would be made manifest. Pablo had envisaged crises in the Eastern bloc as, in part, a consequence of the reforms from above in the Soviet Union. Thus in 1954 the Fourth International had declared:

In no place where the Communist Parties possess a mass base, except in Jugoslavia, have mass breaks with the Kremlin been produced: and, similarly, there has not been any mass break within these parties. The disintegration of Stalinism has begun by assuming the form of penetration into these organizations of ideas opposed to the interests of the Kremlin bureaucracy; and of a process of modification in the hierarchical bureaucratic relations previously established. It is first of all and above all in this manner that the disintegration of Stalinism will proceed for a whole period: the Communist organizations with a mass base will maintain themselves but within these forms of organization there will develop tendencies towards a new content, both as regards ideas which they express and as regards the existing organizational relations through which the tight hold of the Soviet bureaucracy finds its expression.[13]

The FI document anticipates, in general form, the emergence of Euro-communism and reforming tendencies within the Eastern governments such as Imre Nagy and Alexander Dubcek represented. It also predicts profound crises in those Communist parties without a mass base, such as the British. Though the Malenkov reforms had already taken place, the FI resolution anticipates more to come.

With Krushchev's secret speech condemning Stalinism, a great ideological crack for the first time appeared within the Communist movement. In the CPGB a dissident group — the first significant open opposition since the expulsion of the Balham Trotskyists — began the publication of *The Reasoner*. The CP leadership had already begun an inquiry on inner-party democracy headed by members such as Betty Reid, who had long demonstrated their loyalty to the Stalinist version of Communist organization and their implacable opposition to Trotskyism. But before the first rumblings of discontent could be defused by the leadership, the Hungarian revolution erupted. This threw the CP leadership into considerable confusion for they were presented with an uprising against Soviet power led by life-long members of the Communist movement.

Within six days of the start of the revolution the *Daily Worker* sent

Peter Fryer to Budapest to cover the events at first hand. Fryer had previously covered the show trials of Slansky and Rajk to the satisfaction of King Street and was presumably a trusted member of the Party. Yet within days of his arrival in Hungary he was sending back reports for the *Daily Worker* which the Party eventually refused to publish. On his return to Britain, Fryer resorted to the Fleet Street press out of concern that his version of the Hungarian revolution — depicted as a socialist working-class revolution against bureaucratic monolithism — should see the light of day. Soon afterwards this was used against him as a pretext for his suspension and subsequent expulsion from the CPGB.

The Club seized on these events as an opportunity to vindicate the Trotskyist tradition and to intervene actively in the internal affairs of the CPGB in order to win over as many of its members as possible. Healy exhorted that 'all members of the Communist Party and Young Communist League should immediately demand a special Congress to repudiate the leadership line on Hungary. Stay in the Communist Party and fight it out'.[14] This is, in fact, what happened. By 1957 opposition in the CPGB had cohered around the minority report of the Commission on Inner Party Democracy which essentially argued for greater independence from Russia. But the dissidents were heavily defeated at the party's 25th (special) conference of that year. The leadership followed up its victory with 'A political letter to members' which warned that 'it is harmful to give assistance to Trotskyist and anti-Party people who will try to cover up their aims by the participation of one or two Communists as sympathetic contributors to journals or conferences whose main political content is anti-Communist and anti-Party'.[15]

This undoubtedly refers to the Club and the all-socialist 'socialist forums' in which it participated alongside CP dissidents and others anxious to reconsider the socialist traditions on offer. The forums prospered because the CP opposition had no real chance of changing the party's internal regime or even of staying in the party. There were no traditions of open debate which they could draw on since the ideological leaders of the dissidents, like E.P. Thompson and J. Saville, rejected Trotskyism but could only advance a socialist humanist alternative.[16] Most of the 10,000 who left the CPGB as the direct result of Hungary also left organized Marxist politics. Though Healy and Banda of the Club visited many of the leading ex-CP members personally, the highest estimate of defections to the Trotskyists is only 200. The significance of this is better appreciated when it is remembered that Healy's followers numbered about two score only.

Thus the value of these recruits was potentially very high as a disproportionate number had either held leading positions within the CPGB or had the potential for theoretical work.[17] For example, Brian Behan had been the CPGB's industrial organizer and a member of its executive committee. According to his own testimony, Behan had begun to question the leadership because of the CP's complicity in the internment of Edith Bone in Eastern Europe and was mentally prepared — when the Hungarian revolution began — to make a relatively smooth transition to Trotskyism. By joining the Club Behan also brought with him the ability to organize workers and significant contacts in the London building trade. In the case of Peter Fryer the Trotskyists gained not only an able journalist but also the newspaper — *The Newsletter* which he had established after leaving the CP. From May 1957 this became the group's official organ and, for a while, projected a fresh non-sectarian character of open socialist reporting.

Somewhat uncharacteristically Healy pledged himself and advised the first socialist forum to 'examine every point of view'.[18] This line was expedient for the Club to take in view of the heterogeneous composition of the unique audience created by the crisis in the CP. While *The Newsletter* exhorted independent socialists to join the Labour Party, some of them advocated the creation of a new Marxist party (Peter Worsley, Eric Heffer and Ken Coates were of this opinion). But it was unclear as to which tradition or combination of traditions this new party would draw on. What is clear is that the socialist forum movement depended on a level of tolerance for opposing viewpoints and open debate which the Healy organization was not used to: the fact that the Club temporarily adapted to these unprecedented conditions reflects its desire to escape the becalmed state of existence which it had endured prior to Hungary.

The Suez invasion may also have renewed its hope for increased political activity in the CLPs. In fact Bevanism was soon to expire with the conversion of Bevan from unilateral disarmament and from 1958 the Labour left regrouped as 'Victory for socialism'. The Club managed to infiltrate VFS and it even got as far as proposing a successful resolution on unilateral disarmament at the Labour Party annual conference.[19] Within the Club, however, some leading members were beginning to turn against entrism and propose the creation of an independent, openly Marxist party.

It was felt that the gains from 1956 could have been greater — had there been an open alternative to the CPGB. Furthermore, the long-awaited resurgence in Labour politics at the rank-and-file level seemed no nearer despite ten years of entrist activity. On the positive side, the Club had recently gained its first foothold among industrial workers as the direct result of the recruitment of ex-CP members such as Behan.

Yet the Healy leadership theorized that the entrist tactic had more chance of successful application precisely because the Club was set to augment its trade union base. It had long been canvassed in Trotskyist circles that a rank-and-file campaign to democratize the trade unions would result in increased left-wing representation at the national level: this stengthening of the trade union left could then help shift the Labour Party's annual conference out of the grip of the right wing. With these developments the milieu in which the Trotskyists operated would become more conducive to a political polarization within the Labour Party which would lead either to the destruction of the organization or to its transformation into a genuine socialist party: in either case the Trotskyists would increase their numbers and political influence.

There was also an objective basis for militant intervention in the trade unions designed to strengthen the rank and file at the expense of the trade union bureaucracy (as the Trotskyists called it) which was half consciously recognized by the Club. This was the phenomenon of 'wage drift'. Conditions of full employment enabled shop stewards to conduct local negotiations — often via short, unofficial strikes — which won wage rises beyond those obtained for the industry by the national union leadership. Though there was nothing necessarily political in this, the Club calculated that it provided an opportunity to win over those workers who came into conflict with full-time and, frequently, conservative union officials.

The Shell-Mex strike on the London South Bank site in 1957 affords an example in which the Club played a notable part. In retaliation to an unofficial strike MacAlpines sacked 125 building workers and locked out the best part of a further 2,000. Brian Behan was prominent in this dispute and, no doubt via this connection, *The Newsletter* opened its pages to express the strikers' demands. But the South Bank incident was used as a springboard for the Club's highly successful national industrial rank-and-file conference of November 1958. This attracted 500 trade union activists some of whom went beyond the tactical constraints proffered by members of the Club. Behan urged the delegates to build rank-and-file committees in the trade unions which would challenge bureaucratic power in the Labour movement: he also proposed that the Labour Party should be seen as the forum for militant socialist activity. On this latter point there was dissent with Lawrence Daly, notably, calling for the construction of 'a genuinely revolutionary socialist party.[20]

However the conference diagnosed Labour's ills in terms which suggested that the party was basically sound — merely suffering from a usurping right-wing leadership. Its charter of workers' demands stated that 'the main thing wrong with the Labour Party today is that it is controlled by a junta of middle class Fabians and full time union officials'. So despite the misgivings of some delegates the conference adopted a position on the Labour Party and the trade unions which accurately reflected the Club's analysis. According to the charter:

The rank and file in the trade unions and local Labour Parties no longer have a say in determining the policy of the party.

We recall that the basic aim of the Labour Party, as laid down in its 1918 constitution, is to work for the social ownership of the means of production.

The right-wing leaders have abandoned this aim. Only the rank and file can bring the party back to its original purpose and restore the socialist vision and energy of the pioneers of our movement.

The Tory Government can be defeated, and a Labour government pledged to socialist policies elected, only if the industrial workers in particular bring back the fighting spirit to the Labour Party, and turn local parties into organs of working class struggle.

We appeal to industrial workers:

(1)   To ensure that their trade union branches are fully represented on local and constituency Labour Parties.

(2)   To fight for the adoption of militant socialist policies and for the restoration of democracy within the party.

(3)   To make the local parties campaign centres in the industrial struggle, that will give the utmost moral and material help to all workers in dispute in their particular locality.

(4)   To strive for united action on agreed policies without discrimination while freely and openly thrashing out differences where these exist.

(5)   To recognise that the Labour Party was created by the trade unions and is founded upon them, and that major political questions should be regularly discussed in trade union branches.[21]

This passage reveals that the Club put forward an analysis of the Labour Party no different in essentials from those of left social democrats such as, to give a recent example, the campaign headed by Tony Benn and Eric Heffer. (The analysis, by focusing on an allegedly corrupt and usurping middle class leadership, implies that the transformation of the Labour Party in the desired socialist direction merely requires the removal of this leadership. The nature of the rank and file is *assumed* to be socialist.) In Leninist terms, the implication that the Labour Party had merely deviated from a primordially socialist identity, was a case of spreading illusions which could do nothing other than strengthen the forces of social democracy. Yet the group's precarious entrist existence imposed a logic of manoeuvre and adaptation precisely of this sort.

It will be remembered that the FI's rationale for infiltration of the Labour Party rested on that organization's unique relationship with organized labour. The Club's fidelity to this line outlived its affiliation to the FI and the charter it put forward argued that '. . . the rank and file have the power, and the responsibility, to restore trade union democracy' — in order, that is, to shift the Labour Party itself to the left. However the charter does not indicate how this is to be achieved. Instead the Club was reduced to advocating a hodge-podge of economic demands sprinkled by sensationalist and incredible predictions. It expressed concern about the growth in unemployment (which stood at 0.5 million in 1958) and proposed schemes of work sharing and 'nationalization under workers' control' (of engineering, shipbuilding, textiles and land) to deal with it. A token general strike was demanded as a protest against unemployment and the conference noted the rise in racialism as a divisive force within the working class.

In November 1958 the Club drew the attention of the Labour Party establishment and the national press. Healy answered the charges of 'infiltration' with a pamphlet in which he acknowledged the Club's authorship of and allegiance to the charter of workers' demands.[22] If, as we have argued, there was nothing specifically Marxist about the charter it did, nevertheless, bear the Club's catastrophist stamp. Thus readers were assured that: 'unless the Labour Party takes real socialist measures to solve the problems that capitalism places before the British people, then the middle class will be won over to fascism'.[23] Once again a perspective with no apparent basis in either the short or medium term is invoked which lays claim to some special knowledge concerning the demise of parliamentary democracy. This aspect of Leninism and Trotskyism had become an article of faith with Healy who increasingly returned to this theme and measures of authoritarianism to maintain his grip over the organization he led.[24]

From SLL to WRP

Despite their complaints about the witch hunt launched against them, the Club did not attempt to keep a low profile. Indeed within a year of its start, the Club became the Socialist Labour League (SLL). The new name could only signify that the leadership believed that their forces had been significantly strengthened by the capture of ex-CP members since 1956; this was to be celebrated by a less shadowy entrist existence.

Yet by 1959 the organization had already begun to change in some other ways. Peter Fryer left the organization because of misgivings about Healy's style of leadership and because of the latter's personal domination over the Club. From this time *The Newsletter* began to lose its serious and non-sectarian character and *Labour Review* ceased to concern itself with the larger issues of Marxist theory.[25]. It appears that these developments expressed a growing conviction (probably Healy's) that the time was ripening for the creation of an open Leninist organization — understood as a tightly disciplined, self-contained party.

But in the first instance the SLL was specifically committed to the entrist tactic. Thus, 'the aim of the SLL is to prepare and mobilise the working class for the overthrow of capitalism, the establishment of working class power and the building of a socialist society . . . all members of the League must be members of their appropriate trade unions and, where possible, Labour parties and play an active part therein'.[26] However in launching the SLL at a time when its covert predecessor was already under attack, the Trotskyists appear to have been provoking their own expulsion from the Labour Party. Certainly Healy was returning to the rhetoric of the mid-1940s: 'What is the situation in which the SLL is born to inherit and carry forward the best traditions of four Internationals? If we were to choose one word to sum up the salient features of this period, that word would be "crisis"'.[27]

The message of the SLL's leadership seems, therefore, to have been persistence with the old tactic of entrism on the understanding that an economic catastrophe would change the balance of forces to their favour. The foundation conference of the SLL(Whitsun 1959) was told that this was the basis for '. . . a movement to the left inside the trade unions [which] required the formation of an open organization which could recruit trade unionists direct to the Marxist programme and organization while at the same time training them for continuing struggle from their unions into the Labour Party'. So the SLL's 'open' character was conceived merely as a kind of ante-chamber through which recruits from trade union work could pass into entrist activity in the Labour Party. Some members, led by Brian Behan, objected to this continuation of entrism and attempted to amend the draft constitution accordingly — proposing, instead, '. . . that the SLL is an independent revolutionary working class party'.

Since the SLL was proscribed by the Labour Party within one month of its foundation, and since Healy himself envisaged an economic crisis, the conditions might have been thought propitious for an independent party. But Behan's case was not helped by the SLL's internal regime. Peter Cadogan and Ken Coates had already been suspended for arguing for 'a vast united front for peace — a front which cuts across class boundaries because of the inclusive annihilation threatened by atomic warfare'.

Though Behan supported Healy's line on CND (which carried the slogan 'Ban the bomb and black the bases') he came to regret his part in the expulsion of Coates and Cadogan, seeing it as a further reinforcement of Healy's inordinate control over the organization.[28] But this was too late to avert his own expulsion, and that of several of his supporters, *before* the SLL's conference of 1960. This was justified on the grounds that Behan had contravened the correct *procedure* for forming a tendency.

Interestingly the key points in Behan's case for an open, independent party are taken from Healy's stock of preoccupations. Behan argued that total entry '. . . is accepting lock, stock and barrel the Pabloite theory'. This meant that 'in practice the theory of total entry . . . [subordinates] . . . the participation of the movement in the class struggle to whether or not such activity will jeopardise the existence of the movement with the reformist organization'. (This was, indeed, implied in Healy's 'political letter to all members of the SLL' [March 1960] where it was stated that, 'those members who work in the Labour Party should not be expected to sell the literature of the League under conditions where their position inside the Labour Party is endangered.) But for Behan the positive argument for an independent party lay in the prospect of a crisis-torn economy: '. . . all the tendencies towards slump are present . . . [enabling us to] . . . foresee gigantic class struggles waged by the new monopolies against the working class'.[29]

The argument itself merits no examination as it is, by now, all too familiar. But it *is* of significance that Behan and his supporters were dealt with by purely administrative measures. It seems reasonable to assume that the seven dissidents could have been reasoned out of their position and converted to the majority position. That they were, in fact, expelled on the purely formalistic charge of having ignored the correct procedure for launching a tendency, seems entirely unreasonable especially when consideration is taken of the fact that their ideas had been common knowledge inside the SLL since its foundation conference in 1959. The evidence from this and subsequent expulsions from the SLL is that the leadership clique around Healy was inclined to destroy incipient opposition tendencies *before* they could become formally established. This is why the expulsions of 1949 (Deane et al.), 1958 (Cadogan and Coates) and 1960 (Behan et al.) each occurred prior to the conferences at which policy was decided.

Alasdair MacIntyre alleged, before his own expulsion from the SLL, that the organization was completely undemocratic. In a letter to Healy, he maintained

. . . other comrades now allege (with witnesses who corroborate) a whole range of attempts to detach comrades from the minority faction, varying from flattering and political bribery at one end of the scale to talk of violence by yourself at the other . . . it has now been established that minorities cannot exist in your organization. I say your organization advisedly because of your private ownership of the assets and personal dominance.[30]

MacIntyre relates how he was treated as 'a person antagonistic to the movement' after he chose to support Behan's position at the 1959 conference of the SLL. But as with other critics[31] of the Healy group, MacIntyre stressed that he wished to avoid the 'demonology' of blaming Healy personally for all that was wrong with the SLL. In fact because the small size of the Trotskyist organizations permits a handful of individuals to exercise inordinate influence over them, it is not necessarily mistaken to stress the role of individuals in shaping their political character.

Returning now to the SLL's political activities in the late 1950s and early 1960s, I must briefly note its involvement in CND and the Young Socialists (created by the Labour Party in February 1960). As early as 1957 members of the Healy group participated in the Labour

Party's unilateral disarmament debates. But the SLL came to regard CND after its initial alignment as

. . . an indirect reflection of the growth of the class struggle in the ranks of the professional and middle classes. A considerable portion of its membership consists of young people, who find the policies of the reformists and Stalinists repulsive. They are looking for a lead in the fight against the war and their membership of the CND is their first step in this direction. The SLL must retain friendly relations with this stratum of the population.[32]

Nigel Young[33] is correct to observe that in practice this meant that the SLL 'mainly kept aloof' from CND but only in the sense that the Trotskyists resisted the temptation of submerging their organization in the campaign and agitated on a class, rather than on a pacifist basis. From the inception of the Young Socialists, however, the SLL was deeply embedded in that organization and the Labour Party was forced to proscribe *Keep Left* by 1961 because it had become an instrument of the Trotskyists. For the next few years Transport House maintained a running battle to rid the Labour Party of the SLL.

But during the early 1960s the SLL was more concerned with its relations with the American SWP and the ISFI. Since their common response to the invasion of Hungary,[34] the ISFI and SWP had been drawing together for re-unification talks. The SLL, on the other hand, stepped up its tirades against the Pabloites and demanded the same from the SWP. Instead the unity talks identified further agreements between the SWP and the ISFI on the nature of the Cuban revolution. Indeed this was elevated into the acid test of correct revolutionary thinking: did the Cuban experience constitute a socialist revolution? The ISFI and the SWP said 'yes' — the SLL said 'no': 'Cuba represents the most radical of a whole series of petty bourgeois national rebellions in the underdeveloped countries'.[35] For the SLL this was *necessarily* true because the Fidelistra had lacked a Leninist party: therefore they could not make a socialist revolution. The fact that the ISFI said otherwise was only further proof of its 'Pabloite liquidationism'.

When the SWP re-united with the ISFI (to form the United Secretariat of the Fourth International) the SLL remained with the ICFI, which was much reduced in size and influence. The SLL's allies consisted of the French OCI — Lambertistes and a splinter group from the SWP led by Tim Wohlforth. In fact this was tantamount to national rather than international Trotskyism: and yet just as the

SLL's international isolation became clear, the organization left the Labour Party. In the following year (1965) Healy withdrew also from the LPYS and launched an independent Young Socialist organization. The strategy now was to build the party and the SLL increasingly saw itself as *the* alternative to the Labour Party — behaving as if this stance had credibility among at least part of the working class.

The decision to jettison the entrist tactic was implicit in the creation of the SLL in 1959 and in Healy's anti-Pabloism.[36] The move was precipitated by the re-unification of the SWP and ISFI. But since there was no basis in objective conditions which could encourage the growth of a new party the SLL leadership soon faced the choice of either acknowledging its mistake or removing further from reality. In fact the perspective of impending catastrophe was a constant feature of the leadership's rhetoric and increasingly projected as a cure all for the group's stagnation. As a member of the SLL privately confided

. . . I cannot emphasise too strongly the extent to which the SLL is committed to the view that a crisis will develop very quickly and that within months Britain will have six to seven million unemployed and general slump conditions. This is constantly reiterated at branch meetings and aggregates. It follows, (of course!) that a crisis will, at one fell swoop, provide a mass readership for the daily, build the 'Young Socialists', provide forces to flood into the Labour Party, win the unions — and most importantly — provide masses of recruits for the League . . . this line, while guaranteeing a certain amount of enthusiasm in the short term, is bound to produce a backlash when in six months or a year the SLL is no further on.[37]

Given that the SLL was regularly proved wrong in these catastrophist perspectives, the problem is explaining why the leadership was not removed. There are a number of reasons for this which provide insight into the workings of a sect. In the first place members were recruited in an apolitical way.[38] This resulted in a very substantial turnover of members such that, at any given time, only a minority could compare the predictions of one year with those of another. But even this minority could hardly cultivate an alternative to the leadership's perspectives. The almost frenetic political activism required of the rank and file prevented this. If this failed to stop the emergence of an opposition the authoritarian internal regime imposed by the leadership did.

Thus, in 1974 even some of the long-standing members refused to accept the current views of the leadership, so removed from reality had they become. By then Healy was predicting a military coup in Britain headed by the 'Whitelaw-Carrington axis' which, it was claimed, represented the 'squirearchy'.[39] Concentration camps had already been constructed to deal with recalcitrant trade unionists according to members of the group who were interviewed in the national press. But when members of the organization (since 1973 renamed the Workers Revolutionary Party), led by Alan Thornett, objected to this vision, they were summarily expelled from the party.

The bizarre predictions of 1974 were possible only because the leadership of the Club-SLL-WRP had never tolerated dissent in its 24-year history. Thus the leadership group gradually lost touch with reality. Its anti-Pabloism became first an obsession and then a paranoia[40] which swamped its presss with subterranean verbiage almost certainly indecipherable to its intended audience. Parallel with this was the growth of a political arbitrariness and entrenched sectarianism. Thus the group played no part in the Vietnamese Solidarity Campaign because that organization refused to denouce Hanoi,[41] (despite the Healyites' earlier, uncritical support for North Korea in 1950). Likewise the SLL found pretexts for ignoring the women's movement, the students' campaigns and the Troops Out Movement. Today, the WRP is a dwindling force eclipsed by the growth of the International Socialists and the International Marxist Group yet, incredibly, able to produce a daily newspaper, *The Newsline*.

THE SLL-WRP INTERNAL REGIME

Attempts have been made to trace the authoritarian and sectarian tendency led by Gerry Healy back to the WIL[42] and the RCP. While there is some substance in the view that Healyism shares characteristics with Stalinism, it is unjustified to claim that the RCP internal regime bred this tendency. In fact the ISFI was largely responsible for the promotion of the Healy faction and the destruction of a much more open organization, the RCP. Furthermore the characteristics of Healyism were plainly visible in 1947 when the ISFI took Healy under its wing.

We have already established the minority factions pronounced catastrophism so it will not be laboured here except to note Healy's constant return to this theme between 1945 and the present. But Healy was also proposing a Stalinist monolithism as early as 1945. Thus he said:

We are monopolists in the field of politics. To make a successful revolution in Britain, the working class will require to do it through one party and one programme. We are the nucleus of such a party and our programme is the Transitional Programme of the Fourth International. That is why we are out to destroy all competitive parties such as the ILP.[43]

Yet the transitional programme makes no such claim and it is difficult to see how 'monopolists in the field of politics' could ever tolerate the pluralism envisaged in that document by Trotsky. In combination with this error Healy also regarded Marxism as '. . . a precision instrument, that is one that enables us to make *exact* prognoses'.[44] For such a position to be at all seriously intended its author would not only incline towards extreme arrogance in propounding his own views, but also severe intolerance of all dissenters. Everything, for such a person, would be drawn into sharp contrasts between black and white, right and wrong. Peter Fryer provided us with a glimpse of how Healy acted on this principle within the SLL when he wrote:

The denial of democracy to members of the organization is summed up by the general secretary [Healy] himself in two phrases he has employed recently: 'I am the party' and, in answer to the question, 'How do you see Socialism?' — 'I don't care what happens after we take power.[45]

This gives us a picture of a mentality intolerant of all and any opposition and convinced of its own supremely important position in the revolutionary movement.

Once Healy was separated from any potentially moderating influences (that is, from 1953) these personal tendencies came unchecked to the fore. All actual or potential challengers to his personal domination were expelled, while the bulk of the members consisted of raw recruits permanently preoccupied with the chores of political activism. This activism ensured their ignorance of Marxist theory (and of the group's history) and resulted in a high turnover rate of members such that each year's intake was almost completely replaced by the next. This explains why the clique around Healy remained in all the top leadership positions without serious challenge, for the most part, despite the recurring failure of their policies to achieve the wildly optimistic targets which they set for the organization.

Healy's technique for retaining control over the organization was simply to expel dissidents *before* their opposition could crystallize into a coherent tendency or faction. This was achieved by expelling the dissenters before they could appeal to the organization's conference. Thus the expulsions of 1949 (ex-members of the RCP Majority), 1958 (Peter Cadogan, Ken Coates), 1959 (Behan, MacIntyre and supporters) and 1974 (Alan Thornett and supporters) all took place *immediately* prior to the group's next conference (of 1950, 1959, 1960 and 1974 respectively).

Because the expulsions of 1974 have been copiously documented it is possible to probe some of these assertions in detail and shed more light on the nature of the SLL–WRP internal regime. The dissident group led by Alan Thornett was the most significant of those expelled by Healy on a number of counts. First, it was the largest numerically with around 200 subsequently forming the core of a new organization called the Workers Socialist League. Second, its leaders had been prominent members of the SLL–WRP for up to 15 years. Finally Thornett was the group's best known trade union activist and it was largely due to his efforts that the SLL–WRP's only industrial base — at Morris Motors, Cowley — had been built: by 1974 this 'western region' was the group's only area of expansions (with around 700 members).

By his own admission, Thornett's opposition of 1974 was his first vote against the SLL–WRP leadership in six years of central committee meetings. 'At each meeting CC members struggle to make points they know the leadership expect to hear because they know that the slightest deviant contribution will be held as an anti-party position and attacked as such — predominantly by denigration and invective'.[46] Leading party intellectuals such as Tom Kemp and Cliff Slaughter have, according to Thornett, been 'reduced to tears many times in front of CC meetings' on occasions when they inadvertently stepped out of line. The situation had been reached where Healy 'was making all decisions in all fields of work in the WRP'. Thornett's explanation of how this was enabled to come about is worth quoting at length:

The answer is connected with the whole method of leadership of the WRP. At first it seems very hard and political — ruthless decisions are necessary in a revolutionary movement and so on. Members are swayed by the demagogy of Healy's speeches. The decision to challenge Healy in a meeting on any point is a hard one, invoking bitter invective from the leadership and probably resulting in removal from the Committee of the comrade who has made the challenge. Any challenge involves a questioning of the whole of Healy's method and leads directly to his wrong theoretical positions and therefore cannot be tolerated . . . Whilst the party is expanding and Healy appears to be delivering the goods, no one questions the regime.

According to Thornett the nature of WRP meetings rapidly repels potential trade union recruits. It is logical to assume therefore that those who are recruited and remain in the organization are impressed by features of the party's internal regime highlighted by Thornett above. The latter's own opposition was eventually prompted by two facts which he understandably held to be interconnected. These are that the organization was in numerical decline at a time when its political utterances had become completely removed from reality with dire predictions of imminent military coups being the focal point of its 1974 general election propaganda.

Once Thornett stated his opposition to these perspectives, Healy proposed to change the WRP constitution (which had been adopted in 1973 on the basis of the 15-year-old SLL constitution) in order to prevent the dissidents addressing the forthcoming party conference. These changes were duly enacted without WRP branches having time to consider them in advance of the conference itself. It is alleged that Healy took further measures to break up the opposition including the use of 'considerable physical violence' against one long-standing member.[47] Another central committee member, with 14 years' membership of the SLL-WRP, was dismissed and suspended from the organization (subsequent to her expulsion) for merely questioning the authoritarian methods of the leadership. Many others were visited at their homes and variously threatened and cajoled into denouncing Thornett. Finally the whole group of dissidents was expelled from the WRP before its 1974 conference.

The similarities found in the various accounts we have cited concerning the SLL-WRP internal regime are too striking, the accounts themselves too numerous, to be lightly dismissed. The picture that emerges in each of them is of a group dominated by the personality of Healy, a personality which would seem to be authoritarian. The continued dominance of this figure over three decades in the group's history has been attributed to Healy's favoured position as its founder member and to his undoubted organizational abilities.[48] To these factors one may add the organizational and political assistance which Healy received from the leadership of the Fourth International until 1953. After his split with that organization Healy enjoyed the prestige of leading an alternative International (the ICFI) in conjunction with J.P. Cannon of the American SWP. A further split left Healy the dominant figure in this tiny international organization. Clearly one cannot dismiss the significance of Healy's ownership of the SLL-WRP assets, such as the printing press, to which Alisdair MacIntyre alluded after his own expulsion from the group. Likewise the long list of expulsions is itself a contributory factor in accounting for Healy's personal dominance; for anyone who displayed leadership potential was removed from the organization before his or her challenge could crystallize.

However it may not be *purely* organizational factors which explain the authoritarian regime within the SLL–WRP current. In accounting for Healy's personal sway it is necessary to account for the loyalty he received from leading members of the group such as Tom Kemp and Cliff Slaughter (the party's theoreticians), Alex Mitchell (editor of *Workers Press*) and Mike and Tony Banda, the wealthy Ceylonese supporters of Healy. Without such support Healy could not have remained at the head of the organization for so long. Other achievements — such as the daily newspaper, the *Newsline* (since 1976), a monthly theoretical journal, as well as a 'revolutionary college of Marxist education' (opened in August 1975) — would also be inexplicable. The support of this leadership group (which includes a number of well-known members of Equity, the actors' union) may, in part, be attributable to Healy's personal charisma, but it is also likely to result from the conviction that the politics of the organization are worth defending. In particular the Healy group has been concerned since its inception in 1947 with the defence of what it believes to be orthodox Trotskyism. It is to the nature of this orthodoxy that I now turn.

CONCLUSIONS

It seems that Healy and his co-thinkers — more than any other avowed Trotskyists — adhere to a socialist strategy based on a simple breakdown theory in which the capitalist system collapses by virtue of its own inner contradictions and impels the working class to turn to revolutionary politics in an explosion of political consciousness. The leadership of this tendency believes that in the epoch of capitalist decay the political systems of Western Europe are necessarily driven towards forms of authoritarianism and the suspension of democratic rights. The most recent instance of this type of analysis in the case of the WRP was produced in response to the Falklands war. According to the WRP:

Thatcher is assembling the nucleus of a junta in Britain: her inner cabinet, high-ranking Whitehall officials, the service chiefs and chief constables and her ardent supporters in the suburbs. Her aim is to weld these elements into a force which will follow in the footsteps of the notorious German 'Frei Corps' — the predecessors of the SS.[49]

Since this dictatorial process is determined by objective factors of economic decay the struggle for the preservation and extension of democratic rights and institutions is evidently held to be futile. The correct revolutionary stance, according to the Healy group, is to pose maximalist demands for the immediate transition to socialism — since these demands are held to be objectively necessary and free from the illusory quality of reformist slogans.

Just as this version of Marxism regards the state as the instrument of finance capital, so it tends to reduce all non-economic phenomena to the economic base. Thus, in his reply to Alan Thornett, Michael Banda on behalf of the WRP, argues that the real significance of the former's break with the organization results from

. . . the theoretical bewilderment, the deep scepticism and the political disorientation of sections of the middle class and politically undeveloped workers caught in the whirlpool of hyper-inflation and slump. Gripped by this middle-class frenzy and trapped by their own backwardness in the stagnant pool of trade union, reformist consciousness, these revisionists lash out at the philosophy of the party and try to transform it from a guide to revolutionary action into a sterile dogma serving the needs of the reactionary trade union bureaucracy and the bourgeoisie.[50]

Thus is Thornett's refusal to support the WRP's perspectives of imminent *coup d'état* perceived as an unconscious class betrayal ultimately reducible to the economic context of 1974.

Likewise, in his characterization of the International Socialists (now SWP) Cliff Slaughter discovers in their theories '. . . another stage in the perennial middle-class attack on Marxism, concentrated even more directly against the revolutionary party and dialectical materialism.[51] In support of his class–reductionist approach, Slaughter invokes the precedent set by Trotsky which is depicted as the '. . . first great theoretical and political battle against exactly such a petty-bourgeois tendency in the shape of James Burham and Max Shachtman in the Socialist Workers Party (USA) in 1939-40'.[52]

On another occasion Slaughter explains that it is precisely as the economic catastrophe of capitalism draws nearer that

Marxist theory — which has guided the real struggle of the working class and developed through that struggle — has had to be fought for in uncompromising battle against the ideas imported into the working class by these ideologists of the middle class.

More and more this fight has to be carried out against those who *appear* to be themselves Marxists and socialists.

Their task is to say to the workers: we don't challenge the correctness of socialism, of Marx, but we must understand that reality has changed and Marxism must be adapted to it.[53]

Now if we piece these fragments together — and dozens more could be cited of the same character[54] — the picture that emerges is of a group which believes itself to be *the* revolutionary party striving to preserve Marxism from adulteration (in the face of several bogus varieties) and the infiltration of 'bourgeois' and 'petty bourgeois' influences. Because of its conviction in its unique role and destiny to 'make' the socialist revolution, and because of its belief in the imminence of political and economic catastrophe, this group can tolerate no internal — or for that matter, external — opposition. Possessed of unique insight into the political future — based on its correct understanding of the 'precision instrument' that is Marxism — the claims of all other organizations of, or for, the working class are denied. To play a positive role all these must turn to the leadership of the WRP.

Is this merely a simplistic 'reading' of Lenin and Trotsky? Of course we do not believe that these thinkers would subscribe to the vulgar Marxism described above and yet there are elements in the writings of these revolutionaries which lend themselves to such an interpretation. No doubt, in part, the WRP's *Weltanschauung* has come to take its present shape because the organization, being small, has small intellectual resources. It is an organization, too, that has never been linked with great social and political movements — such, that is, which generate new ideas and compel a more subtle, resourceful approach. For these reasons it has been dominated, like all the other groups studied here, by one or two — at the best, a mere handful — of individuals.

Nevertheless the theories which the WRP defends as the central elements of its Leninism-Trotskyism cannot be dismissed simply as simplifications of a 'true' Leninism-Trotskyism, though simplifications they may be. The point is that these simplifications are so tenaciously held and so durable because they accord with the basic thrust and spirit of the Bolshevism which dominated the early Comintern and which Trotsky sought to preserve. The process of simplification has merely made explicit that which was implicit in Comintern (such as the claim of being the sole, legitimate, vanguard of the working class) and asserts bluntly theses which were held a little more circumspectly (as with the perspectives of capitalist economic decay and growing political authoritarianism). In this rather limited though important respect, the WRP really does defend orthodox Trotskyism. Or rather it has petrified this doctrine and kept it from contamination with empirical reality. But it is important to recognize that this is not simply a preservation of the classical texts (contingent prognoses and all): the WRP's orthodoxy also faithfully resonates the certainty, militarism and arrogance of Comintern in its heroic early period.

The mission of the WRP is to preserve what it takes to be the revolutionary message of the Leninist Comintern. It justifies its own centralist authoritarianism in terms of preparation for civil war which is expected to result from ever present tendencies to economic collapse in modern capitalism. Intolerance of opponents is partly a consequence of the conviction that there is only one revolutionary party (on the Bolshevik model) and this is led by those who have truly assimilated the teachings of Lenin and Trotsky whose strategic and tactical thinking is held to be definitive. The task of revolutionaries is simply to apply these lessons. Since it is believed that the leadership is the repository of this definitive knowledge any questioning of it is *per se* heretical. But since heresies, like any other ideas, are held to be merely expressions or reflections of economic categories, the heretics are invariably portrayed as either conscious or unconscious purveyors of class interests inimical to those of the working class.

Of course, it may be objected, this watertight schema is invoked merely because it serves the self-interests of the WRP leadership; the writings of Lenin and Trotsky, let alone Marx, are infinitely richer and more subtle. But this is to overlook that my point is to show why these doctrines — dominant within the WRP and, as we shall see, other organizations of the far left — have credibility within the Trotskyist tradition. If the revolutionary Marxist tradition was free of these arguments it is doubtful that they would command respect and persist for so long. An organization like the SLL-WRP, which has effectively insulated itself from most outside influences on the left — such as the students' and women's movements of the late sixties — has merely preserved the elements of this orthodoxy more successfully than most of its rivals.

5

The International Socialists

Among the first splitters from the Healy organization were the adherents of Tony Cliff's version of the theory of state capitalism. The Socialist Review Group came into existence in 1950 because the founders of the organization believed they had made a theoretical advance which could best be defended outside the Fourth International. This was the justification for a group of only 33 members, most of whom operated within the Labour League of Youth. Sales of *Socialist Review* were only around 350 copies per issue. By 1960 the organization was little bigger.[1] Yet today, according to a rival organization:

The Socialist Workers Party is the largest revolutionary organisation in Western Europe or North America. Of its 3,600 members 33-35% are members of manual unions, 34% of white collar unions, and 14% are students. A quarter of its members are women. Its weekly paper *Socialist Worker* has a paid circulation of 13,000, the monthly *Socialist Review* sells 4,500 copies and the quarterly *International Socialism* sells 3,000 copies.[2]

A history of this organization must be concerned with both the ideas which sustained the group during its propaganda period and the political interventions which enabled it to grow to its present position of challenging the traditional hegemony of the CPGB on the left of the Labour Party. The first task is especially important because this is a self-consciously innovative and unorthodox tradition which has evolved away from Trotskyism. Indeed, such is the scope of its departures from the latter that it is simpler to identify the few points of convergence. According to Tony Cliff,

We accepted from Trotsky . . . that the working class is the agent of the socialist revolution, that [it] is the subject . . . of the socialist revolution, that the criterion to every change in society is what role the working class is playing actively in it . . . The second thing we took from Trotsky . . . is opposition to all rising bureaucracies. Thirdly . . . the theory of the impossibility of socialism in one country. The fact that the pressure of world capitalism distorts development in every workers' state . . . We also accepted from Trotsky the question of the international nature of the revolution.[3]

It is notable that Cliff's list contains very little that is specifically Trotskyist. The theory of permanent revolution, for example, is absent — having been trimmed to an allegiance to the 'theory of the impossibility of socialism in one country'. But in 1950, as Duncan Hallas recalls, 'the founders of the group saw themselves as mainstream Trotskyists, differing only on unimportant questions from the dominant group in the International, but belonging to the same basic tendency'.[4]

The Socialist Review Group, accordingly, sought to reform the Fourth International. This is made clear by the minutes of the SRG's foundation meeting:

. . . being a Trotskyist tendency, and believing that our position on Russia rounds off Trotskyism to the needs of the epoch, we shall fight for the building of the Fourth International as a genuine Trotskyist organisation. We shall apply for membership of the Fourth International.

In fact the 'Russian question' — or the SRG's solution of it — was enough to debar the group from re-entering the FI. It is to the theory of state capitalism, as propounded by Tony Cliff, that I now turn.

THE THEORY OF STATE CAPITALISM

When it first appeared as an internal document of the RCP, Cliff's theory of state capitalism did not have a big impact on the organization. But we have already remarked on the theoretical confusion, concerning the nature of the Soviet economy, which characterized the FI itself in the 1940s. In this context Cliff's theory was neither more nor less useful than the alternatives; it was, however, deviant and unorthodox. In one form or another the concept of state capitalism, as applied to the Soviet Union, was always associated with opponents of the October revolution.[5] It was then taken over, with modifications, by opponents of Stalinism.

Trotsky remarked that 'this term (state capitalism) has the advantage that nobody knows exactly what it means'.[6] His commitment to the defence of the Soviet Union against internal or external reaction, which he placed among the first principles of revolutionary duty, precluded collaboration on this question with adherents of the theory of state capitalism. Despite Trotsky's opposition, the theory was revived among Trotskyists when, after the statization of property in Eastern Europe, the issue of the nature of the USSR became central. In Hallas' view the controversy of 1947 to 1950 revolved on the question of whether Stalinists could overthrow bourgeois regimes. According to the state capitalists such a contingency was specifically excluded by Trotsky and this constituted 'the historical justification for the founding of the Fourth International'. We have seen, in chapter 2, that the ISFI behaved as if the proponents of state capitalism were correct: until 1951 the social formations of Eastern Europe were held to be capitalist despite their obvious 'Sovietization'. It is noteworthy that the ISFI itself introduced the criterion which the SRG held to be fundamental; namely, the '. . . fundamental tenet of Marxism — the conception of socialism as the self-emancipation of the working class'. This was held to be the criterion for establishing the nature of the Eastern European social formations. When the ISFI came to reject this approach, Tony Cliff and his followers decided that it had capitulated to Stalinism.[7]

Cliff advanced his alternative analysis of Eastern Europe when the ISFI concluded that the latter had become deformed workers' states. In *The Class Nature of the People's Democracies* he argues that 'in no way is it possible to demonstrate that the statifications were the culmination of the activities, no matter how deformed, of the working class'.[8] And yet, says Cliff, 'the political supremacy of the working class is a prerequisite for its economic supremacy'. This being the case, he argues that:

where the state, which is a repository of the means of production, is totally alienated from the working class, by this very fact of political alienation the workers are separated from the means of production, they are wage slaves.

For Cliff, then, the Eastern European states are state capitalist. He had already arrived at the same conclusion, by a similar route, on the nature of the USSR which, fortunately, he has chartered for us recently.

> When I came to the theory of state capitalism I didn't come to it by a long analysis of the law of value in Russia . . . Nothing of the sort. I came to it by the simple statement that if the emancipation of the working class is the act of the working class then you cannot have a workers' state without the workers having power to dictate what happens in society.[9]

Trotsky never argued, of course, that the workers of the Soviet Union exercized state power. For him the USSR was a degenerated workers' state precisely because a privileged bureaucracy monopolized state power which — in so far as the centrists of the CPSU were able — was used to defend state-owned property, the major lasting gain of the October revolution. Trotsky's formalistic analysis, which Cliff's was designed to replace, had become, according to Hallas, 'hopelessly outdated', by the early thirties.[10]

The turning point for Cliff and Hallas in the history of the Bolshevik revolution, was the first five-year economic plan of 1928.

> It was now, for the first time, that the bureaucracy sought to create a proletariat and to accumulate capital rapidly. In other words, it was now that the bureaucracy sought to realise the historical mission of the bourgeoisie as quickly as possible. A quick accumulation on the basis of a low level of production, of a small national income *per capita,* must put a burdensome pressure on the consumption of the masses, on their standard of living. Under such conditions the bureaucracy, transformed into a personification of capital, for whom the accumulation of capital is the be-all and end-all here, must get rid of all remnants of workers' control, must substitute conviction in the labour process by coercion, must atomise the working class, must force all social-political life into a totalitarian mould.[11]

It will be recalled that Trotsky viewed the post-1928 events altogether differently. Stalin's terror against the kulaks and NEP-men was analysed by Trotsky as a belated and bureaucratic response to the dangers these represented of a restoration of capitalism. But for Cliff's followers 'that Trotsky could initially see all this as a turn to the *left* (although he was not aware of the full facts until some years later) indicates that he had relapsed into substitutionism so far as looking at the USSR was concerned'.[12] Because, for the state capitalists, the last remnants of workers' control were destroyed in 1928 simultaneously with the bureaucracy's massive violence against the petty bourgeoisie, the economic plans which emerged were the instrument of exploitation, not a step in the direction of socialism.

Indeed Cliff argues that 1928 marks the moment of the bureaucracy's mutation into the 'historical essence' of the capitalist class.[13] But adherents of this theory deny that it has implications for 'world historical perspectives for the next decades if not centuries' (as Hallas puts it). Despite the spread of state capitalism from Russia to Eastern Europe and then to China, Cliff's followers deny that it marks a 'stage' in world political economy. According to Hallas 'it did not follow that if the USSR were indeed an exploitative society in the Marxist sense . . . that it was a *fundamentally new* type of exploitative society'.[14]

Of course if the theory had maintained that state capitalism represented a new type of exploitative society, it would have contradicted the Leninist conception of the epoch and thus removed the, allegedly, objective basis for socialist revolutions. Cliff attempts to avoid this 'pitfall' by regarding state capitalism as a phase in the transition to socialism. Thus 'state capitalism and a workers' state are two stages in the transition period from capitalism to socialism — they are symmetrically opposed and they are dialectically united with one another'.[15]

Cliff argues that state capitalism operates like a single capitalist enterprise. Thus within the state capitalist economy there is no exchange value of commodities because the price mechanism (the law of value) does not act as a regulator of production. Instead the various parts of the state capitalist economy produce use values for each other. However when this state capitalist economy is set in the context of the world economy it behaves like a capitalist enterprise in competition with other enterprises. Thus on a world scale, and by virtue of international competition, the law of value *does* operate. Consequently the pressure of world capitalist economy establishes the priorities of the Soviet economy, in Cliff's schema. The final twist in this theory is that 'because international competition takes mainly a military form the law of value expresses itself in its opposite, viz. a striving after use-values'.[16] So weapons production, for Cliff, has the chief determining role in 'the whole development of the Russian economy'.[17]

THE PERMANENT ARMS ECONOMY

Indeed the centrality of arms production as the major determinant in the development of the Soviet economy also became, for Cliff, the chief explanation of the relative economic stability of advanced capitalist economies during the long post-war boom. Cliff borrowed the idea of a permanent arms economy from Max Shachtman but the thesis reached its most developed form in the writings of Cliff's collaborator Michael Kidron. The basic idea is very simple: 'Insofar as capital is taxed to sustain expenditure on arms it is deprived of resources that might otherwise go towards further investment'.[18]

Because this expenditure is in fast-wasting, end products which constitute a net loss to the circular pattern of commodity production, arms spending represents a 'leak' of potentially productive capital according to the Kidron-Cliff thesis. Just as the great expansion of exports of capital was said to have stabilized the capitalist world before 1914,[19] so arms production, according to the International Socialists, was responsible for the capitalist equilibrium of the fifties and sixties. 'This is because', argues Kidron, 'seen from the angle of the system . . . arms production is the key, and seemingly permanent, offset to the tendency of the rate of profit to fall'.[20]

The proponents of this theory made great claims for it. Kidron argued that the permanent arms economy — the result of 'unrestrained competition' between East and West — marked '. . . the latest, final phase of capitalism'. Kidron maintained that Lenin's concept of imperialism had become obsolete because 'the distinction between empire and colony which loomed so large half a century ago is increasingly irrelevant, politically and economically'.

Likewise, Trotsky's theory of permanent revolution requires revision because, says Kidron:

. . . the national bourgeoisie — or failing it, the national bureaucracy — has been rescued from oblivion by imperialism's withdrawal; national independence has come to it in many cases without a struggle and therewith have come the levers of economic development and its own growth; finally it has gained greatly in strength from foreign capital's new need for willing and active partners in production and from the associated flow of cold war aid.[21]

In practical terms, argued Kidron, the new situation made the emerging proletariat of the Third World the leading class; but not because the bourgeoisie was too weak to lead a revolution of national independence as in Trotsky's theory. In Kidron's view national solutions of any type had become irrelevant. The political primacy of the proletariat resulted from the fact that class solutions only were on the Third World agenda.

However, these would be hard to resolve: for Kidron, capitalism had become less vulnerable to attack in the backward countries: 'to believe now that the short route to revolution in London, New York or Paris lies through Calcutta, Havana, or Algiers is to pass the buck to where it has no currency'.[22] In other words, the International Socialists believed that underdeveloped countries, which had at best achieved state capitalism from ostensibly socialist revolutions (China, Yugoslavia, Albania, Cuba), would now have to wait until their own economic development and revolutions in the advanced world enabled the Third World proletariat to seize state power.

THE VERSATILITY OF THEORY

By the mid-sixties the International Socialists had developed theories which explained a number of problems which had caused discomfort to revolutionary socialists. First they argued that none of the socialist revolutions had achieved anything worth defending: on the contrary they had produced state capitalism. Second, the advanced capitalist world had achieved economic equilibrium and industrial growth by virtue of the technological spin-off from the cold war which had produced a permanent arms economy. Third, the division of the world into two permanently antagonistic camps dominated by the rival capitalisms of the USA and USSR had rendered imperialism obsolete, and had sucked in the backward countries, permitting them a measure of economic growth and national independence.

These three interrelated theories excused the International Socialists from having to choose sides in the cold war; emancipated them from the traditional left-wing habit of predicting the last capitalist crisis (catastrophism); and preserved them from the pitfalls of placing their faith in a foreign centre (Moscow, Pekin, Havana, or the Third World). In preaching that all was yet to be achieved and that there were no short-cuts to achieving it, the International Socialists represented a 'realism' in harmony with the limited political opportunities of Britain in the fifties and the harsh political environment of the cold war.

Cliff's state capitalist theory absolved its adherents from any complicity with Stalinism precisely at a time when Stalinism was equated with communism and the West was hysterically anti-Communist. It is on this basis that some Trotskyists allege that Cliff and his followers succumbed to anti-Communist hysteria when they left the FI in 1950 when the Korean war had just begun. The SRG argued then that

the immediate result of the victory of Stalinism in Korea would be the liquidation of the independent socialist movement and the disorienting of the socialist vanguard . . . We can therefore give no support to either camp since the war will not achieve the declared aims of either side.[23]

It might be supposed that to regard each side as equally reactionary was more comfortable to its proponents than the position of those who were obliged by their convictions to defend North Korea while all those around them were violently anti-Communist. But this is no reason to conclude that Cliff et al were opportunistically ducking their responsibilities. The fact that they subsequently sided with North Vietnam (in the sixties) has been cited as proof of their opportunism but their positions on both Korea and Vietnam are consistent with their fidelity to the principle of proletarian self-emancipation. As Birchall explains: 'The war in Korea . . . was different in nature from the struggles in Vietnam and China . . . [the] national liberation movement in South Korea . . . [was] . . . quickly swamped as the war got under way. After the first few months Korean forces played only a secondary role; the Korean people of the North and South were victims while two great world powers engaged in a trial of strength across their territory . . . there is a sharp contrast with the second Vietnamese war of 1965 onwards. Here both the USA and Russia found the war an embarrassment and would have been glad to stop it years before it in fact ended. While the Vietnamese were the protagonists of their war, the Koreans were victims of theirs'.[24]

Armed with this state capitalist theory the Cliff group could support the Chinese revolution, for example, and yet distance themselves from the post-revolutionary state. The theory is sufficiently elastic to explain almost any eventuality consistent with revolutions in the Third World or semi-advanced world. Indeed save for a socialist equivalent of 1848 the theory *suggests* that any country experiencing a socialist revolution will produce state capitalism: but it does not *say* this and its advocates deny that state capitalism represents a stage in world economic development.

Cliff and his followers have variously advanced the following propositions concerning state capitalism:

(a) '. . . a peaceful transition can be accomplished from a workers' state . . . to a state capitalist regime . . .' because the former possesses 'no bureaucracy or standing army'.

(b) State capitalism was brought about in China by a peasant army led by déclassé elements intent on a bourgeois revolution though armed with twentieth century political innovations such as a centralised party and Marxist ideology.

(c) This 'new civilisation' of state capitalism '. . . was founded on a more systematic exploitation of labour than was possible in the old capitalism of the West'.

(d) 'A regime of bureaucratic state capitalism, with the terrific strain it imposes, needs the blood of a purge to make the wheels go round . . . The contradictions in Russian society are such that nothing could hold the system together except the iron hoops of totalitarian dictatorship'.

(e) In the late fifties this system gave way to 'welfare state capitalism' according to Cliff.

(f) State capitalism is a 'stage in the transition to socialism.[25]

The permanent arms economy thesis is similarly versatile. For while purportedly explaining capitalist equilibrium it paradoxically advances the view that prospects for revolution are strongest in 'the heartland of the system' rather than in its economically backward periphery. Kidron argued that the capital intensive nature of the permanent arms economy creates technological unemployment especially among immigrant workers and (most notably in America) Blacks. By accelerating the concentration of capital and draining resources from the periphery of the advanced capitalist world, the system revives nationalist movements previously dormant or dead. Finally, by displaying unparalleled irrationality, the arms economies stimulate opposition from students and intellectuals. The stability and economic growth which the arms economies facilitated, were bought at the price of greater instability in the future, according to Cliff. This is argued to be the result of the fact that the capitalisms of Germany and Japan were absolved of responsibility for financing the arms economy. While Western arms expenditure stabilized the capitalist world economy for a time, Germany and Japan achieved faster growth rates and began to encroach on the markets hitherto dominated by the USA. Consequently says Cliff:

. . . the US came under increasing pressure to cut the proportion of its own national income devoted to arms. All told the proportion of Western resources spent on arms fell from 7.5% in 1955 to 4% in 1965 and has continued to fall since. The decline in arms spending has meant a decline in its stabilising effect . . . and . . . has pushed us into world recession.[26]

Thus, for Cliff even if no longer for Kidron,[27] the idea of a permanent arms economy dominating both East and West is given the status of *the* major theoretical explanation of both the long post-war boom and the seventies slump. It has, however, been convincingly criticized by representatives of the rest of the Marxist left.[28]

Whatever the theory's scientific status it did at least offer an explanation of the post-war boom when other spokesmen of the far left refused to recognize that such stability even existed. The theory also rather neatly 'fits' with the International Socialists' other distinctive position — the theory of state capitalism. During the years of political oblivion endured from its foundation to the middle sixties, the International Socialists may well have drawn strength from the apparent coherence of its ideology which (unlike the chiliasm of the SLL) taught the membership to expect a long, slow, slog rather than imminent insurrection. And when the first signs of economic slump coincided with the upheavals in Watts, Paris and Prague, the International Socialists were able to explain these 'cracks in the system' within the same theory. This versatility was apparent in the organization's changing self-conception too.

THE NATURE OF THE ORGANIZATION

The Socialist Review Group was active in the Labour Party from the former's foundation until 1965. The organizational weakness of the SRG's entrism is demonstrated by the fact that even after 1959 and in the early years of International Socialism it was forced to combine its meagre forces with two other entrist groups — the Revolutionary Socialist League and the International Group — in the publication of *Young Guard* which unsuccessfully competed with the SLL's *Keep Left* for commanding influence in the LPYS. However the expulsion of *Keep Left* coincided with IS's growing influence over *Young Guard* (at the expense of the RSL and IG) and it was at this time that the state capitalists recruited some basic cadres such as John Palmer and Roger Rosewall. Yet, unlike other entrists this activity was not in any way connected with a perspective of transforming or splitting the Labour Party. Rather, the SRG viewed entrism in the same way as the RCP majority which in 1949 arrived at the conclusion that entrism was the only way of avoiding sectarianism given the prevailing hostile conditions for independent party building. The SRG initially saw itself as 'the nucleus of a Marxist party . . . [which] . . . can be built firmly only on the acceptance of party discipline in the tradition of Bolshevism under Lenin's leadership'.[29] However

Tony Cliff moved to a more permissive model of organization in the course of the fifties, during which time the tactics and strength of the organization remained unchanged. This conception of the future revolutionary party emphasized its role as a servant of the mass movement. In his study of Rosa Luxemburg, published in 1959, Cliff celebrated her 'enduring strength' which '. . . lay in her complete confidence in the workers' historical initiative'.[30]

Of course in so doing Cliff returned to his dominant theme of workers' self-emancipation as the key to Marxist theory. Given the SRG's entrist status it was also opportune for Cliff to applaud Luxemburg's opposition to

. . . abstention from the main stream of the Labour movement, no matter what the level of its development. Her fight against sectarianism is extremely important for the Labour movement of the West, especially at the present, when welfare-statism is such an all-prevailing sentiment. The British Labour movement, in particular . . . can gain inspiration from Rosa Luxemburg for a principled fight against reformism which does not degenerate into flight from it.

In practical terms, Cliff's evolution to Luxemburg from Lenin was apparent in the group's internal regime and journals. When *International Socialism* was launched in 1960 its pages were used by a great number of socialists from outside the organization. An atmosphere of free and open debate also existed within the group which was organized along federal rather than centralist lines. The extent of the SRG's evolution was reflected in the fact that the rest of the far left regarded it as a libertarian-anarchist formation — Marxisant rather than 'Marxist-Leninist'.

In fact, the group was tending away from orthodox Leninism. Cliff had arrived at the conclusion that 'for Marxists in advanced countries, Lenin's original position (i.e. that contained in "What is to be done?" — JTC) can much less serve as a guide than Rosa Luxemburg's notwithstanding her overstatements on the question of spontaneity'.[31]

According to Cliff,

Rosa Luxemburg's conception of the structure of the revolutionary organisation — that they should be built from below up, on a consistently democratic basis — fits the needs of the workers' movement in the advanced countries much more closely than Lenin's conception of 1902-4 which was copied and given an added bureaucratic twist by Stalinists the world over.

This idea — that only a bureaucratic twist separated Lenin's Bolshevik Party from the Stalinist CPSU — is a long way removed from Trotskyism. Indeed the extent of Cliff's departure from this tradition is revealed when he adopts Trotsky's stance of 1904. Referring to *Our Political Tasks* Cliff argued that

In Trotsky's words about the danger of 'substitutionism' inherent in Lenin's conception of party organisation, and his plea against uniformity one can see his prophetic genius, his capacity to look ahead, to bring into a unified system every facet of life.

The only logical interpretation one can put on this statement is that Cliff (at least in 1959) regarded Stalinism as the natural heir of Leninism. But since the rest of Cliff's argument repudiates this proposition one can only conclude that his 'slip of the pen' came about in the course of groping towards a more liberal conception of party organization. By 1962, when the group was renamed International Socialism, it certainly possessed a very flexible, federalist internal regime which Birchall, in his 'official' history of the group, believed to be responsible for the absence of sectarian, introverted tendencies. The group's self-perception was as part of the broader Labour movement rather than as a sect defending its shibboleths.

So Cliff and the SRG had arrived at a non-Leninist conception of the party by the early sixties. According to Birchall 'it was from these years that International Socialism members inherited a somewhat libertarian attitude to organisation, a tendency to distrust discipline or any kind of formalised or centralised structure'.[32]

It was certainly on this basis that the group managed to grow to 200 members by 1964 from recruitment in the Labour Party Young Socialists. The novelty of its ideas and the organization's libertarianism may also account for its growing appeal among young leftist intellectuals. Though the Socialist Review Group had been too small to play a conspicuous role in CND the latter may have been a formative experience in developing Cliff's theory of a 'vacuum on the left' which ultimately resulted in the launching of the Socialist Workers Party in 1977. As David Howell points out 'the unilateralist movement developed outside the (Labour) Party's official channels', and 'the Labour Party seemed marginal to the agitation'. At the same time the crisis in the CPGB in 1956 resulted in the emergence of a Marxist current in the developing new left which permitted 'an emancipation of left-wing thought from the stultifying choice between Stalinism and the acceptance of NATO and the mixed economy'. The IS slogan — 'neither Washington nor Moscow' — and the tradition it represented was at least as attractive as the competing elements in the 'broad, rather incoherent new left'.[33]

In 1965 the International Socialism group withdrew from the Labour Party believing that the time was ripe (and the IS was big enough) to work in the growing number of 'fragmented' struggles which were then developing. Having never had illusions about transforming the Labour Party or of splitting it, the group made the transition to its new role without internal schism and identified the growing number of strikes, tenants' disputes and anti-racist campaigns as its arena for independent political work. The election of a Labour government in the previous year did not lead International Socialism into the self-deceptions common on the rest of the left. In fact the speedy introduction of an incomes policy by the Wilson government coupled with the growth of shop stewards' militancy helped to re-orientate the organization towards industrial activity.

Indeed the shop stewards were regarded by IS as the 'basis of a new revolutionary movement'. It is clear, however, that IS saw this as a potential which had yet to be realized and its break from entrism was not heralded as the formation of a new party. On the contrary, the IS leadership was still open-minded about the organization's relationship to the new shop stewards' movement. Duncan Hallas, some years after the split from the Labour Party, dismissed the Leninist model of 1903 as irrelevant, on the grounds that

. . . the vanguard, in the real sense of a considerable layer of organised revolutionary workers and intellectuals [has] been destroyed. So too has the environment, the tradition, that gave it influence . . . the crux of the matter is how to develop the process, now begun, of recreating it.[34]

In this essay Hallas was clearly rejecting the common mistake of the far left which is 'to imagine that all that is necessary is to build a new leadership around some sect or other and then offer it as an alternative to the waiting workers'. A corollary of this, argues Hallas, is '. . . the assumption that the answers to all problems are known in advance' . . . and so . . . 'to safeguard the purity of the programme is seen as one of the main tasks of the selected few'.

In rejecting these practices, Hallas echoes Deutscher's critique of the Transitional Programme, for he stresses that

. . . the development of a programme, in the sense of a detailed statement of partial and transitional aims and tactics in all important fields is inseparable from the development of the movement itself. It presupposes the participation of a large number of people who are themselves actively engaged in those fields.[35]

Hallas was proposing, then, that the best way ahead was for the IS and shop stewards' movement to grow in parallel since they were co-equivalent in the development of the revolutionary programme.

Both Cliff and Hallas recognized the place of party democracy to facilitate these developments. Hallas observed that party democracy is '. . . fundamental to the relationship between party members and those amongst whom they work' while Cliff stressed its role in developing and preserving the revolutionary cadre: '. . . wide differences of strategy and tactics can and should exist in the revolutionary party. The alternative is the bureaucratised party or the sect with its "leader".'[36] However, the almost federal nature of IS began to change markedly after 1968. One ex-member of the organization claims that Cliff's move back to Leninism was occasioned by the frustration of the spontaneous revolt in France: '. . . the failure of the May events to lead to revolution, together with the confusion caused by rapid growth in IS itself led Cliff to turn right back to Lenin'.[37]

Certainly, the growth in membership between 1965 and 1968 (from 400 to 1,000 in Shaw's estimate) might have led to some internal problems had the organization remained as loosely structured as Birchall describes it. IS's unity call of 1968 (in response to Enoch Powell's inflammatory speech on Black immigration and the enthusiastic support it received among London's dockers) though rejected by the SLL and IMG, led to it playing host to an organization called Workers' Fight which operated as an entrist group within International Socialism for the next three years. Thus the ideological heterogeneity of IS members was increased in 1968. It is doubtful, however, that Cliff's re-conversion to Leninism was simply a question of putting the IS 'house' in order.

Though the Paris events no doubt contributed to the changeover, IS perspectives which pre-date the May uprising also played their part. Kidron's survey *Western Capitalism Since the War* stressed the convergence of the major political parties and the decline of Parliament as a vehicle for the achievement of 'direct, felt reforms'. He argued that the Labour Party no longer promoted significant advances for workers and that strikes were more important in obtaining private fringe benefits. For Kidron, the legislative pendulum had swung against workers since 1964 with the introduction of an incomes policy. IS was moving towards the conclusion that general elections were simply a choice between 'Tweedledum and Tweedledee'.

Since the early sixties Cliff had identified the growing shop stewards' movement as the potential working class vanguard and had seen evidence of its strength in the growing number of unofficial strikes on questions of workers' control (rather than pay) and in the emergence of workplace committees, shop stewards' 'combines' and the accompanying wage drift. To Cliff, the trade union bureaucracy appeared to be weakening while the Labour Party had outlived its reformist period. IS's decision to leave the Labour Party was based on this analysis and its perspective was to establish a leading role in 'the fragments'. After several years' experience and organizational growth the IS, in Cliff's view, was ready for a greater degree of centralization.

Accordingly, in place of an executive committee based on delegates from IS branches, an *elected* national committee (to be determined by conference) was proposed in order to constitute the executive bodies on a political rather than a geographical basis. After fierce debate, Cliff's reforms were accepted. The IS was now geared to a policy of implanting itself in the industrially militant sectors of the working class despite the problem of its predominantly student and white-collar composition.

Not surprisingly then, the first fruit of this policy was the establishment of a rank-and-file group within the National Union of Teachers rather than among manual workers. This caucus set a pattern by producing its own journal which within a few years reached a circulation of several thousand. The significance of this IS group was demonstrated by the election of two of its members to the NUT executive. The success registered here led to a proliferation of IS journals in many other unions including the CPSA, ATTI, NUPE, COHSE and among carworkers and miners.[38] From 1968 the group's newspaper, *Labour Worker,* became *Socialist Worker* (which by 1972 had quadrupled in size to 16 pages). All these developments reflected the growing confidence of the organization which by 1973 claimed 2,667 members (of whom only 200-300 had been in the organization since the mid-sixties).

The 'Bolshevization' of IS would appear to have been a limited success: but it did involve some casualties. Branches involving members of Workers' Fight were formally split in 1969 and in 1971 they were asked to choose between WF and IS at a special conference. Another faction was eliminated in 1973 when a group led by David Yaffe (the so-called right faction) was expelled after months of scholastic disputations which covered every fundamental aspect of IS policy.[39] Cliff's determination to fill quickly the 'vacuum on the left' by building IS piecemeal and arithmetically, however, also caused problems with some of the organization's old guard.

In 1974 Cliff, supported by Paul Foot, moved to the conclusion that a mass audience was potentially available to *Socialist Worker* which should now adopt a more proletarian character. The paper's editor, Roger Protz, had already built up its circulation from a few thousand to 30,000 per week but was opposed to the dilution of its content which he saw as an inevitable concomitant of Cliff's proposal to turn readers into writers for the journal. But Cliff envisaged a circulation of 80,000 by 1976 despite the fact that in the general election of February 1974 only 35,000 copies were sold from a print order of 50,000. Cliff's optimism remained undented despite acknowledging the rather equivocal facts of IS membership figures:

The 1974 registration showed an overall membership of 3,310, half of whom are manual workers, organised into 220 branches, 40 of which are factory or industrial branches. The figures reveal a higher rate of turnover than expected — 48% of registered members have been in IS for a year or less — although we have no figures for previous years on which to make a comparison . . . Recruitment in January and February averaged 150 per month — approximately 40 per month up on the average for the previous three months.

The opposition to Cliff — led by Hallas, Higgins, Protz and Palmer — argued that 'the high turnover of membership proves the need for more serious training and integration' and that though 'there has always been an element of capriciousness and arbitrariness in IS', today 'the membership is unusually uninformed'. However, the argument was to no avail and, significantly, the entire debate remained a national committee affair which excluded the membership (and, no doubt, contributed to its alleged ignorance). Higgins and Protz were sacked, Nagliatti (the IS Industrial Organizer) resigned and Hallas accepted defeat (though he remained prominently in the organization).

Cliff was able to lead the IS along the chosen path of constructing a party which would try to emulate the early CPGB and promote its own version of the latter's minority movement. One major obstacle to this was the poor industrial base of the organization: 70 per cent of the membership were either students, housewives, unemployed, or white-collar workers and of the 3,310 members, only 368 were organized in factory branches. Yet the leadership, according to Cliff, felt that it was objectively possible to overcome this even though the immediate prospect, in 1974-5, was recognized to be 'a decline in the number of industrial disputes':

. . . it is now possible to talk, and to talk credibly, of the need to build a socialist workers' party that will sweep away capitalism. Building such a party is now fully on the agenda. It is a challenge IS willingly accepts . . . such a party has its mainspring in workplace branches. That is where workers' power lies. And that is why last year IS built 38 factory branches and this year the IS Conference decided to aim at 80 factory branches plus a number of white collar branches by autumn 1975.[40]

As part of the proletarianization of IS, almost the entire executive committee was replaced by provincial organizers from the organization's growth areas. But the result of this was that EC meetings became irregular and poorly attended. The logic of Cliff's attempt to transform IS into a workers' party became obvious in other ways too. In 1975 IS members were instructed to terminate their accustomed tactic of collaboration with the broad left in trade union elections and to stand independent IS candidates instead. In the Birmingham AUEW, where the broad left united front had paid off, IS members resisted the change and lined up against Cliff, with Higgins and Palmer, to present the 'platform of the IS opposition'.

It was at this point that Cliff relied on purely organizational manoeuvrings to silence the rebels. By changing aspects of the IS internal structure Cliff pre-empted the attempt to challenge his policies. The national committee of forty was replaced by a central committee of nine which took over its role, while the NC itself was relegated to an advisory function. According to Shaw the delegate system for conference was gerry-mandered so that districts replaced branches as the representational basis of the organization, ensuring that an estimated oppositional minority of one third to two fifths of the membership was reduced to 15 per cent of the 1975 conference delegates.[41] Cliff's position was now virtually unassailable — permitting abuses, such as the decisions to launch the Right to Work campaign (late 1975) and the Socialist Workers Party (late 1976) without consulting the membership.

These practical changes in the IS internal regime were seen by the leadership as necessary alterations to equip the IS for its new role as a national political party challenging the CPGB for hegemony of the left outside the Labour Party. The idea of a socialist workers' party was first floated by Cliff in 1975, but the analysis which gave the idea theoretical justification was worked out long before. In the mid-sixties IS had launched out on its own, leaving the Labour Party and identifying the growing shop stewards' movement as the basis for a new revolutionary party. The upheaval in Paris in May 1968 emphasized the continuing validity of Leninism for Cliff, and as this worked itself out in practice it came to mean the greater dominance of the leadership around him. On the question of inner-party democracy IS spokesmen modified their earlier views accordingly. For example, it was claimed that 'the IS have consistently defended Leninist principles against all those who sought to "revise" them.' In fact we have shown this to be false. IS was converted to Leninism — or Cliff's version of it — in 1968.[42] Hallas, for whom internal democracy had been a *necessary* feature of revolutionary organization in 1971, was more equivocal by 1979. Thus:

. . . the regime must at all times be as open and flexible as possible, consonant with preserving the revolutionary integrity of the party. *The qualification is important.* For unfavourable circumstances weaken the ties between the party and the layers of advanced workers, and so increase the problem of 'factions, groups, and sects' which can be an *obstacle* to the growth of inner-party democracy as Trotsky understood it . . . *it is an indispensable function of the leadership . . . to understand when to close to preserve the core of the organisation from disintegration by unfavourable outside pressures — to emphasise centralism.*[43] [my emphasis]

While these generalizations cannot be dismissed as totally invalid (precisely because they are such generalizations), in the specific circumstances of recent IS history they sound like an apologia for the measures taken by Cliff which, while certainly centralizing the power around him, excluded the IS membership from participation in major decisions. Cliff's own views on inner-party democracy have developed to the point where he applauds Lenin for rejecting '. . . dogmatic schemes of organisation . . .' and is '. . . ready to change the organisational structure of the party at every new development of the class struggle. Organisation . . . should be subordinated to politics'.[44]

Cliff's evolution on this question — from Luxemburg to an instrumentalist conception of democracy — is mirrored by the evolution of IS practice in the 1970s which, among other things, has involved expulsion of dissidents,[45] the suppression of an IS gay group, and a commandist mode of operation in the women's movement. This has been accompanied by a lurch towards 'workerism' — an emphasis on the mainly trade union struggles of

industrial workers which underrates the value of political activity
initiated by other sections of society. Where IS-SWP has involved
itself in these other campaigns it does so in order to build IS-SWP.
Cliff puts the question as follows:

. . . where the question of a rank-and-file, or the Anti-Nazi League being
independent of the SWP was a problem for us a few years ago, at the present
time it's not a problem at all. We simply always say quite clearly that the
leadership of the Rank-and-File is the SWP. The leadership of the ANL is in
reality the SWP and we don't give a damn.[46]

The organization's attempt to build itself piecemeal, until it surpasses
the CPGB in influence over trade unionists and the whole Marxist
left, has been conducted by the IS-SWP leadership in such a way as to
repel organizations seeking collaboration (IMG) or organizational
autonomy (the women's movement and the defence organizations of
ethnic minorities). As the SWP was launched in order to fill the
vacuum which Cliff located to the left of the Labour Party, it has had
to try and live up to his over-optimistic projections and fallen into
sectarianism as it failed to do so. An examination of the IS-SWP
strategy will reveal the reasons for this evolution.

COMPONENTS OF THE RANK-AND-FILE STRATEGY

The IS-SWP theory of rank-and-filism is both an industrial strategy
to build the IS-SWP and is seen by the organization as a
revolutionary strategy to overthrow capitalism. As the strategy
developed the IS simultaneously elaborated an argument against the
entrist option which involved a characterization of the Labour Party
as Tweedledee to the Conservatives' Tweedledum. IS writers played
down the role of the Labour Party in obtaining reforms which, they
argued, were either the product of the post-war economic boom or
of extra-parliamentary pressure in the (most notable) form of strikes.
This made the Labour Party superfluous in either case and could
stand as an argument against entrist infiltration designed to capture
the party. Furthermore 'the only time the Labour Party could be so
captured would be at a time of massive struggles when it is
irrelevant. More than that it would be a positive danger — by
switching the struggle from the factories to the polling booth'.[47]

    To this argument of Kline's Cliff added that the Labour Party
membership — largely inactive, middle-aged and middle-class
servants of an electoral machine — was simply not worth the trouble

which entrism involved.[48] Again it was stressed that in a recession, when the route to parliamentary reforms was closed, the Labour Party became irrelevant as a forum of socialist activity. Hallas also observed how this activity became grotesque by contamination of the Labour milieu:

[entrism] is based on a false identification of the Labour Party and the labour movement . . . it fails to take into account the obvious facts that there is no connection between the Labour Party membership organisations and any actual working class *struggle* (with very rare exceptions like Clay Cross), that the vast bulk of the individual membership (which, incidentally, has declined by a third over the last 20 years) is a purely paper membership never seen at any party meetings, that the active membership is much less working class than the card-holders and that much of it (both left and right) represents a political *selection* of individuals firmly wedded to the Labour Party-type politics, municipal and national, by *conviction* as well as habit . . . finally it ignores the deleterious effects of the Labour Party environment on those who enter it in order to change it . . . entrism is a parasitic activity . . . the entrist's political activity is necessarily dominated by the rhythms of Labour Party life, the conferences, the resolutions won or lost, the elections for this or that post or delegacy.[49]

The IS view, then, is that the Labour Party is basically an electoral machine, generally absent from working-class struggles, which is liable to corrupt socialists who operate in its routinist milieu. Moreover it could only be transformed by conditions which would make this transformation less than vital: for the rest of the time it is either a secondary factor in achieving reforms (during periods of economic boom) or incapable of resisting the roll-back of existing reforms (during economic depression). For the IS the industrial struggle, by implication, would enable socialists to avoid these drawbacks by interventions of an independent character.

It will be simply noted that the IS argument tends to equate the *organizational* absence of the Labour Party in extra-parliamentary conflict with its (supposed) *ideological* absence in the minds of the participants. Likewise the CP's influence in the trade unions — which IS would need to displace — is seen to be on the wane, since it is committed to '. . . a reformist strategy characterised by parliamentary cretinism, a reliance on the Labour Party and an abject kow-towing to the 'left' trade union bureaucracy'. The strength of the CP has been further weakened according to IS, by polycentrism in the Communist movement and the advent of the nuclear stalemate which renders the Party superfluous as a tool of Russian foreign policy. By the IS's own account, it would seem that both the CP and the Labour Party can be by-passed by an organization deeply involved in militant industrial struggles. As we shall see, the 'trade union bureaucracy' is identified as the chief obstacle against which the IS must mobilize if the rank-and-file strategy is to succeed.

THE OBJECTIVE CONDITIONS

We have already seen that the IS strategy was predicated upon the emergence of shop stewards' power as this developed in the industrial circumstances of the fifties and sixties. According to (then) IS member Richard Hyman, the decades of economic growth and full employment were years in which 'over 95% of recorded strikes [were] unofficial' and a significant number, as at Pilkingtons, were anti-official.[50] A growing number of strikes, it was observed, were purely local affairs often resolved before the union's national leadership had even been informed of their existence. This was the basis of growing shop stewards' influence: the Donovan Commission on industrial relations in 1965 estimated that 175,000 stewards existed in British industry. By 1975 Tony Cliff argued that the number had grown to 300,000.[51] By then, however, the contraction of the economy was beginning to undermine the shop stewards' position by once again centralizing trade union bargaining at national level. As Middlemas points out this was also an ideological offensive against shop stewards as '. . . public opinion turned against "shop stewards' militancy" as if that alone had been responsible for the country's failure of economic achievement'.[52] The IS understood that this development was also designed to restrain rank-and-file militancy '. . . whether government strategy towards trade unionism is 'hard' or 'soft' its basic logic — dictated by the constraints of contemporary capitalism — remains consistent: to curb the influence of independent shop-floor organisations.[53]

It seems clear, however, tht Tony Cliff regarded both the rise in shop stewards' power *and* the offensive against it as evidence of the growing politicization of the 'economic struggle' in industry. In 1970 he argued that 'both the rise of the shop stewards' organizations and the number of unofficial strikes are symptoms (among other things) of the common aspiration of the working class: towards workers' control'.[54] But he also saw in the 'employers' offensive' against shop-floor militancy — that is, in national incomes policies, wage freezes and productivity deals — measures, which, by leading to a collision between the unions and the government, would pose questions about the purpose of production, the division of the social product and control over the means of production.

Cliff's argument was that 75 per cent of all stoppages of work between 1940 and 1960 were concerned with questions other than pay. Typically, he argued, the intensity of labour, the duration of work breaks, conditions of employment and such were the main areas of contention in industry. But, argued Cliff, the economic crisis forced the state and the employers to launch an attack on rank-and-file power. In this offensive, the defenders of capital attempted to enlist the support of union officialdom — the trade union bureaucracy.[55]

In the early seventies — when IS made its 'turn to industry' — Cliff's rank-and-file strategy was baptized in circumstances which appeared favourable to its success. In Hyman's words, workers were pursuing '. . . ambitious demands . . . with unwontedly militant methods . . . when the predicament of British capitalism makes even the traditionally limited patterns of union action increasingly intolerable'. Apart from militant innovations such as the 'flying pickets' of the miners' strike in 1972 and the wave of occupations — most notably at Upper Clyde Shipbuilders — political strikes had also reappeared in significant numbers. Though the defeat of the Industrial Relations Bill and the fall of the Heath government are the most celebrated examples of this, political strikes were also called in support of old age pensions (September 1973), against phase two of Heath's pay policy (May 1973) and in solidarity with the 'Shrewsbury Three' (in both 1973 and 1974). For Hyman, as for IS, these features of the industrial struggle demonstrated:

. . . that collective action represents a reaction against the economic exploitation and deprivation of control inherent in the institution of wage-labour, and possesses a dimension of revolt which can never be wholly suppressed.

The IS initiative in launching a rank-and-file movement was intended to politicize further these elementary sectional struggles (which were tending to overcome the traditional constraints of trade union action anyway) and make of them one national movement which would form the basis of a new revolutionary party.[56] The first national rank-and-file conference was called in March 1974 with 500 delegates representing 300 sponsoring bodies. An organizing committee was established consisting entirely of IS members. At the time revolutionary optimism was high within IS. For the first time since the 1920s an alternative to parliamentarianism had been adumbrated which threatened both the trade union leadership and the Labour Party. The direct action which Saltley and Clay Cross symbolized seemed to hold out the prospect of a revitalized socialist movement based on the apparent radicalization of leading sections of the working class. The IS tended to make the equation between economic and political militancy imagining that one followed the other in a straightforward fashion which would transform IS into a revolutionary party. The model it sought to emulate was also taken from the 1920s, namely, the minority movement.

The minority movement was set up by the Communist Party in order to overcome the craft consciousness, apoliticism and sectionalism of the shop stewards' movement and with the intention of transforming the reformist trade unions into 'efficient organs for the suppression of capitalism', as the Second Congress of Comintern posed it. In order to accomplish this, the Communist Party sought to develop rank-and-file factory committees within the unions based on the shop stewards' movement. Yet by 1926 the CPGB, despite worthy efforts, had organized only 17 per cent of its 6,000 members in factory cells. A study of this episode by two IS members was forced to conclude that the CP failed with the minority movement because of hostile 'objective conditions'.[57] Clearly the IS, which in 1974 had only 11 per cent of its members in factory cells from a total only half the size of the CP in 1926 and far less proletarian in composition, started from an inferior position with its rank-and-file initiative. Furthermore if, as Hinton and Hyman conclude, the CP erred in the 1920s because it tried to identify with a non-revolutionary mass movement and in consequence 'the Party's own theoretical level (degenerated) to that of a militant defensive reformism', the IS soon found itself in a similar position. Thus one year after the national rank-and-file movement was set up, the IS defined its objectives primarily in defensive terms: 'these rank-and-file organisations linked together in a national movement which will act *primarily in defence* of workers' interests'. [my emphasis][58] This was reflected in the pages of *Socialist Worker* which, in the 1970s, became almost exclusively preoccupied with championing workers in pay disputes. The politics of the IS weekly were reduced to a celebration of trade union militancy and to attacks on those who defaulted on this. All other issues were subordinated in its propaganda to the struggle it depicted between the rank and file and the trade union bureaucracy.

The Trade Union Bureaucracy

Leninists have always regarded a revolutionary strategy based solely on the transformation of reformist trade unions into revolutionary *trade unions* as a syndicalist error. IS writers, in their confusion as to the nature of the rank-and-file strategy, have produced statements which smack of this syndicalist 'deviation'.[59] Yet, Cliff, Hinton and Hyman have all identified syndicalism as a weakness of the early shop stewards' movement.[60] Andreas Nagliatti, while he was IS industrial organizer, viewed the national rank-and-file movement as a mainly defensive working-class organization, while Ken Appleby argued that it was a means 'of increasing the radicalisation of the working class'.[61] Cliff, as we have seen, regards it as the basis of a new revolutionary party.

This confusion of perspectives probably results from the fact that, as the IS left opposition observed, the national rank-and-file movement '. . . is not the product of the realisation of leading sections of the class for unity in struggle, but rather the result of the behind-the-scenes activity of IS'.[62] The movement, whatever its original (uncertain) conception, quickly became a means of building IS and was conducted in a way which reduced the rank-and-file organizations to a composition of IS members and sympathizers only. The failure of the NRFM to strike deeper roots is also a failure of IS theory.

The IS argued that the objective need for a NRFM stemmed, in large measure, from an alleged conflict of interests between the 'trade union bureaucracy' and the shop floor. Despite innumerable references to this bureaucracy, IS literature fails to provide any detailed analysis of the stratum. Though national leaders of trade unions are commonly cited as instances of the union bureaucracy, even shop stewards who leave the bench too frequently for union business are considered potential bureaucrats by IS.[63] It is clear, however, that IS explains bureaucratization in terms of the embourgeoisement of union officials.[64] The 'two souls' of the trade union official are explained by Cliff as follows:

Trade union officialdom is caught in a contradictory position. Their trade unions are organisations for the defence of workers against the employers; but they themselves live completely differently and separately from the workers they represent. Even the most 'left' of the top union officials is trapped by his social environment. Worse still, he has to work through an official machine whose personnel is very much a prisoner of this same environment. The official is, and feels that he is, a member not of the working class but of the middle class.[65]

The IS emphasis on embourgeoisement as the cause of bureaucratization in trade unions overlooks the fact that the *function* of trade union officialdom is the main source of tension between the leadership and the rank and file because it encourages, even necessitates, that this leadership views each industrial conflict as a problem to be solved within a given framework. The rules of the game are such that every trade union negotiator must become skilled at compromise. Indeed the very existence and goals of trade unions are proof of the centrality of compromise and that unions *reflect* class differences rather than seek to abolish them. By stressing the syndicalist theory of leadership betrayal due to embourgeoisement, the IS unwittingly places its own members in an embarrassing contradiction since those of them who become full-time union negotiators must eventually compromise ('sell out') if they are to be credible trade unionists. Significantly, the IS nowhere explains how it is possible both to work within the sphere of official trade unionism and to construct independent rank-and-file organizations. Since, as IS argues it, this process affects both left and right wings of the trade union leadership it is pure folly to suppose that the left–right distinction can be of determinant significance in the way conflicts are resolved between workers and management, or workers and state.

IS was very critical of the CPGB precisely because the latter proposed that left trade union leaders were its natural allies and that the industrial militants at shop floor level should prioritize the election of left wingers in to leading positions. By making this activity the chief plank in its industrial strategy the CP, according to IS, makes the rank and file prey to illusions and victims of sell outs. The 'conversion' of Scanlon and Jones to the last Labour government's pay policy is cited by IS as an example of the CP's blunderings since the latter championed the 'terrible twins' as leading lefts with whom the militants should collaborate. Hence the need, according to IS, for a strategy based on the independent organization of the rank and file within the trade unions. This is argued to be of special significance in periods of economic downturn when the tendency to incorporate the unions into the state is accelerated: '. . . the role of the trade union leadership is to come to terms with government economic priorities — even though these priorities reflect the essentially capitalist (and anti-trade unionist) rationale of enhanced profitability and more intensive exploitation of labour'.[66] Under these conditions, the choice facing the trade unions is, according to Cliff, between integration with the state or control by the rank and file.[67] That IS's preferred alternative has strongly syndicalist overtones is indisputable.[68]

For in order to organize a revolutionary rank-and-file movement it is held by Leninists to be necessary for this rank and file to come under the leadership of a revolutionary party. IS, however, launched the NRFM *in order* to create a revolutionary party. Though this initiative failed to establish more than the semblance of a national industrial base for IS, the organization was carried by its own logic, rather than the logic of real developments into re-naming itself the Socialist Workers Party at the beginning of 1977. The organization then tried to live up to its new nomenclature by acting as if it was already the acknowledged leader of a significant, vanguard, section of the working class. The result was a sectarian refusal to join in united front activity with other organizations in elections, in the Right to Work campaign and in the Anti-Nazi League.

This pass was reached via a determinist reading of the conjuncture which, in the early seventies, imagined that the economic depression combined with shop floor militancy would mean that 'pure-and-simple trade union activity *does* pose a substantial threat to the stability of the capitalist economy'.[69] There is no doubt that Cliff believed that economic circumstances would politicize the rank and file towards a revolutionary consciousness

when workers ask for a few shillings a week in a single shop, the ideological veil covering the system as a whole is not pulled aside but when 100,000 workers demand a 20% rise to keep up with rising prices the class struggle moves to the centre of the stage.[70]

Socialist Worker reflected this argument by presenting the strike news and pay demands as if the larger the quantity of pay demanded the greater the socialist consciousness of the trade unionists involved. Yet this emphasis and the IS's workerism did nothing to prevent the decline in membership between 1974 and 1976. Ironically the IS was revived by its campaign against the National Front when the Anti-Nazi League was formed in 1976. Though 'politics' rescued the IS, temporarily, from its economistic blind alley, the organization remained formally committed to its rank-and-file strategy until the SWP Conference of 1981.

ABANDONMENT OF RANK AND FILISM

By 1982 the SWP Central Committee outlined its reasons for

abandoning the rank-and-file strategy. In some respects its analysis is similar to our critical remarks above. The practical collapse of the SWP's rank-and-file groups, it seems, ultimately forced the organization to revise its formal perspectives. This collapse is illustrated by the figures for rank-and-file newspaper sales (table 5.1).[71]

TABLE 5.1 *Rank-and-file newspaper print orders (,000)*

	1973	1982
Carworker	6	—
Collier	5	1.6
Hospital Worker	6	2
Platform	3	—
Textile Worker	1.5	—
Case-Con	5	—
Journalists Charter	2	—
NALGO Action News	6	2.5
Rank and File Teacher	10	3
Scots Rank and File	2	—
Redder Tape	3	1
Technical Teacher	2	1.2
Dock Worker	5	—
GEC Rank and File	8	—
Building Worker	2	—

These figures demonstrate the failure, in particular, to establish a base in heavy industry which, as we have seen, was central to the SWP strategy.[72] According to the party's leadership:

. . . as soon as the National Rank-and-File Movement was launched at the March 1974 delegate conference the conditions which would have permitted it to flourish ceased to exist. The election of a Labour government took the political edge off wage-militancy, which in any case collapsed thanks to the Social Contract. One sign of this was the collapse of most of our factory branches. In practice we abandoned the strategy, shifting to the Right to Work campaign. However when there was a revival of Rank-and-File militancy in 1977 we tried to relaunch the NRFM refusing to recognise the changes in the objective situation. This led us into ultra-left substitutionism . . .'

The SWP's failure to consolidate its factory branches has forced the leadership to acknowledge that 'the geographical branch is the key to our organisation and intervention in this period'. This is explained as a consequence of the downturn in trade union militancy which is seen as a move to the right within the working class. The SWP Central Committee likewise identifies a move to the right within the Labour Party since the beginning of 1982 concluding that:

We cannot substantially influence that process. We are, quite simply, too small and too marginal to influence the direction of the Labour movement.

What we can do is to argue patiently and carefully . . . we can begin to rebuild the socialist consciousness which is essential in the current period.

While this would seem to imply that the erstwhile Socialist Workers Party is in reality able to play the role only of a propaganda group, no such firm conclusions are reached, though it is recognized that to persist with the rank-and-file strategy (an essential component of the SWP's claim that the objective basis for party building exists) would merely result in 'substitutionism and sectionalism'. The SWP's auto-critique also makes clear its concern with the level of political sophistication within the group. I suggested above that this was an early casualty of the group's economism during the period when the NRFM was thought viable.[73] Now — in recognition of the failure of this project — the central committee stresses the need for a deepening and expansion of the group's ideology, this being the SWP's last defence and sole claim to distinction in a period when it is, once again, forced to 'swim against the current':

Only people who are confident of revolutionary politics can really hope to be able to put forward the arguments which are needed . . .

The thing which holds a revolutionary organisation together during the pressure of a downturn is the clarity of its politics.

The political discussion in the branch is the most important item of the week. Every branch works better the more all of us understand about the general ideas of Marxism. . .

Together with a number of exhortations to improve the quality of branch politics, these remarks seem to indicate concern that the SWP membership, faced with few opportunities for the practical preoccupations of the 1970s, will grow despondent and fall away from the organization.

However the SWP leadership appears to remain committed to the perspective of party building despite its abandonment of rank-and-filism. Just as there is no critique of this, there is no mention of the economistic assumptions on which this project was based. While it is recognized that the NRFM was initiated on the basis of assumptions which ceased to be relevant after 1974 there is no recognition of the shortcomings of the industrial militancy *before* 1974.

CONCLUSIONS

In reality the trade union militancy of the early 1970s was in the narrowest sense concerned with economics. The militants were not so much concerned to transform society or — like the syndicalists of 1900-14 — to pose alternatives to 'politics', as to ignore politics altogether. Though the syndicalist attitude of hostility to bosses and bureaucrats was evident and the technique of spontaneous militancy in direct industrial action was certainly present, the syndicalist strategy and hope were absent.[74] In a sense the IS-SWP attempted to foster the political radicalization of the working class and to this extent it departed from the classical syndicalist strategy which sought to raise class consciousness by multiplying the number of militant strikes (leading, ultimately, to a revolutionary general strike).[75] But the IS-SWP, as we have seen, did believe that the economic struggle of trade unions was, in the conditions of the 1970s, leading objectively to the goal of political radicalization which the organization desired. This economism underpinned the IS-SWP initiative of rank-and-filism and, indeed, the launching of the SWP itself.[76]

The ability of the SWP to correct its errors, is not helped by the kind of internal changes recorded above which have augmented the power of the leadership at the expense of internal democracy. We have seen that each of the major ideological and practical developments in the organization's history began with Tony Cliff whose intellectual dominance over thirty years was reinforced by greater organizational control. His organizational manoeuvres of 1974-5 led to the departure of many of the group's leading intellectuals.[77] This, combined with the high turnover of membership, has weakened potential countervailing tendencies to Cliff's intellectual and organizational hegemony within the SWP. Indeed Cliff's greater control of the SWP coincides with the political isolation of the group.

For we have seen that since its break with the Fourth International, the 'state capitalist' tendency has been a purely national formation without the benefit of organized and regular forms of international collaboration.[78] In fact the state capitalist theory has acted as a barrier to such connections since this is a shibboleth with few organized adherents outside Britain. While recognizing, intellectually, the need for an International, the followers of Cliff reject the FI and have come to conclude that national mass parties must be built first. Yet the piecemeal construction of a mass revolutionary party, which the SWP has attempted, has no successful precedents and is far more likely to produce a national sect.

Cut adrift from any tradition which might have provided some theoretical anchorage the IS-SWP tendency produced a number of novel though questionable theories which justified the twists and turns of its practical politics. It is noteworthy that Cliff's lengthy study of Lenin locates the latter's genius in his readiness to 'bend the stick', or adapt to circumstances.[79] Cliff's recent enthusiasm for this Lenin, for centralism and for the 'intuitive sense' in politics coincides with the centralization of the IS-SWP. More recently this centralism — or at least the form that it takes — has been relaxed as the existence of an organized faction within the SWP indicates, as do also calls from the membership to adopt the entrist tactic.[80]

However this may be, the synchrony of these internal changes of organization with certain political developments is noteworthy. Discounting the Workers' Fight episode of 1969-71, the IS-SWP internal battles intensified in the mid-1970s. In 1973 the right faction was expelled to form the Revolutionary Communist Group; in 1974 Roger Protz was removed as editor of *Socialist Worker;* further expulsions in 1975 resulted in the formation of the Workers' League and Workers' Power. At the same time the IS-SWP lost many individuals who had been part of its basic cadre.

We have noted Cliff's return to Leninism after 1968. But the actual changes that were designed to bring IS-SWP into line with this model were undertaken in the mid-1970s; that is, during the same period in which the expulsions and splits from the organization took place. At the same time the International Socialism group began to emphasize a simplistic economic determinism. It was stressed that the Labour Party had become an irrelevance because of the economic crisis. Parliament was no longer an arena of political significance: 'direct, felt reforms' were no longer possible there. Yet the group believed that 'pure-and-simple' trade unionism was a 'direct threat to the system'. This conviction led the organization to overstate the political significance of strikes and subordinate aspects of its politics of direct concern to other social categories (students, women, tenants, etc).

The launching of the SWP completed this process of 'Bolshevizing' IS. From this point the organization began to assert its exclusive mission to lead the working class. Accordingly relations worsened between the SWP and organizations which occupy the same part of the political spectrum. The SWP worked alongside or within these groups (such as the Anti-Nazi League, CND, Right to Work campaign, women's movement and so on) in a manner which subordinated the campaigns to the project of building the SWP. The usefulness or worth of these independent groups was measured according to how far they furthered the growth of the SWP — where they were seen as rivals (as with Socialist Unity) they were spurned.

The return of this organization to Leninism would seem, then, to have involved a return to sectarianism, economism and centralism. It is surely of some significance that this once heterodox, libertarian political current — which formerly viewed itself as a *tendency* within the Labour movement — should display the characteristics, noted earlier in this study, of Healyism, from the moment its leaders believed that conditions were ripe for party building. In fact the perspective which led to the SWP posing as *the* revolutionary party was nothing other than the vision of revolutionary political consciousness arising directly out of frustrated trade union and reformist politics in a period of economic crisis. As such — and for all the group's theoretical eclecticism — this was simply a restatement of faith in the perspectives of the early Comintern.

This is all the more ironic in view of the group's theoretical stress on the centrality of self-emancipation in Marxism. In practical terms too, the experience of this group is of relative success in pursuing single-issue campaigns such as those of the Anti-Nazi League and the Right to Work. These elements of the group's politics suggest that its strengths lay in its contribution to a redevelopment of socialist theory and a practical impact as a catalyst of mass movements beyond the confines of the traditional working-class organizations. Both aspects found appeal among recently politically activated sections — in particular youth, women and intellectuals. In the 1960s and 1970s in particular the Labour Party had lost much ground in this quarter and seemed incapable of revitalizing socialist politics and theory. To that extent the IS-SWP was correct in identifying a political vacuum to the left of the mass working-class organizations. However, in its zeal to build an alternative, the IS-SWP resorted to political categories and perspectives resonant of the Leninist Comintern. Whatever the qualities and strong points of this earlier experience, it seems to have been ill suited to the conjuncture and political culture of the period since 1968 on the British extra-parliamentary left.

That the IS–SWP turned to arithmetic party building based on economistic assumptions and a tighter internal regime after many years as a federalistic, theoretically permissive propaganda group is testimony to the powerful pull which the Bolshevik experience continues to exercise. The magnetism of the latter's 'success' perhaps accounts for attempts, such as that of the SWP, to apply such formulae even in conditions where a minority revolutionary socialist culture does not exist within the working class as in Britain. Conversely, the shortcomings of this tradition — such as the absence of a rigorous critique of factors once removed from the primary economic organization of capitalism (mass culture, sexism, racism, etc) — are overlooked or neglected even when the first steps towards such a critique are being formulated (as by the women's movement). Reference to the preoccupations of the early Communist movement, then, would seem to be essential in accounting for the preoccupations of the IS–SWP in the 1970s.

6

The New Left and the Politics of the International Marxist Group

In this chapter I will examine the Trotskyist response to (and initiation of) political movements and campaigns which either originated outside, or were ignored by, the traditional mass organizations of the working class and their members. The emphasis so far has perforce been on the far left's pre-occupations with catastrophism, the Soviet Union, the Communist parties, the Labour Party and the trade unions. In part this reflects the pre-war legacy of Marxist theory and political practice. But it also arises because the far left had virtually no other reference points during the forties, fifties and early sixties. By the late sixties, however, the political situation was transformed as a great number of political campaigns and causes began to mobilize significant numbers of students, youth, women and ethnic minorities in Britain. As this was by no means confined to Britain and occurred in an increasingly explosive world political context the sections of the FI developed a political practice informed by the ISFI's thesis of 'the new rise in world revolution'. This period of FI history begins, however, with the re-unification of the ISFI and the American SWP, a process which began in 1956.

THE RE-UNIFICATION OF THE FOURTH INTERNATIONAL

The 1953 split in the FI, it will be remembered, was explained by the seceding organizations in terms of the ISFI's alleged 'liquidationist' tendencies and adaptations to Stalinism. The basis for these allegations was the optimistic analysis of the Malenkov reforms as proffered by Michel Pablo who, it was said, envisaged the self-reform of the Soviet bureaucracy. The tactic of entrism *sui generis* and the ISFI's mild condemnation of the Russian repression in East Germany were alleged to stem from Pablo's heretical response to the Malenkov thaw.

However, the ISFI was more guarded when, in 1956, Kruschchev's 20th congress speech became known in the West. Though the secret speech was taken as confirmation of the bureaucracy's retreat in the face of 'pressure from the masses', the ISFI argued that the bureaucracy's self-reform could not be fully concluded unless '. . . the politicisation of the masses, going over to direct action, combines with a sharper differentiation, an actual break between the developing revolutionary wing and the more and more isolated thermidorean wing of the bureaucracy'.[1] In other words, the ISFI recognized the continuing validity and necessity of a 'political revolution' as Trotsky had posed it. The ISFI discounted the prospects of a return to the Stalinism of the Stalin era on the grounds that the international balance of forces made such a return 'impossible'. At the same time, the ISFI definitely excluded the possibility of the CPSU becoming a genuine Leninist organization by a series of reforms from the top. It saw the Krushchev reforms rather as a bureaucratic self-defence: a return to Leninism would require a qualitative break involving whole sections of the CPSU rank and file.

The report of Ernest Mandel (alias Germain), from which this analysis is drawn, prophetically observes of Hungary (where it is acknowledged that '. . . the masses . . . seem more passive than in other countries') that '. . . the whole situation seems ripe for [it] to be one of the first countries where a more or less open struggle between tendencies will take place inside a Stalinist party which holds power'.[2] Mandel was clear that 'the decisions of the 20th Congress favour the unleashing of . . . a violent movement of criticism and anti-Stalinist opposition'.

When the Hungarian revolution finally erupted, the ISFI drew the lesson, again, that a revolutionary party was needed if such elemental upsurges were to lead anywhere. But the ISFI also used this occasion to produce its fullest statement yet on the necessity for a plurality of political parties in the post-revolutionary state as a precondition for realizing the original intent of Marx's 'dictatorship of the proletariat'.[3] It was Mandel, again, who wrote this statement.

Beginning by noting that the ISFI's fifth world congress had reaffirmed its commitment to the 'freedom to organize all parties which place themselves within the limits of Soviet legality', Mandel proceeded to argue that:

It is on this point that Trotsky, and ourselves still more clearly, go one step further than the fundamental documents of the Third International, and the Left Opposition. We believe that this step is justified by the Soviet experience. If the proletariat does not have the right to organise different parties, the tendency struggle inside the class party itself is inevitably stifled, for sooner or later this struggle threatens to end up by splitting the party. It is only if the revolutionary party honestly accepts the rule: all power to the workers' council, if it acts within the framework of these councils as an organised vanguard fighting for the triumph of its ideas, only then does the idea of the *dictatorship* of the proletariat take on its true meaning. Therefore, any other solution *ends up in bureaucratic arbitrariness* in which the party takes the place of the class, the Central Committee takes the place of the party and the secretary general of the Central Committee.

The ISFI did not limit itself to pedagogic productions either, since it did what it could to intervene through agitation in the Hungarian uprising via the distribution of propaganda within Hungary which expressed solidarity with the insurrectionists and called for a government of soviets. Both the theoretical and practical responses of the ISFI to the Hungarian revolt gave the lie to the ISFI's claim that the International Secretariat had become a liquidationist and Stalinist tendency. The analyses put forward by the American SWP and British SLL were substantially identical to those of the ISFI.[4]

Yet when, in 1957, the British Trotskyists moved a resolution on 'the situation in the world Trotskyist movement' it reiterated Healy's belief that there were two distinct wings — one orthodox (ICFI) and one 'Pabloite-Deutscher' (ISFI) — in the world movement.[5] The American SWP, however, had already re-established links with the ISFI via the good counsels of Leslie Goonwardene, a leader of the Ceylonese LSSP, the only mass Trotskyist party in the world. But the Healy organization had, if anything, hardened its attitude against the ISFI, maintaining that the latter 'could no longer be regarded as a trend within Trotskyism'. The Healy group reached this conclusion because of the ISFI's assertion that the epicentre of world revolution had shifted to the Third World. Healy's 'Euro-centrism' — another dispensable feature of his 'orthodox' reading of Trotsky — made him see this as the ultimate step in 'liquidationism'. For Healy, the ISFI had '. . . abandoned Lenin and Trotsky's positions on independent working class actions and organisations, subordinating themselves to "progressive" nationalist leaders'. Healy's continued opposition to the ISFI was based on the latter's persisting commitment to entrism *sui generis* and its recent emphasis on Third World struggles. On the question of entrism *sui generis* the Fifth World Congress of the ISFI had attributed the numerical strengthening of its national sections to the Pablo strategy. In 1961, the Sixth World Congress argued that entrism *sui generis* had given the Trotskyists access to 'oppositional formations tending to organise themselves to carry out a tendency struggle' within crisis-ridden Communist parties in the wake of 1956.

A more recent development concerned the ISFI's recognition in 1959 that the European working class was 'the *de facto* rearguard of the world revolution.[6] The ISFI's attitude towards the Algerian and Cuban revolutions, in particular, was regarded by the SLL as final proof of its departure from Trotskyism.[7] Yet for the American SWP and the ISFI the Cuban revolution — or rather one's attitude towards it — became the 'acid test' for the re-unification of the FI. Having already agreed on the nature of the Hungarian revolution, its destruction and implications for revolutionary strategy, the ISFI and SWP had drawn close enough to regard agreement on Cuba as a final resolution of the differences of 1953. Even the SLL, sensing this convergence, proposed a parity commission which would begin talks on re-unification. But it also recognized that the differences of 1953 were being circumvented. Healy's response was to intensify his polemics against the ISFI's alleged deviations from orthodoxy and chastise the SWP for '. . . treat[ing] . . . [Pabloism] as an accidental, theoretical deviation using wrong organisational methods. It [the SWP] is not able to give an account of the social and historical roots of this deviation . . .' In other words, for Healy the ISFI had become the representative of alien (that is, bourgeois) class forces. Healy warned against purely organizational means for re-unification and desired that the parity commission discuss the differences between the ICFI and ISFI.[8]

However, the enthusiasm of the SWP and ISFI for the Cuban revolution swept the differences of 1953 to one side: in fact they even held out hopes for the conversion of Castro to a genuine (Trotskyist) socialist internationalism.[9] The isolation of the SLL was made complete as it adopted a position on the opposite extreme — regarding the Fidelistra as 'petty bourgeois nationalists' who could not lead a socialist revolution because a Leninist vanguard party was absent in Cuba. For the same reason, the SLL denied that a dictatorship of the proletariat existed in Castro's Cuba: '. . . the Castro regime is and remains a bonapartist regime resting on state capitalist foundations.' According to the SLL, the Castro regime was not qualitatively different from the Batista dictatorship. Castro's seizure of power was, for Healy, merely '. . . a political revolution which has transferred power from the hands of one class *to another section of that same class*'.[10]

The contrast between Healy's analysis and that of the parties to re-unification could not have been more acute since the SWP and the ISFI claimed that Castro had 'unconsciously' realized the programme of permanent revolution and had forged a revolutionary party in the process of revolution. On this basis the SWP and ISFI re-unified in 1963 to form the United Secretariat of the Fourth International (USFI). The SLL regarded this fusion as totally unprincipled and directly responsible for the capitulation in July 1964 of the LSSP which entered the bourgeois coalition of Mrs Bandaranaika in Ceylon. Though this move was taken against the instructions of the USFI and though the LSSP was promptly expelled from the International, Healy regarded the whole affair as symptomatic of the theoretical and political bankruptcy of the International leadership.[11]

It was certainly true, as Healy contended, that the re-unification talks between the ISFI and SWP did not confront the reasons for the split in 1953. What the re-unification did demonstrate, however, was the theoretically insubstantial nature of the original differences — differences which ten years later were patched over via agreement on the Cuban revolution. The sense of great expectations behind the re-unification of 1963 complements the sense of frustrated impotence which fuelled the split of 1953: the common element in both events was the desire to overcome the FI's political isolation, by short cuts.

ORIGINS OF THE INTERNATIONAL MARXIST GROUP

The split of 1953 left the ISFI without a section in Britain. It was for this reason that the Committee for the Regroupment of the British Section of the Fourth International was set up in 1955,[12] by sympathizers of the ISFI and several members of foreign sections of the ISFI who happened to be resident in Britain. Together these published a mimeographed journal called 'Fourth International'. In 1956 the committee joined forces with the International Socialist Group — an organization led by Ted Grant, Jimmy Deane and Sam Bornstein, who had all been members of the old RCP Majority. The new group became known as the Revolutionary Socialist League and worked within the Labour Party attempting an entrism which avoided the mistakes of Healy's Club. The fifth world congress of the ISFI in 1957 recognized the RSL as the British section of the International.

However this arrangement did not last long, for despite the fusion of the two groups, the ISG worked independently of the committee. Tactically the groups were confused, with entrism being conducted in the Liverpool and Glasgow Labour parties around the journal *Socialist Current* and independent activity elsewhere through the journal *Workers International News*. During 1958 and 1959 these organizational differences became openly political and tactical in content. The old ISG leadership opposed the ISFI's line on the colonial revolution and the danger of world war while the committee members supported it. The latter argued for united work with other entrists within the Labour Party and CND, while Grant's followers clung to perspectives of economic slump and political crises within the Labour movement (which they assumed to be causally connected).

Of those who opposed Grant most left the RSL to join Healy's organization. Only six people, incuding Pat Jordan, withdrew from the RSL in 1961 to distribute a Fourth International journal called *The Internationalist* and it is from this group, based in Nottingham, that the present IMG can trace its history. In 1961 they called themselves the International Group and became the *de facto* section of the FI in Britain despite the fact that Grant's RSL continued to receive financial assistance from the American SWP. This confusion persisted until the USFI engineered their re-unification in 1964. Once again, however, the ostensibly fused groups worked independently with the former International Group members publishing *The Week*. This time the RSL did work with other organizations — most notably the Socialist Review Group — in joint entrist work organized by the journal *Young Guard* which they sold in competition with the SLL's *Keep Left* in the Labour Party's Young Socialist organizations.[13] Competition between the RSL and SLL is alleged to have caused the latter to use intimidatory methods in Wandsworth Labour Party Young Socialists. It was for this reason, according to Pat Jordan, that RSL did nothing to assist the SLL when it was subsequently 'witch hunted' out of the Young Socialists in 1965. Certainly this occasioned the formation of a faction, which opposed the Grant leadership in the same year. Led by Jordan, this opposition became known as the International Marxist Group; but both this and the RSL were reduced to the status of sympathizers with the USFI by the Eighth World Congress in 1965, causing the RSL to sever all remaining links with the International. Thus the IMG remained the sole sympathizing section of the USFI in Britain, and consisted of those who had set up the committee, of 1955, and who had subsequently formed the International Group. Since 1965 the RSL, which currently promotes the Militant Tendency within the Labour Party, has had nothing whatever to do with the USFI.

The IMG tendency at first channelled its energies into the Nottingham city Labour Party where, according to Jordan, it 'won hegemony' and elected Ken Coates to the presidency. This was used as a base from which to launch national campaigns in the Labour movement such as the Medical Aid to Vietnam Committee. According to Jordan, 'by this means we circulated the whole of the Labour Party and trade union movement with an appeal to give money to a fund which was linked with the NLF . . . as a result dozens of contacts with sections of the Labour movement were made which were extremely useful in the early days of the Vietnam Solidarity Campaign'. Indeed, for such a small group of people obscurely connected with the FI the IMG tendency was extremely successful in promoting campaigns which drew widespread support from within the mass organizations of Labour and won the sponsorship of notables in the movement.

The Week gained the support of Bertrand Russell, Ernie Roberts MP and Laurence Daly, among others. The IMG's position in South Nottingham CLP enabled it to forward a motion calling for solidarity with the Vietnamese National Liberation Front, which *The Week*'s editor Ken Coates spoke to at the Labour Party Annual Conference in 1965. Coates and *The Week* were also deeply involved from the beginning with the publication of *Voice of the Unions* and its offshoots which developed from an initiative by Ernie Roberts and Frank Allaun. In April 1964 the *Voice* newspaper promoted a conference on workers' control which won the support of Hugh Scanlon and Jack Jones. In addition to these activities the IMG emphasized Vietnam Solidarity work to which it had been directed by the USFI in 1965. In this the IMG members joined forces with the Bertrand Russell Peace Foundation and the War Crimes Tribunal. Russell collaborated with leading IMG members in launching the Vietnamese Solidarity Campaign (VSC) in June 1966.[14]

Despite the prominence of IMG members in these public activities, the organization itself was still virtually unheard of in consequence of its entrist status.[15] The perspective of *The Week* was that '. . . a mass left would arise in the Labour Party once Labour was in power'. Even after four years of Wilsonism the IMG's perspective remained unchanged. Yet during this same period the propaganda campaign which the IMG waged in VSC paid off in several respects. It succeeded in destroying the pacifist line of the Communist Party and the latter's vehicle (the British Council for Peace in Vietnam) and replaced these with its own slogan ('Victory to the NLF') and a mass campaign led by the VSC. The first VSC demonstration of 22 October 1967 mustered 5,000 supporters. In March 1968 25,000 were called on to the streets before the massive show of strength in October of the same year when over 100,000 marched under the slogan 'Victory to the NLF'. Most of those mobilized by the VSC were students and youth outside of the Labour Party; indeed the trade union and labour movement — far from showing any initiative on the Vietnam issue — displayed, if anything, a waning interest. Labour Party conference agendas for the years 1965 to 1968 show amendments on Vietnam numbering 19, 51, 13 and *one* respectively.[16]

The strains between these two wings of IMG activity — its engagement with the traditional mass organizations versus its success in mass mobilizations of a seemingly new vanguard — soon caused splinters within the group. The organization split in October 1967 when *The Week* supported an unofficial dock strike opposed by the TGWU leadership. According to Pat Jordan, Coates favoured Jack Jones' stand against the strike. Because of the latter's importance to the campaign for workers' control, Coates is alleged to have temporized on this issue.[17] With Coates' subsequent departure from IMG, the latter lost its influence over the militants it had done much to mobilize in the workers' control conferences and since 1968 — when the conferences were formalized as the Institute for Workers' Control — the IMG has played no part in that movement. The fact that IMG failed to recruit even a handful of these trade union militants prior to the split must, in part at least, be attributed to its clandestinity as an entrist formation.

For the same reason the IMG gained fewer recruits from the VSC than the International Socialists. The IS was, like the IMG, at first connected with VSC through its involvement in the Labour Party Young Socialists. But unlike the IMG, the IS quickly withdrew from the Labour Party when it became clear that VSC supporters were, in the main, non-members of the LPYS. Paradoxically it was the IS which wanted the VSC to orientate for working-class support while the IMG fought to keep it a single-issue campaign. In the event IMG won on this question and the logic of its commitment to the VSC forced it to give up entrism in 1969. By this time the IMG identified the student movement as its best field of activity and, in belated recognition of this, launched a youth organization — the Spartacus League — in 1970. The IS, which succeeded in gaining far more recruits from student campaigns, departed from the Vietnamese Solidarity Campaign in order to concentrate on the trade union struggle against *In Place of Strife*. In this way the IS was able to avoid becoming a purely student organization by constructing a trade union base. Once again, the IMG only belatedly sought a similar route (during the miners' strike of 1972) and paid the price for its tardiness. But the IMG's major weakness in these years was part of the legacy of British Trotskyism which can be summarized as the view that any upsurge in working-class consciousness would automatically channel itself into the constituency Labour parties and trade union branches. The concomitant error was the belief that any tendency struggle inside the Labour Party reflected an upsurge in workers' class consciousness. The IMG supposed, therefore, that protest struggles would be led by the working class. Though this was belied by the experience of VSC (and even, to some extent, CND) the IMG persisted in this mistake until the former became a spent force.

THE NEW RISE IN WORLD REVOLUTION

A *New Society* survey of 1968 showed that a majority of the VSC's rank and file had been active in CND.[18] Apart from personnel the two campaigns share a number of other characteristics which were to become typical of far left political interventions in the late sixties and seventies. Such movements tended to arise around single-issue campaigns of loose, *ad hoc* organization. They relied, for the most part, on the impact of mass demonstrations and appealed principally to the young. The political convictions of the 'membership' of these campaigns can best be described as liberal/libertarian — at least, for the majority. Within VSC, for example, Pat Jordan identified three tendencies, including those represented by IMG and IS. Since IMG and IS combined forces numbered no more than 1,000, it is instructive that the third tendency, according to Jordan, consisted of 'spontex' devotees imitating the American new left. It is likely that the latter were more numerous than the Leninists among VSC's rank and file. Their social composition was, in the main, lower middle class, rather than proletarian. Far from relying on the membership of the mass working-class organizations, these campaigns drew on new agencies of protest such as women, students, youth and ethnic minorities. The new rhetoric tended to be culturalist, anti-bureaucratic, idealist and anti-technological in content, rather than economistic. In complex ways these movements were connected with revived interest in alternative life styles and even the fashion and popular music of the 1960s.

The IMG's involvement in such campaigns virtually comprised the whole of its independent activity after its withdrawal from the Labour Party. By 1970 its problem was how to relate the predominantly student base of its organization to the working class. The answer appeared to lie in the slogan 'from the periphery to the centre' — a slogan which echoed the USFI's conviction that revolutionary advance was proceeding from the Third World to the advanced capitalist countries. On this basis the IMG activists became preoccupied with campaigns on Ireland, racism, feminism, Vietnam, the organization of school students etc. aimed at immigrants, women, youth and the unemployed. By 1971 IMG had accumulated over 30 front organizations, approximately one for every eleven members of the organization.[19] The cost of this was an ultra-activism which reduced IMG to a federation of campaigns instead of a stable cadre.

The amount of political activity required of IMG members in these years can only be guessed at but it may assist the reader's imagination to note that the following areas of activity expected of a member in 1978 (by which time activism had become 'normal' again and, therefore, typical of the far left as a whole). Assuming that the member is a teacher and female she might be expected to engage in the following three areas of work:

(1) *Activity Related to Work*
    (a) Trade union activity (branch meetings, trades council, official positions)
    (b) Attendance of IMG teachers' fraction meetings (fort-nightly)
    (c) Attendance of *Socialist Teacher* public meetings (monthly)
    (d) *Socialist Teacher* sales campaigns among colleagues
    (e) *Socialist Challenge* sales campaigns among colleagues
    (f) Sundry conferences, demonstrations, lobbies etc.

(2) *Activity Related to IMG* (internal life and external work)
    (a) Branch meetings and 'aggregates'

   (b) *Socialist Challenge* public sales (weekly)
   (c) Private study of journals (*International, Inpresor, Labour Focus on Eastern Europe*)and internal bulletins
   (d) Pre-conference discussions, literature and meetings (every two years for periods of three months)
   (e) Branch educationals
   (f) Sundry mobilizations for various campaigns

(3) *Special Activities*
   (a) Women's caucus within IMG
   (b) Feminist literature (*Socialist Woman,* etc.)
   (c) Women's movement (autonomous) meetings
   (d) Sundry conferences, campaigns, demonstrations etc.

Such activism leaves little time for anything else and may account for high membership turnovers within the groups. It is also possibly both cause and consequence of the disproportionately student and recently ex-student compositions of the organizations. But, more importantly, the activism required of members — and even sympathizers — of the Marxist left underlines the 'otherness' of these organizations in the context of the British political culture. The commitment which is required of those transferring their political loyalties to revolutionary socialism involves a change in political style which transforms aspects of the recruits' life-style. This undoubtedly acts as a barrier to the recruitment even of those who are further left than the Labour left. The high turnover of membership on the far left suggests also that even those who make the break with conventional politics have enormous difficulties in sustaining it (notwithstanding the strict selection procedure of groups like the IMG which operate a six-month candidate status for new members).

   Both the IS and the IMG had missed whatever opportunity for organizational and political advance CND might have afforded them. CND itself, of course, must be regarded as a failure, not simply measured against its own objectives but also by virtue of the fact that the call for disarmament was driven underground again for nearly two decades as the campaign petered out. Nigel Young pinpoints the cause of CND's demise in the absence of any theory of change or positive strategy, a failing which was '. . . reflected in and reinforced by the theoretical lack, and absence of strategic vision, in CND as an organisation'. It was this absence, argues Young, '. . . which enabled Marxist sects or organisations to successfully take over or supersede some of the offshoots of nuclear pacifism in the later 1960s moving into a vacuum of ideas and tactics'.[20] However since the SLL mainly kept aloof from CND after its initial involvement and the CPGB only became involved three years after the movement began, it was the latter which was left in control of British pacifism as the campaign for nuclear disarmament fizzled out. By 1966 both the IMG and the IS had emerged to lead CND's past support successfully away from pacifism under the militant pro-Vietcong slogans of VSC.

From this development the IMG and the IS attempted to launch youth organizations which would win support for Leninist ideas. On the basis of the spontaneous student unrest of the late 1960s the IS launched a Revolutionary Socialist Student Federation in 1968 to rival the explicitly apolitical National Union of Students. In this the IS was supported by the IMG. Indeed the success of the French section of the FI — The *Jeunesse Communiste Revolutionnaire* (JCR) — in the events of May 1968 in Paris inspired the IMG to envisage a similar scenario in Britain which it described as '. . . toward the concept of Student Power'.[21] The desire to imitate the French events was present at the first conference of the RSSF which 'adopted an action programme around the Student Red Base concept'. The full measure of the IMG's preoccupations and enthusiasm for 'student power' is revealed by its support for the notion of universities transformed into 'red bases'. In the late sixties the organization projected an image and style of politics not dissimilar to the politics of 'extra-parliamentary opposition', which for a time took root in Germany. The IMG's collaboration with libertarians in the publication of *Black Dwarf* (between 1968 and 1970) and the Third Worldist and student emphasis of *Red Mole* after 1970 were symbols of a political practice which gave *de facto* support to the view that the European working class was no longer a revolutionary force. The political style of IMG at this time was suggestive of Marcuse rather than Lenin.

This political style was never, however, given theoretical justification. Indeed it was simultaneous with these practical orientations that the IMG launched a propaganda campaign to promote Leninism. The old *Black Dwarf* editorial board split because of the IMG's determination to create a Leninist youth organization — the Spartacus League — in 1970.[22] When *Red Mole* was launched it was a specifically IMG publication — its first — and it immediately promoted a Leninist line. The FI had developed an explanation of the student revolt which attempted to situate the phenomenon within an orthodox framework.

As early as 1965 Mandel had attempted to theorize an alternative strategy for socialism which escaped the bounds of catastrophist perspectives. He had argued that 'as far as economic crisis or catastrophe is concerned . . . there are strong reasons why this can be avoided by neo-capitalism for a considerable time to come'.[23] Mandel argued that while, 'for the next decade', catastrophic crises would probably be avoided in Western Europe, the system would periodically face other economic and social problems. Mandel instances high wages, automation, increasing alienation, income policies, 'managed' or provoked unemployment and so on as examples of the 'new' problems of capitalism. These would provide opportunities for a strategy of 'structural reforms' as advanced during the Belgian general strike of 1960-1. Such changes, he maintained, would be anti-capitalist in nature and part of a transition to socialism. The 'explosion' of May 1968 was, for Mandel, a vindication of this analysis.[24]

According to Mandel the role of students had been to 'detonate' a crisis in late capitalism by their fight to reform the system of higher education. This crisis had developed into a pre-revolutionary situation when the political and economic demands of 10 million striking workers were added to those of the students. For Mandel the May events had vindicated the central political positions of the Fourth International.[25]

Mandel explained the student revolt in terms of the insufficient material conditions and facilities of the institutions of higher education combined with the authoritarian structure of such institutions and the ideological bias of academic courses. This amounted to no more than a description of the students' avowed grievances; but to this, Mandel added an analysis of the long-term changes which the capitalist economy was beginning to place on the universities. He argued that this amounted to 'the demand for technically specialised labour and (the demands of) the swelling state apparatus'.[26] According to Mandel (and, for that matter, most of the revolutionary left) the universities were subordinating themselves to the requirements of capital and, at the same time, failing to expand fast enough to satisfy the burgeoning demand for higher education. The result, according to this analysis, was overcrowded campuses of disaffected students who were increasingly critical of the material and ideological shortcomings of their education. Mandel also stressed the proletarianization of post-graduate occupations and the disenchantment and alienation which resulted from it. He advocated that the 'revolutionary student movement' should use the university for the benefit of anti-capitalist workers' movements in need of information and research which would weaken the system.

The IMG echoed Mandel's conviction that the universities could in this way become 'centres of opposition to the capitalist system'.[27] This faith was reflected in the RSSF's 'six point action programme' which demanded 'an end to bourgeois ideology . . . in courses and lectures'. Alongside this giddiness IMG reaffirmed the Marxist conviction that '. . . at present there is no perspective for the development of a mass revolutionary base outside the traditional working class movement'; and it spoke of '. . . our long term perspective for the emergence of a mass revolutionary party [which] remains a split in the ranks of social democracy involving, necessarily in Britain, a really significant section of the trade union movement'.[28] There was, however, a growing gap between such statements and the IMG's political practice. For despite its entrist status (which it terminated in 1969) the IMG was clearly preoccupied with movements and campaigns without significant connections to the Labour movement. The gap between the IMG's formal and actual policies was resolved in favour of its *de facto* practice when it became an independent organization and launched *Red Mole*.

The first issue of *Red Mole*, in 1970, declared its intention to help 'the student left . . . to generate a far greater self-consciousness', though it also spoke of a 'long-term aim' to create a 'revolutionary youth organization rather than a purely student one'.[29] The importance which *Red Mole* ascribed to its largely student readership was quickly attested by a proliferation of articles on the 'campus revolt' (the first issue carried articles on Lancaster, Oxford and Warwick Universities plus coverage of Jerry Rubin's trial and Japanese students' struggles). The second issue of *Red Mole* was entirely devoted to an exposition of Leninism but this very quickly gave way to an ultra-leftist version of 'vanguardism'.

This latter took the form of a long article by Robin Blackburn entitled 'Let it Bleed'.[30] According to Blackburn '. . . the only principled course for revolutionary socialists during the coming election will be an active campaign to discredit both of Britain's large capitalist parties'. The FI's conventional wisdom which justified entrism by reference to the organizational ties between the trade unions and the Labour Party was specifically rejected. '. . . to say that the Labour Party is "organically" linked to the working class is thoroughly confused and confusing . . . because it has a totally bourgeois leadership [it is] *organically* linked only to the political institutions of the ruling class'.

For Blackburn, only the cash nexus linked the Labour and trade union bureaucracies. But, he argued, the significance of the Wilson governments lay in the fact that this experience had '. . . further weakened the hold of the Labour Party over the British working class and it is this fact that is of capital importance to any Marxist evaluation of this Party and the coming election'. Furthermore, says Blackburn, the Labour left, equally discredited, cannot, given the contraction of the economy, pose a serious alternative to the Tories. In these circumstances, he argued, there is no reason to suppose a Tory government would be worse than Labour.

Blackburn's article — a personal statement — is of interest here for the response it drew from the IMG leadership. Pat Jordan criticized some of its points but argued against a Labour vote just as Blackburn had. Later, with the election of a Tory government, *Red Mole* declared 'the old Tories are back' and Tariq Ali explained that

For the workers the electoral victory of the Conservative Party represents a marginal set-back: marginal in the sense that it cannot be predicted categorically that the policies which the Tories adopt will be any different from those practised by Mr Wilson's government, but a set-back nonetheless because a Labour Party in opposition will once again be able to sustain the illusion that it is the only alternative to Toryism and in the absence of a real alterantive it will not be easy to combat this illusion. For this reason alone a Labour victory would have been preferable.

In thus minimalizing the differences between Labour and Conservative Ali, like Blackburn, argued as if the party's working-class constituency was merely the dupe and passive victim of an elaborate con-trick. There is no doubt that IMG's sectarian attitude to Labour (which is subsequently repudiated via Blackburn's and Ali's self-criticism)[31] was a manifestation of a wider ultra-leftism which affected the USFI in the early 1970s.

As noted, the USFI, since its formation in 1963, had come to emphasize the importance of struggles for national liberation in the Third World.[32] The significance it attached to the Cuban model of revolution became clear through the FI's uncritical support of guerillaism in Latin America.[33] By the Ninth World Congress, in 1969, it could declare that 'the only realistic perspective for Latin America is that of armed struggle which may last for long years'.[34] According to an international oppositional tendency led by the

American SWP and some Latin American Trotskyist leaders like Hugo Blanco, this line, in practice, sanctioned kidnappings, ransoms, 'Robin Hood' redistributions by armed cliques and such like and stemmed from the FI's idolatry of Guevara's Bolivian adventure and the 'style' of 1968. This, they claimed, had infected the IMG since 'the same line of reasoning is apparent in the uncritical view taken of the use of terrorist tactics in Ireland, particularly those involving the Provisionals, the more extreme and less political wing of the IRA'.[35] The IMG's attitude to the Labour Party during the general election of 1970, then, must be viewed in this context. The FI's ultra-leftist mood had developed, by 1973, to the point where it could claim that socialist revolution was approaching in Europe '. . . not just in broad historical perspective . . . but even from a conjunctural point of view'.[36] Before pursuing this, however, it is important to trace the development of the far left's attitude to Northern Ireland — especially that of the IMG.

NORTHERN IRELAND

The far left was as unprepared as any other section of the British political spectrum for the eruption of generalized political struggles in Northern Ireland in 1969. This accounts for the confused and shifting slogans and sympathies which these Marxist groups produced during the subsequent decade. An instance of this is the response of the IS to the anti-Catholic pogroms of 1969 in which it called for the intervention of the British army to defend the minority. The IMG roundly condemned the International Socialists for committing the basic error, in the Marxist view, of entrusting the coercive arm of the bourgeois state with the defence of the 'anti-imperialist' section of the Northern Ireland community.

The IMG's response to the political crisis of the Stormont regime was to declare 'Permanent revolution reaches UK'.[37] The editorial of *International* however, recognized that 'a revolutionary leadership has yet to be built and no working-class organisations have won any honours in the recent situation'. If a contradiction exists in simultaneously proclaiming the existence of permanent revolution and the absence of a revolutionary party, the IMG ignored the problem by asserting that 'the left must support the right of the Irish people to use whatever methods they think fit in the struggle for self-determination'. From the beginning, the IMG was aware that such support would include justification for the armed struggle against B-specials, Paisleyites, and British troops. Pat Jordan argued that apart from support for such struggles as the Catholics felt fit to undertake in promotion of their own interests, British socialists must regard as their main task an agitation for the withdrawal of British troops since the latter will 'inevitably be . . . used against the Irish people'.

During 1970 the IMG devoted much of its energies to the education of its own membership and sympathizers on the historical background to the Northern Ireland crisis.[38] As with the rest of the organized left (excluding, of course, the Labour Party), the IMG viewed the conflict as a crisis of British imperialism. On this basis the IMG formed the slogans 'Self-determination for Ireland' and 'Withdraw all British troops now'.[39] Otherwise, we have observed, the IMG had resolved to support *any* tactics adopted by the Republican movement and had reduced its role to that of a cheer-leader for the Catholic minority. This became clear when the IRA campaign moved from defensive to offensive postures.

In response to these developments the IMG began to publish articles by Lenin and Trotsky in which the Bolsheviks had taken a sympathetic view of terrorism. Despite the rather exceptional nature of these extracts it is now clear that they were intended to prepare the IMG's supporters for a position of support for the Provisional IRA's terrorist campaign. In *International* the IMG's preamble to articles by Trotsky (on the murder of a Nazi official by a boy named Grynszpau) and Lenin (on Friedrich Adler's attempted assassination of the Austrian Prime Minister) warns against:

those who simply condemn terrorist actions out of hand and forget the obligation of Marxists to defend those who are struggling against exploitation and oppression even when those who are actually engaged in the struggle adopt methods which Marxists know will not attain the aims which are being fought for. (p.48)

The question of classical Marxism's general attitude to terrorism was also dealt with in an article supporting the Quebec separatists.[40] By 1971 the IMG insisted that revolutionaries '. . . must uncondition-ally support the struggle of the IRA against British imperialism and its puppets'.[41] IMG's principal slogan was now 'Victory to the IRA'.

Though, at first sight, the slogan 'Victory to the IRA' appears to be a logical extension of the IMG's initial 'unconditional support' (for whatever methods the nationalist Irish might choose to adopt) it in fact committed the IMG to a new political position. For it implied that victory *could* be achieved by terrorist tactics. This evolution in the IMG's understanding of the Northern Ireland conflict was helped along by the USFI's enthusiasm for guerilla warfare in the Third World. The IMG's relatively successful Vietnam Solidarity Campaign appears to have been the model for the Irish Solidarity Campaign, which it launched in 1970. 'Victory to the NLF' was replaced by 'Victory to the IRA'. And yet the IMG had earlier displayed an awareness of the political shortcomings of the Provisional IRA in so far as it recognized that 'Liberation for the North cannot be seen except in the *general* context of a republican movement throughout the country'.

The same article went so far as to claim that 'the fate of the Irish revolution in the immediate future will depend on the ability of the Irish revolutionary groupings to capture the leadership of the republican movement and to indivisibly weld together that movement with the struggle in the North'.[42]

As it became clearer that the Provo campaign was politically backward and confined to terrorist offensives in the North of Ireland so, paradoxically, was the IMG's support for this campaign increasingly uncritical. While, in late 1970, the IMG was still awaiting the '. . . constitution of the Irish revolutionary vanguard party', by 1971 it had seemingly discovered it in the Provisionals.

To some extent the change in political line may express the IMG's frustrated attempts to find alternatives to the IRA.[43] However the fact that these were also described as 'urban guerilla' groups attests to the IMG's generally favourable view of that tactic. This was given some plausibility by the Provisional IRA's own early emphasis on *defence* of the Catholic ghettoes.[44] It may also have been that the IMG was unclear about the real situation in Northern Ireland. This is suggested by the statement that the Official IRA '. . . will play a much greater role in liberating Ireland than will the Provisionals'.[45] At the same time the IMG's principal slogan ('Victory to the IRA') aligned it with the Provisionals — since it was they who promoted the military campaign. Furthermore all IMG statements on Ireland stressed the obligation *unconditionally* to support the IRA. Indeed the IMG castigated other far left organizations which distanced themselves from Provo terror.[46]

This was the situation, then when the Provisional IRA extended its bombing campaign to London in 1972. The IMG had already isolated itself from the rest of the far left by its insistence on the centrality of unconditional support for the Provos. The refusal of the IS to go along with this logic made joint work on Ireland impossible. Despite the fact that the Anti-Internment League (set up by IS in the summer of 1971) also stood for 'Troops out now' the IMG stood apart from it:

We would argue . . . that it is necessary to transform the present campaign against internment and for the withdrawal of British Troops into a campaign which is in active solidarity with those leading the fight against British imperialism. And in the meantime we will continue to build and support the Irish Solidarity Campaign.[47]

In practice this meant that in defence of its shibboleth of 'unconditional support' the IMG *was* the Irish Solidarity Campaign, and vice versa.

Occasionally the IMG's own statements demonstrated the illogic of its slogans on Ireland. Thus, according to *Red Mole* 'it is now clear that the split in the Republican Movement was the tragic and politically confused result of an attempt to graft a reformist programme on to the Republican tradition by the Officials'.[48] The same authors were equally clear that: 'the Provisionals . . . are bourgeois nationalists'.[49] Justification for the latter's bombing campaign was provided by the (spurious) argument that the Provisionals received mass support from the Catholics of Northern Ireland. According to Bob Purdie and Gerry Lawless (the IMG's authorities on Ireland) this meant that the campaign of bombings was 'not terroristic'.

It was this reasoning which prevented the IMG from supporting the Anti-Internment League (which had proved capable of mobilizing 20,000 around its democratic slogans). In self-justification the IMG argued that 'we reject a campaign on self-determination and Troops Out because it can be very easily taken up and transformed into a "Bring the boys home" campaign based on *liberal* issues with only a negative impact'. It is difficult to take this argument seriously since both demands appeared among the six-point programme of the Irish Solidarity Campaign. Clearly it was the IMG determination to support the military campaign of the Provisionals which cut the organization off from all significant forces concerned with Ireland. Instead of fighting effectively against the conspiracy of silence on Northern Ireland by taking up specific issues (such as internment) the IMG's efforts were consumed in sectarianism.

The imposition of direct rule in 1972 took the ground away from the Anti-Internment League. Strangely it was precisely at this point that the IMG entered the campaign. By now the AIL had degenerated to a political introversion obsessed with programmatic matters and, for what it was worth, was won over to the IMG's modified slogan: 'Solidarity with the IRA'. In 1973 the IS withdrew from the League. The IMG's 'Solidarity' slogan was put forward in recognition of the illusory content of its predecessor: that is, in belated recognition of the fact that the IRA campaign could not achieve 'victory'. The IMG continued, however, to be purblind concerning the Provos' use of terror. The AIL's 'Statement on the London bombing' makes this clear: 'We refuse to condemn *any* [my emphasis] action carried out in Britain by the IRA'.

Within the IMG there were voices of dissent from this policy but they failed to change the leadership's line.[50] The members of 'the tendency' desired an orthodox Marxist line on IRA terrorism which would put the IMG political position closer to that of the International Socialists. The latter regarded the IRA's bombing campaign in Britain as an instance of the contempt displayed by the 'middle class' Provisional leadership towards the working class of Britain. As for the IRA campaign in Ireland the IS had this to say:

The attitude of socialists towards both wings of the IRA has to be similar: support for them insofar as they protect the Catholic population against the British troops and sectarian attacks, unconditional support for their right to throw out the British troops even if we do not agree with the tactics they use, but no illusion that 'Victory to the IRA' is possible in modern Ireland on the basis of the republican ideology.[51]

However, even this statement ignores the *indiscriminate* nature of Provo terror in Ireland itself during the early seventies. It is this aspect of the IRA campaign of that time which renders the classical Marxist position on terrorism inapplicable.[52] This 'classical' line was largely developed in Tsarist Russia in relation to acts of violence against leading members of the governing class under political conditions in which legal politics were severely constrained. In this situation Marxists declared the futility of individual acts of terror and the impotence of terrorism as a method for achieving social change. At the same time their political sympathies were clearly with the oppressed who were driven to such acts of violence. But the Provisional IRA offensive in Northern Ireland during the greater part of the 1970s involved the bombing of bus depots, hotels, restaurants, public houses, and so on, and led to the deaths and maimings of people who could in no sense be described as the oppressors. Thus even the IS's political line on IRA terror — in eliding the indiscriminate nature of the Provisional campaign in Northern Ireland — was well wide of the mark. It thus demonstrates the even greater political confusion of the IMG, whose unconditional support for the IRA aligned it with an organization which engaged even in openly sectarian killings.

Both IMG and IS began, from late 1973, to stress the slogan 'Troops out now' in their work on Ireland.[53] The 'Troops out' movement was launched at Fulham Town Hall in October 1973 by individuals, acting on their own account, from IMG, IS, Big Flame, and the CP. Ironically, it seems that the IMG came to rediscover the potential of 'Troops out' slogan only after an army wife collected 46,000 signatures supporting this demand which was posed along racist and chauvinist lines. The press publicity received by the campaign did something to raise the issue of British military involvement in Northern Ireland — an issue chiefly ignored by the mass political organizations.

In taking up the 'Troops out' slogan the IMG devoted less time and space for discussion on the character of the Provo campaign. Though its advocacy of 'unconditional' support for the IRA remained formally intact, the London fire bombings of August 1973 were described as 'tactically mistaken' by *Red Weekly*.[54] Yet in reporting the second TOM Conference nine months later (May 1974) *Red Weekly* described the Marxist Fred Halliday (a principal speaker at the conference) as a liberal for publicly disassociating himself from the IRA's military campaign.[55] Any evolution towards a new position on IRA terror was, therefore, rather *ad hoc* and empirical. The Birmingham bombings in late 1974 drew an unequivocal condemnation from IS while IMG continued to stress the exclusive culpability of the British government.[56]

The first TOM conference (which attracted only 40 individuals) had decided to give priority to pressurizing left Labour MPs to break with 'bi-partisanship'. Jeff Rooker, Maureen Colquhoun and Stan Thorne were among the first successes of this tactic. By the second conference trade union notables such as Mike Cooley and Dave Bolton (vice-president of the Scottish NUM) had been won over. It was probably the growing affiliation of trade unionists to the TOM which eventually persuaded the IS to throw its weight behind the campaign in the wake of the Ulster Workers' Council 'lock-out'.

Both IMG and IS (together with much smaller Trotskyist groups such as Big Flame and the Revolutionary Communist Group) have, since 1974, continued to stress the 'Troops out' slogan in their political work on Ireland. Others, such as the Militant Tendency[57] and the Communist Party, have backed campaigns like the peace movement and the 'Better life for all' campaign. Their (IMG and IS) earlier excesses on the question of IRA terror have gradually given way to a more sober estimation, both of the Provisionals and of the Republican ideology.[58] At the same time the Provisionals themselves have moved away from their Catholic-Nationalist ideological legacy and this has been reflected in changed tactics and a stricter selection of military targets. What is perhaps most significant about the IMG's and IS's political agitations on Northern Ireland was that they did genuinely attempt to find a revolutionary position in a context of enormous hostility. Apart from the ultra-leftism to which this attempt gave rise in the case of the IMG, it is perhaps even more disturbing that such efforts have occasioned an arrogant authoritarianism in groups such as the Revolutionary Communist Group which continues to proclaim that even *criticism* of IRA tactics is reactionary.[59] But this should not be allowed to detract from the invaluable role of the Marxist left in forcing the 'Irish issue' on to the British political agenda. This is a clear illustration of the need for independent socialists organized outside the Labour Party, since for most of the relevant period the latter collaborated in the conspiracy of silence on Northern Ireland. Only within the period since 1979 has the Labour left given this situation any of its attention and there is every reason to believe that this came about because of the persistent agitations of the Marxists demanding troops out.

LENINISM AND FEMINISM

It has been remarked that the events of May 1968 gave rise to a 'great revival of interest in non-Leninist traditions on the left'.[60] Yet we have seen that the International Socialists came to emphasize Leninism precisely because of these same events. Likewise the IMG for all its youthful enthusiasm for 'studentism', resisted the temptation of becoming a British equivalent of Lotta Continua. Throughout its short history the IMG has been an avowedly Leninist, vanguard organization. As we have seen, this seemed to involve bouts of ultra-leftism but, notably has never involved departures from the widest internal democracy. In part this may be attributed to the IMG's very recent origin as a mainly student, intellectual, organization expecting and obtaining high rates of political activity from its membership. In part, also, the IMG's democratic record is attributable to its connection with the Fourth International which may have learned the error of its own past mistakes in this field.[61]

It is more likely, however, that the IMG's commitment to a genuine internal democracy is the result of its formation during a period in which many important political struggles on the left were waged by militants deeply suspicious of all organizations on the grounds that organization necessarily involved conservatism and bureaucratism. Since the leadership of IMG was largely drawn from this same cohort it might be expected to be particularly sensitive to feelings on this issue.

Of all the new forces radicalized in the late 1960s the women's liberation movement was both the most important and the most critical of traditional forms of organization. Of the two major objectives which the first conference of WLM set itself, the first was 'to develop an organisation that in its form and content would eradicate the relevant faults of the other preceding radical groups'.[62] Ideologically the WLM included elements drawn from 'the spontaneist methods of anarcho-syndicalism and the Situationists, the separatism of Black Power, socialist theories of the unity in struggle of oppressed peoples' and the psycho-politics of Laing and Cooper. Its organization, like its syncretic ideology, was a challenge to the orthodoxies of Leninism, emphasizing loose, non-hierarchical, grass roots collectives and the necessity for all oppressed groups to develop their own autonomous organizations and 'their own understanding of their own situation'. The women's movement, from its inception, self-consciously resisted the leadership principle by promoting a pre-figurative politics which attempted to begin now (by strict application of the collective principle and 'consciousness raising') that which some Socialists imagined would happen automatically *after* the socialist revolution.

Some organizations on the far left deride the women's movement as a middle-class pastime: this is the position of the WRP and the Militant Tendency. The SWP, while recognizing the importance of women as an agency of revolution, sees iself as *the* nucleus of a revolutionary party to which all revolutionary forces must rally. Thus,

. . . a socialist feminist consciousness can only be created when there is a *fighting* organisation which has real roots among women workers and housewives. The women's liberation movement is not a fighting organisation. Because it puts the question of consciousness first, not the taking of power by the working class, it has its own distinctive structure: there is no clearly defined membership . . . no unified politics (it embraces women with very different views) and no centralised organisation . . . because of its politics, its structure and its middle class orientation the

women's liberation movement can have little left to contribute in practice
. . . our emphasis (the SWP) has to be on women workers.[63]

Accordingly the SWP's *Womens Voice* is concerned primarily with
women as workers or strikers and with both in so far as they are
potential recruits to the SWP.

The IMG, like the CP, was quick to recognize the value of an
autonomous women's movement and its cadres played leading
organizational and practical parts in campaigns which the women's
movement mobilized for, such as the National Abortion Campaign.
Its relationship with the women's movement has been described
most clearly by IMG leader, John Ross.[64] According to Ross the
Leninist party concentrates its energies and channels its forces in the
struggle against the 'bourgeois state'. For Ross, the political is that
which participates in or affects the affairs of the state: 'only if they are
questions impinging on the state do they [personal relationships] . . .
become specifically political as opposed to social'. Ross argues that it
is here that the WLM errs — in conflating the personal and political
— and it is this which leads some feminists to anti-Leninist positions.
Just as a Leninist party would not attempt to take over the trade
unions so, says Ross, it also recognizes '. . . the necessity of the
distinction and organisational independence of the women's
movement and the party'.

A party, and party members, can attempt to persuade or *urge* a course of
action on the women's movement or a union but they must never be in a
position to *impose* anything.

The IMG decided at a political committee meeting of July 1975 to
inaugurate a written debate on the subject of internal caucuses for
women, Blacks, and homosexuals. This resulted in the pursuit of a
resolution, 'Women's caucuses within the revolutionary
organisation', at the IMG's 1978 Conference, which said

Sexism in society finds its reflection inside the IMG. It finds expression in a
number of ways: inadequate educational development and integration into
the leadership structures and insensitivity to women's level of development
and confidence in their own abilities, fed by dismissive male assumptions
and insensitive methods of debate and discussion; insufficient sensitivity to
women comrades' responsibilities for children etc . . . caucuses of women
comrades are therefore an important element in the steps taken by the IMG
as a whole to understand and adopt measures to remove sexist barriers in
the development and integration of women comrades.

In keeping with Ross's argument the same resolution also argues

. . . it is not the place of a revolutionary organisation — or caucuses within it — to substitute for the WLM by structuring discussions on . . . aspects of personal liberation, that is, *it is not* the place of a revolutionary organisation to structure discussions on how comrades should *conduct their lives* for example, discussions on comrades' personal relationships and attitudes to marriage, monogamy, children, etc.

However the resolution was forced to recognize that the distinction between the personal and the political is not always very clear, because it argues that where the former are '. . . a barrier to the development of a revolutionary organisation it is the responsibility of the whole organisation to structure discussions on these questions, with women's caucuses preparing contributions for discussion when it is necessary'. This, the most advanced position on the far left regarding the relationship between Leninism and feminism, is still regarded as unsatisfactory by leading socialist feminists.

Sheila Rowbotham, for example, complains that 'sexual relationships between men and women or between people of the same sex have been seen by Marxists as either decadent and diversionary or as personal questions outside politics'.[65] Against this,

Feminists have insisted that how we live, now, has a practical significance for how we organise. Such an assertion of subjectivity and the need to find organisational means to unlock structures of feeling as part of political practice is quite alien from the traditions of Leninism. Indeed Leninism was explicitly opposed to earlier social preoccupations with ethical questions and the new forms of life.

It is noteworthy that this critique of Leninism comes not from a radical feminist or a supporter of women's rights but from a socialist and ex-member of IS: as such it illustrates the estrangement of the women's movement from the politics of the far left. This follows from the WLM's preoccupation with prefigurative politics, since according to Rowbotham,

Within Leninism there is no conscious commitment to struggling against the forms of relationship which are created by the division of labour under capitalism, as part of the effort to make socialism. It is assumed that the existence of a revolutionary party itself can transcend the particular interests of sections within the working class.

Rowbotham's argument against Leninism was developed, in

conjunction with Hilary Wainwright and Lynne Segal (both socialist feminists) to the point where it was claimed that, like Stalinism, Leninism deals in 'the manipulation of people' and assumes a superior knowledge. This arrogance is alleged to stem from a notion of the scientificity of Marxism held by Marxist organizations.[66]

Before taking up some of these issues it is worth examining the lengthy resolution, 'Socialist revolution and the struggle for women's liberation', which the Fourth International adopted at its world congress in 1979. This represents the first full resolution on the question of women's liberation ever discussed by the Trotskyist movement and certainly its most sophisticated attempt to deal with the relationship between Marxism and feminism. It begins by acknowledging the independent origins of the women's movement which forced the existing mass organizations of the working class to respond to its emergence. Arising in the context of 'the death agony of capitalism', 'the development of the women's movement has thus become an important factor in the political and ideological battle to weaken the hold of the bourgeoisie and its centrist, social democratic and Stalinist agents within the working class'.

The Fourth International — while warning of attempts to 'integrate the leadership of the women's movement into the accepted patterns of class collaboration' — envisages itself 'winning the leadership of the struggle for women's liberation'.[67] Yet the resolution clearly states that since the feminist struggle is not identical with the struggle of the working class 'women must wait for no one to show them the way' and '. . . even after the revolution the independent women's liberation movement will play an indispensable role in assuring the ability of the working class as a whole . . . to carry this process through to a successful conclusion'.[68]

The FI statement clarifies the relationship of its sections such as the IMG with the independent women's movement.

By independent or autonomous we do not mean independent of the needs of the working class. We mean that the movement is organised and led by women; that it takes the fight for women's rights and needs as its first priority, refusing to subordinate that fight to any other interests; that it is not subordinate to the decisions or policy needs of any political tendency or any other social group; that it is willing to carry through the fight by whatever means and together with whatever forces prove necessary . . .

Our support for and work to build the independent women's liberation movement distinguishes the Fourth International today from many sectarian groups that claim to stand on Marxist orthodoxy as represented by their interpretations of the resolutions of the first four congresses of the Third International. Such groups reject the construction of any women's organisations except those tied to and under the political control of their party.[69]

The role of the Trotskyists *vis-à-vis* the women's movement is to contend for the support of the best socialist feminists 'in a framework of democracy' by arguing the Marxist analysis. The function of the revolutionary party is to time and formulate the raising of demands within the women's movement. Indeed the party is tactician and leader of the whole class and seeks to orient all facets of the class struggle to the abolition of capitalism. Armed with its superior understanding — enshrined in the Marxist programme 'that represents women and the working class' — the party seeks to overcome the deep divisions fostered by capitalism by synthesizing the experience and demands of all oppressed groups. The organizational norms of the Leninist party are derived from this programme. These incorporate the widest democratic rights but, it is argued, the formation of women's caucuses within the revolutionary party merely reproduces the divisions which the party seeks to overcome. Democratic centralism, on the other hand, can avoid the centrifugal dynamics implicit in the party conceived as a federation of interest groups. Thus the decision to allow women's caucuses within the IMG is specifically repudiated.

It will be noted that the case for democratic centralism ultimately rests on a conviction that the revolutionary programme of the Trotskyists, since it is based on the science of Marxism, is an actual synthesis of the multifarious interests and experiences of all the oppressed. But the objection of many socialist feminists, often Marxists themselves, is that 'a correct analysis of the subordination of women cannot be provided by Marxists unless Marxism itself is transformed'.[70] The Trotskyists seem blissfully unaware of even the possibility that the Marxist tradition to which they subscribe is inadequate for the task. Let us see how the Fourth International attempts to come to terms with the sexual division of labour and confront the specificity of women's oppression.

According to the FI the patriarchal nuclear family is one of the central pillars of class society; in other words it is 'rooted in private property'. for the bourgeoisie, we learn, the family provides for the transmission of private property between generations. But

for the working class while the family provides some degree of mutual protection of its members, in the most basic sense it is an alien class institution, one that is imposed on the working class and serves the economic interests of the bourgeoisie not the workers. Yet working people are indoctrinated from childhood to regard it . . . as the most natural and imperishable of human relations.[71]

Several elements of this argument are worth noting. First, the Fourth International asserts that 'the family system is an indispensable pillar of class rule. It must be preserved if capitalism is to survive.[72] In fact it is not at all clear that domestic labour, for example, is a functional prerequisite of capitalist production. To maintain that this and other aspects of the 'family system' are in some essentialist sense pre-given by the logic of capitalist development merely serves to deny that major advances towards women's liberation can be made within a capitalist system. As such it is just a more subtle way of claiming that women must trust in socialism if they are to achieve anything.

It can be further objected against this Marxist functionalism that it fails to see that the family and the sexual division of labour as presently constituted are to a very great extent products of class and gender struggle. Such functionalism effectively ignores the conflict and choices which led to the present social arrangements. Moreover, the crudest instances of this logic purport to show that since the family is an effect of the economic causality of capitalism, feminists and socialists have identical interests best served by promoting the working-class struggle. This amounts to saying that all sectional interests can be aligned in terms of the labour-capital contradiction.[73] The FI does not explicitly draw this conclusion, unlike the SWP, the Militant Tendency, and the RCG, but in linking the family system and capitalism as mutual dependents it promotes an all-or-nothing view belied by historical experience. After all, if the accumulation of capital were so dependent on domestic labour as the cheapest way of reproducing labour power, how could we explain the removal from the family of so much which formerly came under this heading?

The FI not only informs us that 'the family system is the institution of class society that determines and maintains the specific character of women as a sex': it is also argued that only the bourgeoisie has a material interest in the preservation of this institution. As we have seen, the FI attributes the support for the family within the working class to the pernicious influence of bourgeois 'indoctrination'. Thus the family, in this view, exists by virtue of false consciousness. It is not even acknowledged that the conventional male control over the family wage has normally provided a very solid basis for working-class sexism. The FI is too concerned to deny a male self-interest in the oppression of women and insist that 'it is the capitalist class, not men in general and certainly not male wage earners, which profits from women's unpaid labour in the household'. This argument places the FI's analysis very firmly within the orthodoxy established by Engels' *Origin of the Family, Private Property and the State*.

Engels' argument stressed the coincidence of class and sex antagonism. His basic insight retains its validity in showing that as pre-historic, more egalitarian forms of society broke down in response to developments which created an economic surplus in society, classes and stable hierarchies emerged. Once class property was established, women's labour was privatized within the monogamous family in order to secure the inheritance of property. The subordinate position of women is thus attributed to their exclusion from socially productive labour. The clear implication of Engels' argument is that the liberation of women will coincide with their re-entry into socially productive work. Only the property-owning bourgeoisie has an objective stake in the preservation of the family, the site of women's oppression.

Indeed, in Engels' argument the social position of women is an effect of the family which is itself a product of private property. No wonder then that Socialists impressed by this argument believed that the abolition of capitalism was synonymous with the liberation of women. The Fourth International has broken with this tradition in so far as it now recognizes the falsity of this conclusion. But it retains the economistic argument right up to this point before concluding that ideology — albeit a false consciousness produced by indoctrination — plays a determining part in maintaining the working class's allegiance to the family. It is presumably the pervasiveness of this ideology which brought the independent women's movement into existence and which — together with the persistence of sexism in non-capitalist societies — has alerted the FI to the need for such an independent anti-sexist movement. However, it should now be obvious that the Trotskyists regard this ideology as a product of the exploitation of labour by capital. This is an explanation in which gender plays no part at all. Such an analysis, argues Michele Barratt, 'can be of little use to feminist analysis'.[74]

This is because the position of women in any society is closely bound up with the gender constraint of wife/motherhood. To understand the oppression of women, therefore, it is necessary to use gender system as a basic category of historical analysis. But in the analysis of the Fourth International the concept of gender is not utilized at all. If we examine the FI's dissection of the 'family system' — which it makes the fundamental institution of women's oppression — we see that the burden of the Trotskyist analysis is uncomplicatedly economic. The five functions of the family system are:

(1)   a cheap method of maintaining labour power;
(2)   a mechanism for property inheritance;
(3)   the most inexpensive and ideologically acceptable mechanism for reproducing human labour;
(4)   the enforcement of a social division of labour in which women are fundamentally defined by their child-bearing role and assigned tasks immediately associated with this reproductive function. 'Thus the family rests on and reinforces a social division of labour involving the domestic subjugation and economic dependence of women';
(5)   the family is a repressive and conservatizing institution which 'fosters the possessive, competitive and aggressive values of capitalism' which are 'necessary to the perpetuation of class divisions'.

It can be seen that some concession of the importance of gender is made in point (4) but this is never developed while the values attributed to the family in point (5) are simply designated capitalist values. To have acknowledged the association of these values with masculinity would have undermined the FI's whole analysis which effectively confines the oppression of women to the material interests of the ruling class. Yet one can insist on masculinity as a problem without reducing the issue to a simple power struggle between the sexes, as in radical feminist accounts. If we reject the idea that the condition of women can be deduced derivatively from the economy, it is possible to analyse it as a complex structure of different elements — of which gender is one. This approach would dispense with the view which sees family ideology as a mere con-trick and give due weight to the importance of gender constraints in explaining the oppression of women.

The dominant gender system in any society provides authoritative versions of masculinity and femininity. And the sexual division of labour is presented as a natural extension of gender identity. This does not just apply to the rules of the family system;

The role they perform in conditions of legal-economic dependence as

domestic labourers has followed women into industry reproducing the
sexual division of labour or the larger terrain of socialised production,
depressing their wages to a norm well below that of male labour,

concentrating them within a narrow occupational range generally at the
bottom of the job hierarchy and making them an easy prey for trade union
opportunism.[75]

This being the case we are not simply talking about a division of
labour between men and women but a division that places men in a
superior and women in a subordinate position.[76] A material interest
in the maintenance of this system extends far beyond the
bourgeoisie. In the trade union concept of the family wage, for
example, the ideology of familialism and the economic supremacy of
men are both at work. The general failure of the FI's resolution on
women stems from its refusal to recognize that the sexual division of
labour is structured in such a way that relations between the sexes are
relations of domination and subordination. In this respect its analysis
remains 'sex-blind'.

It may be possible by emphasizing the role of ideology and thereby
situating the problem of gender to understand the oppression of
women within a Marxist problematic. For a number of reasons some
of the most ambitious attempts to do this have sought to utilize
psychoanalysis.[77] This is principally because it privileges the
problem of gender construction and recognizes the profound nature
of these identities. Psychoanalysis has thus been seen as a useful
approach to understanding the deep hold of ideology on the
individual and a method of investigating the nature of ideological
representation. It is not our intention to advocate this particular
approach to the union of Marxism and feminism, merely to
emphasize that such a rapprochement is unlikely to develop within a
Marxist tradition characterized by economism and an exclusivist
insistence on the labour/capital contradiction. For it is the tendency
of the Fourth International to reduce the political and ideological
levels of the capitalist mode of production to mere mirror reflections
or derivations of the economic base. This clearly emerges in its
analysis of the family system and its hold on the working class. The
Trotskyist approach is thus to trivialize the role of ideology just as
most socialist feminists have come to emphasize it. In practical terms
the functionalism of the Trotskyists points to little progress under
capitalism (because the family is necessary for it) whereas leading
feminists conclude that 'it is perfectly possible for feminism to make
more intermediate gains under social democracy than it does in the

first years of socialism'.[78] On the other hand, the Trotskyists are sanguine that the working-class family is in any case in process of dissolution while feminists observe the pervasiveness of familial ideology and conclude that this 'common-sense' is as in need of challenge within the working class and its institutions as it is anywhere.

This discussion shows the extent of the differences between the Trotskyist and socialist feminist analyses of women's oppression and indicates some of the practical ramifications of these varying approaches. In so doing it suggests some explanations for why even the most advanced far left analysis of women's oppression is unlikely to impress the growing body of socialist feminism within the women's movement. In particular, the posture of vanguard and the concomitant claim of the superior status of the Trotskyist programme will be treated with suspicion if the Marxist theory which underpins them is manifestly defective. Not only were the Marxists absent when the women's movement began its recent second phase; since then most Marxist groups have had little to say to people increasingly aware of the ideological and cultural dimensions of their oppression — be they women, gays, Blacks or youth. The social divisions which these new movements have drawn attention to, while expressing real material divisions in society, are not confined to the workplace or specific to capitalism.

While the Trotskyists have been prepared to champion the economic demands pertinent to these campaigns (equal pay, equal work, crêches, maternity/paternity leave) and take up less obviously economic issues (abortion) which have created mass mobilizations, they have not embraced the more difficult problems (of sexuality, pornography, domestic violence) which are, nevertheless, of central concern. This may to some extent reflect the narrowness of the Trotskyists' theoretical base and a failure to address (even recognize) its limitations. We have seen, for instance, that the Fourth International evades the problem of gender (and provides no convincing analysis of patriarchy). It may well be that in terms of its analysis of women's oppression the Trotskyist movement simply inherits the deficiencies of classical Marxism which so conceptualized the field of production as to exclude women (and the production of the species and its labour power) from its central theoretical category.[79] But even so the mode of Trotskyist intervention in the politics of the new movements compounds these problems because this practice consists of importing externally derived policy positions into the organizationally autonomous movements. The result is not simply that these interventions take on an alien, manipulative character, but that the Marxists thereby reduce their chances of enriching their theory by learning from the experience and politics of the mass campaigns. Thus when, for example, the elected leadership of Youth CND was suspended because of alleged irregularities at its Manchester conference in July 1983 the Socialist League (alias IMG) was held responsible. Whether the specific charges are true or not, the very fact that the mode of operation of the Socialist League within these campaigns resembles that of entrists within the Labour Party creates an impression of duplicity and bad faith which leaves it vulnerable to charges of undemocratic practices. This practice owes a good deal to the widespread Trotskyist conviction that the main problems of theory have already been solved and that the task in hand is to apply the correct tactics and preserve the revolutionary strategy. We have seen that even the FI (and, therefore, its British section) is characterized by this conviction and assumes a paternalistic attitude vis-à-vis the women's movement. However, it also needs pointing out that the Fourth International has made very real advances over other Trotskyist formations in this respect. If it is less doctrinally rigid than the others this owes something to its *international* character and the democratic conditions which now prevail within it.

The IMG Organization

Ten years after 1968 the IMG membership stood at a mere 750, yet the organization was confident enough to launch a new youth organization, called 'Revolution'. The group had grown during the previous two years (from 650 members in 1976) and since the launching of *Socialist Challenge,* in 1977, paper sales had increased by 60 per cent; the paid sales stood at 5,500 with a print run of between 8,000 and 9,000. At this stage in its 'socialist unity' appeal IMG optimism seems to have been high. The self-imposed project of uniting the revolutionary left had attracted some small groups (such as Big Flame[80] and the Marxist Workers' Group[81]) to engage in joint work with IMG: the refusal of the SWP to enter the spirit of this initiative had yet to wreck it.

Despite these positive signs the IMG remained an organization confined to the student and white-collar sectors and almost wholly lacking in a working-class or industrial base. Its trade union work was, to practical purposes, only possible in the National Union of

Teachers, the CPSA and NALGO. In industry it had achieved token visibility only at British Leyland (specifically in the Rover factory, Solihull). Even the group's pentration of larger *political* organizations was unusually feeble. By 1978 IMG members seem to have decided spontaneously that their column of entrists in the Labour Party and the Labour Party Young Socialists were wasting their time and such activity dwindled to nothing. While rebuking this, the group's Central Committee was forced to admit that '. . . the stranglehold of Militant is almost impregnable, especially when other small revolutionary forces . . . refuse to help us build a revolutionary alternative tendency'.

In fact IMG held the initiative only in respect of certain campaigns in the women's movement and in its socialist unity drive. Even in connection with the National Abortion Campaign and the Working Women's Charter, which it had done so much to sponsor, the complaint was heard that this activity did nothing to build IMG but only consumed its resources. The group's national 'periphery' (ie. sympathizers) was estimated at just 500 — a poor showing for all the time it had spent promoting single-issue campaigns of wide appeal.

If the IMG was in any way sounder and more stable than the rest of the far left, it was in respect of the organization's internal regime. For throughout its existence the IMG has avoided the kind of internal disruption and authoritarianism which we have encountered elsewhere on the Trotskyist left. From its origins in the mid-1960s to the end of the seventies no factions were expelled from the IMG. The only exception to this pattern came in 1980-1 when a group of entrists were discovered to have created a faction with the purpose of splitting as large a section of the membership away from the organization as possible.[82]

The IMG sets high standards of political behaviour for its members. The rank-and-file is expected to be very active politically. New members must first endure a six-month period of candidate status during which both member and organization can scrutinize each other. The group's norms insist that the recruit gives priority to party work, the only exception being when 'leave of absence' is granted on occasion of ill health or for purposes of vacation. While the IMG (as we have seen) does not attempt to structure the private lives of its members it clearly does expect the personal behaviour of members to accord with certain (ill defined) revolutionary principles. Certainly sexist or racist behaviour would not be tolerated. Indeed the group has taken measures designed to encourage 'oppressed layers' — such as by admitting a certain validity to the principle of 'positive discrimination', though not one based on quotas; these are firmly rejected as apolitical. For IMG no special status is attached to a member's social background but rather to his or her politics. Thus the organization positively discriminates in cases when the collective politics of the group are enhanced. This is why, as we have seen, women's caucuses were permitted within the organization but not as a replacement for the discussion of 'women's issues' at branch level. The IMG's commitment to measures designed to augment the collective nature of the group's politics also lies behind its guarantee of members' tendency, and even factional, rights.

The individual rights of IMG members command their own cost in terms of greater political activity. The model of participatory democracy which the IMG internal regime seeks to achieve exacts a price as can be seen from the following analysis of the group's 1978 conference.

The IMG conference is a two-yearly event spread over four or five days. It is preceded by a three-month discussion period. During this time members are expected to conduct discussions at branch level around the dozen or so areas outlined by the central committeee. They are also required to convene three regional aggregates at which these and other issues (suggested by individual members) are debated. Members are encouraged to write contributions to the discussions which are printed in internal bulletins. Of course the informed member needs to read these reports which average 32 pages each (approximately 20,000 words per bulletin). Only the technical capacities of the IMG National Centre restrict the number of such bulletins to about thirty; otherwise this, and the 5,000-word limit per contribution, would undoubtedly be lifted. Bearing in mind that other activities are not suspended during the pre-conference discussion period, it is obvious that an enormous effort is required of individual members.

The right to form tendencies and factions increases this commitment of time and energy whenever it is taken up. On these occasions tendencies and factions produce reports and analyses of their own which are printed nationally and freely distributed throughout the organization. These, inevitably, prompt counter-arguments and alternative platforms. They also require tendency meetings, caucus activities and the co-ordination of supporters (which invariably involves travelling the country). Since the organization of conference is scrupulously fair, the right to form a tendency or faction involves the right to proportional representation of delegates. For every five members, a branch may elect one conference delegate so long as the members concerned have paid their subscriptions and the conference levy (which was £6,600 in 1978 or £9 per member).

The IMG conference is the sovereign political assembly of the organization though the norms of democratic centralism permit *International* bodies to qualify this sovereignty. Conference elects a nominations committee which draws up a list of candidates for the central committee: the conference then chooses from this list and elects the central committee. Executive work is performed by a smaller political committee elected by the CC. Both these bodies may appoint subordinate committees: both are open to members of dissident tendencies elected on the basis of proportional representation.

Clearly these formal rights are extensive. Furthermore the IMG's political practice — which is relatively free from instances of authoritarianism — shows that these rights are real; that, in other words, the organization's political culture is genuinely democratic. We have already attempted to account for this in the previous section. Here it will simply be observed that the small scale of the IMG (IMG membership stood at 40 in 1968, 400 in 1972 and around 800 by 1978. See *Socialist Challenge*. 2 February 1978) and its intellectual composition are both congenial to the functioning of a participatory democracy. It must remain a matter for speculation as to how it would fare if either of these factors were changed.

To the Socialist League

The IMG's emergence in the late 1960s from the clandestinity of entrism together with its very success in VSC and among students ensured its character as an organization of the young and educated. Its distance from the struggles of the British working class — which reached new heights of militancy and innovation in the early 1970s — was perpetuated by the International's orientation summed up by the slogan 'from the periphery to the centre'. Once the student revolt had faded, the International Socialists sought a new orientation — the 'move to the class' — which marks the start of its attempt to construct a trade union base to the organization.[83] At the same time, 1970, the IMG's major initiative was launching the Spartacus League, a new youth organization which confirmed its status as a student formation. It was not until the miners' strike of 1972 that IMG made a serious attempt to intervene outside this milieu and even then it was confined to pamphleteering and calling for a general strike[84] (for which there was no resonance at all).

However, the IMG's isolation from the heavy industrial working class was not such a problem as traditionally depicted by Marxists. The ninth world congress of the Fourth International had after all justified IMG's withdrawal from entrism by reference to the recent upsurge in militancy among sections of the population outside the mass workers' parties and trade unions. It believed that a new opportunity had been created for the construction of a mass vanguard party capable of challenging the hegemony of the traditional workers' parties. In fact an anti-capitalist element could be perceived in many of the campaigns and movements which sprang up to the left of the Labour Party in these years. But it was extremely foolish and arrogant to suppose that the tiny and youthful IMG (with approximately 200 members by 1969) should act as vanguard to these groups. The chief ideological weakness of the IMG stemmed from its refusal to recognize that the Leninist model of a vanguard party deeply entrenched within the manual working class did not and need not apply to it. While there was no prospect of the IMG becoming a workers' party of this sort, it did have the chance to develop a close relationship with the new feminist ethnic and student politics of the period. Together with these and other forces that had either rejected labourism or been neglected by it, the IMG had the opportunity to develop a socialist subculture through serious educational and agitational activities. Though at first confined to the periphery of British politics a Marxist group of this sort would have gained in influence as a variety of vanguardist illusions elsewhere on the left were shattered and confidence in the Labour Party repeatedly depressed. Already, by 1970, it was becoming apparent that, (as Miliband has recently expressed it)

. . . 'organised labour' must now be taken to include a vast number of people in teaching and other forms of communication: here is to be found, for the first time in British history, an 'intellectual proletariat' which is insecure and often disaffected. Its contribution to the political culture of labour is already considerable and is likely to grow further.[85]

Unfortunately, the IMG in common with all other Trotskyist groups was wedded to conceptions which prevented it from too close an identification with these forces. The underdeveloped state of Marxism in relation to sexism has already been noted. A similar barrier disposes the Trotskyists to think of most white-collar workers as either middle class or strategically less significant than other wage earners. Both assessments are wrong. But it is common for such workerism to downgrade all struggles and agencies at one remove from the industrial militancy of the traditional proletariat. Thus, although the IMG is by no means the worst exponent of such notions, it strove to rid itself of an embarrassing non-proletarian image. In this respect the development of the International Socialists (via the struggles against the Industrial Relations Act) into a bigger force with an industrial base was looked upon as a model to be imitated. Dissatisfaction with IMG's performance in the recruitment of manual workers led to the removal of Pat Jordan and Tariq Ali from the leadership in 1972; both were closely associated with the perspectives of 1969.

Though this change was intended to help IMG gain a foothold in the manual trade unions, in practice it led to a sterile campaign for a general strike and the election of a Labour government with a socialist programme. In fact the call for a general strike was a completely futile pose but the fact that it was thought credible within the IMG is attributable to the re-emergence of catastrophism within the Fourth International.

For the general line adopted at the ninth world congress of the FI argued that the downturn in Western economies was the context in which '. . . the political positions of Trotskyism, not merely against social democracy and Stalinism, but also against all centrist deviations within the vanguard, will be strikingly re-affirmed'.[86] Of course, this was not to be a mere academic vindication of Trotskyism but was expected to have very tangible results. The period is characterized as one of political victories (starting in Vietnam) that have turned the balance of forces decisively against imperialism and though defeats occur (as in Chile) they run counter to the general tendency. The world situation is described as exactly the opposite of 1923-43 when the general picture was one of working-class defeats. As for Britain, the IMG concluded that in effect the economic pre-conditions for the post-war consensus no longer obtained. Its analysis was given substantial support by Mandel's *Late Capitalism* (1972) which predicted a long recession in the capitalist economies rooted in the preceding 25-year boom.[87]

Thus initially the 'new rise of world revolution' was described in very general terms. But by the early seventies the FI was sure that the approach of socialist revolution in Europe could be identified '. . . not just in broad historical perspective . . . but even from a conjunctural point of view'.[88] Within IMG, however, a series of shifting tendencies, alignments and re-alignments developed after

1972 as the militants tried to fashion tactics appropriate for those perspectives. Internationally the FI was split between tendencies based in the Americas (the Leninist-Trotskyist faction) and in Europe (the international majority tendency) partly over the pros and cons of guerilla movements. The IMG debate — at times very fierce — revolved on the claims made for united fronts on single issue campaigns (on the model of VSC) versus the leadership's rather abstract faith in a general strike. As already mentioned this general strike line was pursued by those desirous of emulating the International Socialists' 'turn to industry'.

In fact despite the explosion of industrial militancy under the Heath government the IMG was not able to establish an industrial base comparable to that of IS. In some measure this was no doubt due to the IMG's overwhelmingly student composition which, despite Narodnik-style forays into factory work, was always unlikely to appeal to trade union militants. Moreover the IMG's style of politics was still informed by its experience of the late sixties. One important feature of this was the abiding conviction that a significant cohort of militants, organized in a variety of radical campaigns outside the Labour Party and trade unions, was the raw material of a future Marxist party. Despite its so-called 'industrial turn', a large proportion of IMG members preferred an orientation aimed at those already breaking with Labourism. As the IS's industrial strategy unfolded in the mid-seventies and it became increasingly apparent that rank-and-filism actually amounted to little more than a prolonged celebration of wage militancy, those in IMG concerned to avoid such economism were even more disposed to emphasize the importance of *political* consciousness.

By 1977 the project of gathering together all those prepared to fight on a platform of class struggle gained majority support inside the IMG. One aspect of this orientation — and perhaps an aspect that was over-emphasized — was the conviction that the myriad Trotskyist groups could be won over to a unified revolutionary organization.[90] It was now argued that the doctrinal differences dividing these groups were not of sufficient importance to justify separate organizatons. Indeed the IMG were clearly prepared to include the 'state capitalists' of the SWP in this category of potential unifiers. However, the very fact that the International Socialists had become the Socialist Workers *Party* was symptomatic of that organization's determination to regard itself as the core of any future revolutionary organization. That this was an entirely sectarian attitude is evinced by the refusal of the SWP to field candidates under the banner of Socialist Unity as proposed by IMG in a number of by-elections in the seventies. This not only resulted in the SWP candidate standing against Socialist Unity, but also permitted the National Front to beat both in the Hull and Newham contests. And in the Ladywood by-election of August 1977 the Socialist Unity candidate polled almost four times the SWP vote.

However, these experiences did nothing to bring the SWP to a revaluation of its position and the IMG unity initiative only succeeded with much smaller groups like Big Flame. Ironically by 1979 it had become apparent that both the Socialist Unity initiative and the SWP rank-and-file strategy had failed. But the IMG and SWP drew different conclusions from this mutual failure. As we have seen the SWP recognized the need for ideological consolidation while remaining an independent organization. The IMG, on the other hand, came to stress the importance of the Benn campaign to democratize the Labour Party and increasingly submerged itself in entrist activity. Finally, the organization — by now completely absorbed in entrism and CND — re-named itself the Socialist League and at the start of 1983 brought out *Socialist Action* to replace *Socialist Challenge*.

CONCLUSIONS

By the mid-sixties the Fourth International had acknowledged the *de facto* rearguard position of the Western working class and increasingly emphasised Third World struggles as the epicentre of world revolution. The IMG's politics were formed around this time and the growth of the organization coincides with the exodus from the Labour Party and the explosion of extra-parliamentary struggles of the period 1965-70. From the time of its emergence as an independent organization in 1969, the IMG's political orientation was towards students, feminism, Third World solidarity campaigns, Northern Ireland and other 'peripheral' causes and groups. The very fact that these struggles were regarded as in any sense peripheral was, of course, attributable to the conviction that serious revolutionary work must ultimately be based on factory cells and the industrial working class. But IMG was singularly unsuccessful in establishing an industrial base despite resort to several 'turns to industry' such as that of August 1983 which resulted in politically motivated sackings at British Leyland's Cowley plant. In practice IMG politics were bound up with the 'new left' of 1968.

For the political milieu in which IMG operated, from the moment it abandoned entrism, was heavily influenced by the anti-bureaucratic thrust of the women's movement, student radicalism, community politics, the squatters' and claimants' movements. IMG's greatest success was in helping to catalyse single-issue campaigns like VSC, NAC and the revived CND. But it sought to build a Leninist party from its involvement in these mass mobilizations and that it emphatically failed to do. Instead its attempts at channelling diverse organizations in the same direction resulted in the IMG becoming an ultra-activist group championing more issue campaigns than it had members. A feature of the organization's politics was its tendency to react to radical causes such that consistent, patient work was mostly out of the question. Instead the group was more likely to take up an issue once it had become the focus of attention only to drop it when the mood passed.

This practice eventually led the IMG, now called the Socialist League, back into the Labour Party in pursuit of the same radical forces that it had failed to organize independently. The decay of the Labour Party which occasioned the withdrawal of IMG from entrism in 1969 now, more advanced, took it back in 1982. Paradoxically, the steady decline of labourism, responsible for the 'successes' of Thatcherism, has frightened a good many radicals into a last desperate attempt to salvage something from the wreckage. At the very moment when a socialist alternative is both possible and necessary, Marxist energies are consumed in trying to strengthen the Labour left. For whatever its intentions, this is what an entrist group must end up doing as we shall see in the next chapter.

7

The Militant Tendency

If the Labour Party cannot be turned into a socialist party, then the question which confronts us all is, how can we form a socialist party? If we are not ready to answer this question then we are not ready to dismiss the party that exists.[1]

The answer to Ken Coates' question continues to elude British Trotskyism which has so far been unable to construct an open socialist party capable of challenging Labourism for the allegiance of trade union and socialist activists. Indeed this problem was first confronted by Trotksy as early as 1933. The problem of how a tiny group becomes a pole of attraction for class-conscious workers (who may have never even heard of it) prompted Trotsky to suggest that his British followers enter the ILP as a 'secret faction': this short-term, tactical move was expected to gain the Trotskyists an audience — a political milieu in which they could work — and enough quick recruits rapidly to resume the building of an open Leninist party. The demise of the ILP, however, led the Trotskyists to withdraw and turn their attentions to the Labour Party. For, as Trotsky noted in 1936 '. . . a revolutionary group is not a revolutionary party and can work most effectively at present by opposition . . . within the mass parties'.[2]

As we have seen, Trotsky expected catastrophic events to transform political conditions so radically that the tiny Fourth

International would emerge from the war a mass world party of socialist revolution. It was the failure of this perspective and the prolonged marginality of the Trotskyists since then that has kept the entrist tactic at the forefront of Marxist debate and practice. In fact the post-war decades have seen the Trotskyists justify entrism in several different ways. In the 1940s the RCP minority proposed entrism in anticipation of an imminent economic and political crisis that was expected to find its first expression in a growing polarization within the Labour Party: hence the latter was reckoned to be the most useful arena for revolutionary activity. Entrism has also been employed in order to boost recruitment in open Trotskyist groups. Such forays were even in 1982 being executed by organizations seeking to benefit from the radicalization of the CLPs. The International Marxist Group, the Workers Socialist League and the Workers Revolutionary Party have all resumed a significant level of entrist activity since the rise of the Bennite movement in the Labour Party. But we have also seen that entrism has been utilized by Trotskyists when revolution has seemed such a distant prospect that the dangers of sectarian degeneration await the builders of open independent parties. This was the rationale advanced by the RCP majority in 1949. In the 1950s the FI added the perspective of war-revolution to the growing list of conditions which made entrism propitious. The 'entrism *sui generis*' of Michel Pablo foresaw decades of secret faction work on the part of the Trotskyists within the hostile environs of the European Communist Parties. In Britain the diminutive nature of the CPGB, together with the 'unique structure' of the Labour Party provided, respectively, the negative and positive reasons for entrism *sui generis* applied to the latter.

The entrism of the Militant Tendency has similarities with a number of these models but conforms to none of them. It shares with the Pablo variant the intense secrecy which has earned it the name 'deep entrism'. Like the perspectives of the RCP majority, Militant's orientation to Labour is long term: its forerunner, the Revolutionary Socialist League initiated Militant's present course in 1955. The RSL, as we saw in the last chapter, was itself the product of a fusion which involved members of the old RCP majority such as Ted Grant and Jimmy Deane. Today's Militant Tendency is led by the former. But though the connections with the RCP continue to be stressed, Militant has evolved a characteristic perspective on the Labour Party. In 1973, that is after almost 20 years of entrism, a Militant internal document declared 'we are only just at the start of real entry work with the outline of those conditions laid down by

Trotsky just beginning to take shape'.[3]

These conditions are specified as the development of pre-revolutionary situations characterized by 'ferment in social democracy' and the growth of a left wing within which there is the possibility of a rapid crystallization of 'the revolutionary tendency'. It is clear, from an analysis of Grant's 'Problems of Entrism', which was first written in 1959, that this scenario is expected to terminate in the transformation of the Labour Party into 'a revolutionary party'. Though it is declared that 'this is the historical justification for the policy of entrism', the Militant Tendency is the only major Trotskyist group which believes in this possibility. For Militant, entrism has become a strategy.

It is characteristic of Militant that it explains the Labour Party's reformism and parliamentarism in terms of a politically corrupt leadership which arose because of the economic corruption of a section of the working class. Both arguments are culled direct from Lenin's *Imperialism*. Thus Militant's 'History of the Labour Party' maintains that:

Relying on the double exploitation of workers in the colonies, British capitalism was able to buy off a small, skilled section of the working class by conceding above average living standards to them. It was upon this section, plus the growing numbers of trade union officials and middle class 'Lib-Labs' who found their way into the leadership of the Labour Movement, that the ruling class were to depend to hold the movement back'.

In this way Militant conceives of reformism as a problem of leadership. Likewise the socialist revolution is a matter of the political will:

Then as now it was the lack of a clear Marxist leadership, prepared and determined to draw together the separate strands of industrial and political struggle to achieve a definitive solution to the destruction of the moribund capitalist system and the building of a socialist society.[4]

Already it will be apparent that the Militant Tendency perceives itself as a Leninist and Trotskyist current and that it has pared the problems of socialist politics down to the question of who leads the Labour Party. In order to situate the Militant Tendency within the Trotskyist tradition, however, it is necessary to consider its analysis of this movement. This will provide us with a better understanding of its distinctive politics.

TRADITIONS

The Militant Tendency traces itself back to the RCP majority and, beyond, to the WIL. More generally, the following statement reveals Militant's theoretical legacy:

We stand on the foundations of the ideas of Marx, Engels, Lenin and Trotsky, of the decisions of the first four congresses of the Communist International and of the Founding Conference of the Fourth International and of the documents of the Marxist movement in the last 30 years. We stand for the creation of the Fourth International and reassert our confidence in the industrial proletariat as the decisive force in the struggle for socialism in every country'. Quoted by R. Underhill (1980) in *Entryist activities of the Militant Tendency,* report to the CLPs, March, p.21.

Ted Grant, who is a leader of Militant, was also a leader of the RCP and a member of the WIL. The Militant Tendency attempts to keep these traditions alive by educating its supporters in the history of the FI and, particularly, the course of the British section. This history consists, in the main, of cataloguing the errors of the FI leadership which are alleged to be so numerous and fundamental that

Even to dignify this tendency by calling it centrist would be a compliment . . . twenty five years [history] . . . has indicated that they are organically incapable of transformation organisationally and politically in the direction of Marxism.[5]

Thus, at bottom, the Militant Tendency regards the Fourth International as a non-Marxist organization. The start of this decline seems to be located in the attitude of the FI to the RCP, as far as Militant is concerned. Because the RCP was led by ex-WIL members 'J.P. Cannon . . . pursued a vendetta against the leadership of the British organisation'. According to Ted Grant, Cannon's dislike of the WIL was based on the latter's criticism of the 'unprincipled fusion' of 1938 which Cannon contrived among rival Trotskyist groups in Britain.

From these petty and personal beginnings the campaign against the RCP grew as the latter openly criticized FI analyses which it considered wrong. Thus according to Militant, the RCP developed superior insights to the FI on a large range of issues. For example, on the stabilization of bourgeois democracies post-1945, on the nature of Eastern Europe and the survival of the USSR, on the post-war boom, on all these issues and more the RCP promoted superior analyses to those of the FI. In Militant's view 'the collapse of the RCP dealt a blow to the movement nationally and internationally which we are now in the process of repairing'.

Militant hold the FI responsible for the destruction of the RCP: and in Militant's view the FI's own history has been one of opportunist zigzags devoid of Marxist perspective. Hence Militant has no intention of rejoining the FI and holds out no prospect for the regeneration of that organization. Instead it seeks to 'develop and broaden . . . work among contacts, groups and even individuals that we can reach in other countries'. But also Militant believes that '. . . an important part of the international work consists of building a viable tendency in Britain'. There is evidence that Militant has established such contacts in Spain, France, Greece, Sweden, Ireland, West Germany, Belgium, Canada and Sri Lanka. However in 1975 the Irish section of this entrist International could claim only sixteen members in the North and fifteen in the South where they were confined to a single branch in Dublin.[6]

Militant has been more successful in establishing a significant base within the Labour Party though, as I shall argue below, this has been much exaggerated too. What concerns us now is its attitude towards the other Trotskyist groups in Britain. Given what we have discovered about its depiction of the FI, its references to 'the anti-Marxist sects'[7] is entirely consonant with its complete disdain for that organization. Militant invariably refers to all other Marxist groups in Britain as 'the sects'. The leadership of the Militant Tendency lose no opportunity to arouse contempt for their rivals. Thus of these groups it alleges 'they are not educated in the essential ideas of Marxism partly because of the ingrained contempt of their leaders for the working class. All the sects have this in common'. It is noteworthy that Militant has learned to use an ethos of class resentment to stigmatize all its opponents — Marxist and non-Marxist alike. Its chosen enemies are always 'middle class' and the good and wholesome are always working class. This particular Manicheism, which is far less intellectually demanding of its devotees than Marxism, may strike a chord in a specifically Labour and trade union milieu which has itself nurtured just such a limited and parochial 'class consciousness'. We will have occasion to comment on the Militant Tendency's 'workerism' in other contexts below.

While Militant expresses total disapprobation for 'the sects' and most other organizations and tendencies in and around the Labour

movement, this is equalled only by the similarly exaggerated sense of
its own significance which is to be found in its internal bulletins.
Thus

What guarantees the superiority of our tendency — the tendency of
Marxism — from all others inside and outside the labour movement is our
understanding of all the myriad factors which determine the attitudes and
moods of the workers at each stage. Not only the objective but the
subjective ones too.[8]

Once more it is necessary to observe a combination of beliefs
which may be inimical to democratic practices both within the
Marxist group and between it and other political organizations. This
combination of theoretical arrogance and contempt for all other
political tendencies has particularly authoritarian implications among
Marxists who express a greatly exaggerated faith in the centrality of
political leadership. The Militant Tendency share this conviction
with organizations such as the WRP and its forerunners. For
Militant, 'cadres — Marxist cadres — are the key to the Socialist
revolution in Britain'.

When Militant uses terms such as 'Marxism' or 'the Marxists' it
refers to its own analyses and supporters. As we have seen, it regards
all other Trotskyist and Communist organizations as 'anti-Marxist'.
From this we can legitimately deduce that it regards itself as the
essential and sole political leadership of the coming socialist
revolution. Indeed the Militant Tendency is not shy of making this
singular claim explicit. Thus 'we consider that our organisations are
alone in upholding the banner of Marxism . . . we repudiate every
sectarian fragment appropriating the name of Fourth International'.[9]
Militant's conviction concerning the 'anti-Marxist' theories of 'the
sects' is revealed in the following advice to its supporters who are
warned that '. . . some of the best elements of the Sects can be won
as we succeed in building a powerful tendency. But experience has
shown that the task of re-education especially of their middle class
elements takes so long and is such an exhausting process that it is not
worth the effort'.[10]

In practice Militant abjures contact between its supporters and 'the
sects'. While other Marxist groups attempt to recruit from and
persuade each other, the Militant Tendency thinks this is 'not worth
the effort'. Its insularity is reinforced by its clandestinity, by the
absence of other Marxist groups from the Labour Party during the
1970s and by its own absence from Trotskyist-inspired campaigns.
There is some evidence that Militant has failed to take root where the

socialist tradition is strong and has grown in areas of traditionally low working-class political activity in the Labour Party. Thus it is weak in Scotland and relatively implanted in Liverpool.[11] It could be, then, that Militant's small appetite for recruitment from the sects is motivated by considerations of self-preservation. If so its growth in the 1970s owes much to the lack of ideological contestation within the Labour Party, that is, to the absence of alternatives. But this is not to deny the possibility that Militant offers a dynamism or *élan,* a campaigning zeal and an idealism of positive appeal, especially to youth. This can be better gauged by a look at its principal policies.

POLICIES

The Militant Tendency has no strategy for socialism — just a list of demands. These demands are seen as transitional demands — that is demands which can only be implemented if the capitalist system itself is dismantled. Militant campaigns for the adoption of these demands by the Labour leadership. Its focus on the leadership reflects its conviction that this is the central issue before socialists: namely the transformation of this leadership into a revolutionary force. All the other factors making for a socialist revolution are either assumed to be already present or in the process of ineluctably becoming so. Two observations are in order here. First this mechanical determinism inclines the Militant Tendency to neglect actively involving people in actual struggles that can change people and circumstances. The Militant Tendency's commitment to working within the organizational framework of the Labour movement and its contempt for other Marxist organizations together explain its absence from many campaigns and its corresponding emphasis on 'resolutionary socialism' (i.e. an emphasis on winning votes and official positions within the Labour Party and trade unions). Rather than support, for example, the Campaign Against Youth Unemployment — initiated by the Young Communist League and the Young Liberals — it launched its own campaign via the LPYS. It ignored the National Abortion Campaign until the latter received official TUC support. A desire for 'respectability' may also have occasioned the Tendency's almost total silence on the Falklands War. It is, perhaps, this proclivity to adapt to the Labourist ideological milieu which accounts for its erstwhile support for the Irish Peace movement and the 'Better life for all' campaign together with its shunning of the far left-inspired 'Troops out' movement (despite Militant's formal support for the 'Troops out' slogan). Of course the Militant Tendency's focus is one of changing the leadership of the Labour Party: until this is achieved no serious political advances can be made. When the group finally took a stance on the Falklands crisis its leadership emphasis was clearly illustrated in an argument *against* active interventions prior to the establishment of a socialist government in Britain. Thus Ted Grant argued that the Argentina-Falklands problem would be solved once the top 200 monopolies had been nationalized. Then,

If necessary, British workers and the Marxists will be able to wage a war against the Argentine junta, to help the Argentine workers to take power into their own hands. But only a democratic socialist Britain would have clean hands. A Labour government committed to socialist policies would probably not need to wage war, but could issue a socialist appeal to the Argentine workers to overthrow the monstrous junta, take power, and then organise a socialist federation of Britain and the Argentine, in conjunction with the Falkland Islands.[12]

Second, Militant is inclined, because of this same mechanical determinism, to reduce all political problems to problems of capitalist economics. Issues which do not readily lend themselves to this reductionism are neglected. Thus, as Pete Duncan has noticed, 'the first 267 issues of *Militant*, up to 1975, contained four articles on women'.[13] The same author notes that Miltant failed to adopt an attitude on the Corrie Amendment (to David Steel's Abortion Act 1967) *until after the TUC took up this issue*. The implication is that Militant's economism downgraded this issue until the TUC action made it respectably workerist.

The foundation of the Militant Tendency's beliefs is the conviction that Trotsky '. . . shows the organic tendency of the decay of capitalism everywhere'. We shall see the use this idea is put to later: here it is enough to note that the Militant Tendency perceive '. . . unmistakeably a perspective of new revolutionary developments in the advanced capitalist countries, the underdeveloped lands of the ex-colonial world and the deformed workers' states of Russia and Eastern Europe'.[14] For Ted Grant this is the coming to pass of Trotsky's prognoses of the 1930s: 'The period which Trotsky confidently foresaw in the immediate pre-war period now opens out in different historical conditions'.[15] For the Militant Tendency 'the organic crisis of British capitalism demands further attacks on the already reduced standards of the working class'.

Britain's 'irreversible decline' is regarded by Militant as the context in which the attitude of the Tendency to all political issues is determined because

On a world scale capitalist economies not only find themselves in a crisis, they find themselves ensnared in an epoch of crisis, stagnation and decline . . . short-lived half-hearted booms, followed by downturn and recession in an ever tightening cycle — these are the characteristics of the new period of general decline of world capitalism . . . the search for lasting consessions and lasting reforms is now as futile as the search for flesh on an ancient skeleton.[16]

So Militant's general analysis of world capitalism predicts more frequent, more intense and longer lasting slumps punctuated by short, weak revivals that preclude the wresting of meaningful reforms from the system. Indeed for Militant reforms are not merely unattainable:

The 'reformist' alternatives of the leaders of the trade unions and Labour Party are attempts at . . . shoring up decrepit and decaying capitalism. They do not see that by doing so, they are merely prolonging the death-agony of the system and lending it a more violent and convulsive character.[17]

Militant also assert that a catastrophic fall in the rate of profit is at the root of this generalized crisis of capitalism.[18] For this reason 'in order to "solve" the crisis of British capitalism, living standards must be cut to the bone and all the social and economic gains painfully won by organised labour over the last 150 years will have to be destroyed'.[19] Thus though Ted Grant occasionally castigates the sects for their 'apocalyptic ravings' and reminds his readers that capitalism can always find a purely economic solution to its problems, the main thrust of his and his comrades' writings contends that 'the whole of British society is heading for a gigantic explosion'. The apocalyptic vision of the Militant Tendency ultimately rests on a mechanical determinism in spite of Grant's disparaging of the sects for this same theology: 'There are no capitalist solutions to the problems of world capitalism let alone to the acute difficulties facing the British capitalists'.[20]

On another occasion an internal bulletin refers to '. . . the crisis of [the] system, for which there is no way out — except possibly for a period at the expense of the working class'. But the salvation of capitalism will be at the price of barbarism according to Militant. The period of class struggles that is now upon us will,

. . . end either in the greatest victory of the working class achieving power
and the overthrow of the rule of capital with the installation of workers
democracy or we will have a military police dictatorship which will destroy
the labour movement and kill millions of advanced workers, shop stewards,
ward secretaries, Labour youth, trade union branch secretaries and even
individual members of the Labour movement.

Written in 1977, this dire warning specifies a period of ten to fifteen
years in which this issue will be resolved.

I have sought to establish that Militant regards the current crisis as
a long-term condition of capitalism — especially British capitalism
— which will either issue in socialist revolution or a collapse into
barbarism within the foreseeable future. Given this analysis, it will
now be easier to appreciate the organization's attitude to groups such
as the Anti-Nazi League and the Women's Liberation Movement.
The Anti-Nazi League is criticized by Militant for aiming
'. . . simply to combat racism without linking it to an overall
socialist programme'. Tony Cliff's argument that the ANL, by
raising political activity and boosting confidence and consciousness,
ultimately helps to increase socialist awareness is rejected by Militant
on these grounds. Despite the ANL's success in mobilizing upwards
of 80,000 people for its demonstrations, Militant regards the
organization as a blinkered, sectional and hysterical response to
fascist organizations of negligible proportions. No doubt some of
this argument is deduced from the fact that the ANL was inspired by
the SWP which is, in Militant's terms, an 'anti-Marxist sect'. But
such conclusions are also reached by deduction from Militant's
general economic and political analysis of British capitalism which
posits either a socialist revolution or a collapse into the worst
reaction as the choice facing the Labour movement over the next
decade or so. Hence Peter Taaffe's argument against the ANL insists
that 'only the Labour movement mobilised on a socialist programme
is capable of eliminating those conditions which breed racialism and
fascism and can combat this poison'.[22]

This also, of course, accords with Militant's chosen strategy of
remaining within the Labour Party and focusing its energies on a
change of leadership and programme. The SWP by virtue of its
'sectarian' independence is regarded as lacking seriousness in its
avowed anti-racism. Likewise, for Militant 'the liberation and
emancipation of women, and the main sector with which we are
concerned, working class women, lies in struggle . . . within the
framework of the organised trade union and labour movement'.
Within these confines Militant pursues the feminist cause

according to its lights. This ensures that it attends only, in the main, to bread-and-butter issues: 'The big movements among working class women will . . . be economic issues — low pay, prices, rents, nursery facilities and the like'. The women's movement itself is described as 'divisive' and is elsewhere condemned by Militant as a corrupting force in class and ideological terms: 'While standing firmly against all discrimination against women, especially working class women, Marxism rejects the hysteria of the petit-bourgeois dominated women's liberation movement, echoed by the sects, which tends to portray the male sex as "the enemy"'.[23]

Just as Militant nowhere recognizes the political, social and economic specificity of women, so it collapses issues of especial concern to students into its workerist and economist perspectives. In the wake of the student unrest of the late 1960s the Militant Tendency concluded unenthusiastically, 'a certain amount of attention should have been paid to the students but with the main purpose of educating them to understand the need to turn towards the Labour movement'. Militant perceives real politics taking place 'outside the artificial environment of the Universities'. Its student bulletin — distributed to members of the tendency only — advises that 'comrades, where possible, should move out of college accommodation and find housing in the town'.[24] The bulletin implies that the politics of student unions is unimportant: '. . . our priority must always be the winning of workers to Marxism and the role of our student comrades is to use the extra time they have towards this end'.

But Militant not only subordinates student politics to its objective of establishing a working-class support in industry and within the Labour Party: it places its own organizational goals above those of specific campaigns and issues. A 1977 issue of the *Student Bulletin* makes this clear: 'The success of an occupation . . . as far as we are concerned is measured in paper sales and new members for the student and youth organisations'. As we have seen Militant regards itself as the sole, *bona fide* Marxist organization in Britain. Since it also stresses the crucial role of leadership in the transition to socialism, it follows that the chief criterion of success in this enterprise is the strengthening of the Militant Tendency. Political activity which distracts from this project, let alone that which obstructs it, is *per se* reactionary when looked at from Militant's vantage point. Once possessed of a Militant leadership however, anything is possible for the British Labour movement: 'With a Marxist leadership, the trade unions *could assume power peacefully,* as was possible in France in 1968'.[25] Indeed Peter Taaffe argues that this could be accomplished once the Labour movement adopts 'a clear Marxist programme'. It was the absence of this in Chile and Portugal, according to the editor of *Militant,* which brought defeat to the workers of those countries.

The rise of a mass campaigning movement such as CND does not aid this process as far as Militant is concerned. Taaffe assures his readers that '. . . a war between Russia and the capitalist West . . . is completely ruled out in the foreseeable future'.[26] The enthusiasm of the sects for mobilizations around this issue is seen by Militant as a consequence of their lack of understanding of Marxism. For

the capitalists do not wage war for the sake of waging war but in order to extend their power, income and profit . . . to destroy the working class which nuclear war would mean would be to destroy the goose that lays the golden eggs. Consequently it is only totalitarian fascist regimes, completely desperate and unbalanced which would take that road.[27]

It seems that the Militant Tendency cannot conceive of the relative autonomy of political factors (indeed of any non-economic factors except political leadership in the shape of a Marxist vanguard party armed with the 'correct' programme) except under circumstances where the temporary neutralization of class factors permits the precarious dominance of a dictatorship. Such 'exceptionalism' is of course only acknowledged because it was explicitly analysed by Marx: the Militant Tendency is simply content to reiterate Marx's analysis and unable or unwilling to conceive of novel applications or new instances of it. In practice this means that Militant employs an economic reductionist method in all of its analyses.

The key points in Militant's programme are the demands for the nationalization of 'the 250 monopolies', a 35-hour week without loss of pay, a socialist plan of production, the introduction of a minimum wage of £70 and an end to wage restraint. It also calls for no redundancies, a retraining programme run by the trade unions, earlier retirement and longer holidays for all workers. Militant seems uncertain about the nature of these economic demands. On the one hand we are told that, '. . . in spite of all the propaganda of the bosses, if the pressure is sufficient, they will be forced to make concessions', but on the other, it seems that even the introduction of the 35-hour week will require 'the socialist reorganisation of society'.[28] In fact the Militant Tendency regards these as transitional demands and, as such, incapable of being realized under capitalism. But given that Militant's greatest successes have been among students and young people there are no obvious reasons in its programme to explain the progress it has made. It seems unlikely that the students and youth who have joined Militant did so because of the latter's economistic demands. A *prima facie* case would seem to suggest the remoteness of these issues from the lives of full-time students, school children and unemployed youth. Rather this programme of economic demands tends to confirm Militant's reputation for an uninspired and routinist politics and even a measure of puritanism.[29] To account for its relative strength requires, therefore, a closer look at the milieu in which it operates — the Labour Party and the LPYS.

AN ORGANIZATION WITHIN AN ORGANIZATION

The 1970s, it it increasingly argued, saw the Labour Party become the victim of 'creeping Marxism'. *The Times* alleged that the party was 'infiltrated to a terrifying degree by crypto-communists and fifth columnists' while defectors from its ranks perceived 'a growing emphasis on class war and Marxist dogma'. Some commentators envisaged that if the process of radicalization continued 'the successor Labour government would be openly ultra-Left Wing' and 'set up shop with the title "people's socialism" in the window'.[30] The key explanation for Labour's drift to the left, in most accounts, is 'the extraordinary revival of Trotskyism in Britain'.[31] According to some recent analyses Labour's constitutional changes since 1979 '. . . are a direct result of [a] persistent campaign' waged by the Militant Tendency.[32] However in all these accounts hard evidence to support these statements is remarkably sparse; a close examination of the available facts is therefore in order. For this purpose it is analytically convenient to consider the Labour Party and its Militant Tendency according to two distinct periods: 1955-70, and since 1970. Only then will we look at the LPYS.

1955-70

In 1959, after four years of entrism, Ted Grant wrote an essay called 'Problems of entrism' in which he admitted that Trotsky's conditions for entrism were 'still not present'. While acknowledging a lull in the Labour Party, Grant sought to persuade the 'tiny handful' of his co-thinkers that the prospects for open party building were even worse:

Our job . . . is the patient winning of ones and twos, perhaps of small groups, but certainly not the creation of a mass revolutionary current which is not possible at the present time.

The task is to convert this handful into an integrated group with roots in the mass movement and then, from a cadre organisation into a wider grouping, leading to the development of a mass organisation.

Militant hardly grew at all in the 1950s and even by the mid–sixties it still rested on a 'mere handful'. In the last chapter I described the Revolutionary Socialist League's ill-fated attempts at joint work with the International Group (forerunner of IMG) and the Fourth International. The RSL published *Socialist Fight* until *Militant* was launched. The following year Ted Grant recruited Peter Taaffe who became editor of the newspaper in October 1964. However the first ten years (1955-65) of entrism did not advance the organization very far. Since Healy's secession from the FI in 1953 there had been no official British section. If there was any pole of attraction for Trotskyists in Britain after 1959 it was the Socialist Labour League and its youth organization. As these organizations were also entrist and as the doctrinal differences between Grant and Healy were fairly esoteric, it was difficult for the RSL to project a distinct profile. Furthermore, Grant's organization had also to contend with similar-sized groups around Tony Cliff and Pat Jordan respectively.

The Labour Party was far from being a congenial host to the entrists. In 1961 it proscribed both the SLL and its youth journal *Keep Left*. Until 1965 Transport House fought a running battle against Trotskyist infiltration of the Young Socialists. Under these circumstances, it may be presumed that the other Trotskyist groups were loath to risk their own expulsions by too obvious activity. In any case the Militant Tendency's forerunner, the RSL, was confined to a few CLPs only until the mid-1960s, especially Swansea, Brighton, Norwood (South London) and Bradford. Here its activity was particularly cryptic — in accordance with the requirements of deep entrism or entrism *sui generis*. Not until the 'student revolt' of the late 1960s did the Militant Tendency begin to grow and even then its progress was restricted to the campus.

Despite the lack of progress registered, in terms of its avowed objectives, the Militant Tendency did not seriously question the assumptions on which they were based nor did it reconsider the nature of its host, the Labour Party. Yet as a political parasite this latter question is of vital importance to it. While Militant rejects the socialist credentials of Labour's leadership and of labourism it does assume that the Party is a genuine workers' organization. It also assumes that the politically advanced workers belong to the Labour Party and that any upturn in radical consciousness will be refracted through it. Finally, Militant Tendency's political practice assumed that exclusion from the Labour Party would only exacerbate the isolation and marginality of revolutionaries in Britain. These assumptions are far from being obvious today.

Between 1951 and 1981 the Labour Party had been in decline in some important respects. In the 1950s and 1960s in particular, Labour's world view had become especially threadbare in a context of ideological convergence between the two main parties. Labour's 'reformist conservatism' as Bauman called it shifted in emphasis '. . . away from traditional welfare demands towards economic growth, efficiency and technocracy' under the first two Wilson governments.[33] Some political analysts regard the convergence of the Labour and Conservative Parties during this period as a cause of rising political apathy. Political activity fell both in terms of voting and of party membership. Those who remained party members were less involved in campaigning, while voters became significantly less inclined to support either of the main parties.

Though it may be precipitate to conclude with Crewe that 'public allegiance to [the] system has weakened',[34] party identification has been eroded and Labour can no longer rely on the old loyalties.[35] If voters are becoming more selective and fastidious when casting their votes, there is evidence that the accompanying decline of party loyalties results from the failure of these parties to find new issues and campaigns with which to build new electoral majorities. In the last chapter I described the rise of mass campaigns on a wide range of issues which Labour failed to take up and the emergence of issues which may have become of mass concern had Labour fought strenuously for them (anti–racism and workers' control are examples of the latter). Militant's chosen strategy ensured that it was also absent from these campaigns which were insufficiently 'working class' in composition or economistic in demands to warrant its attention. Though its contempt for the sects may have inclined Militant to ignore movements which they inspired (such as the National Abortion Campaign and the Right to Work Campaign) its clandestine existence in the Labour Party was not designed to favour a leading role in them anyway. But it is *as* important to recognize that Militant's absence from the 'new left' concerns of the late-1960s is an ideological, as well as an organizational matter. As we have seen, Militant regards the women's movement, the student radicalization of this period, the Anti-Nazi campaign and CND (to name just some) movements as at best peripheral, at worst distracting, 'middle-class' issues. Its recruitment among students in the latter part of this period (1955-70) may be due to the exodus of socialists from college Labour clubs at the high point of student militancy which, paradoxically, left Militant the field to itself. Certainly all significant rival organizations had established themselves as independent 'parties' by 1969.

The rise in political activity and militancy among the young in the late 1960s seems to parallel the decline of Labour partisanship — which by the early 1970s was at its weakest among this same cohort. This moved Crewe *et al,* to speculate on 'the possibility that increasing numbers will be ready to support small, extremist parties'.[36] Certainly the decline in Labour's grass roots activities[37] and the number of its activists was not discouraged by those, like Crosland,[38] who believed that an army of activists was irrelevant under modern conditions of party campaigning and even potentially dangerous. Considering the evidence — which indicates that the constituency party organizations 'shrivelled to a skeleton' between 1966 and 1970[39] — the rationale for entrism, even on a 'lesser evil' basis, is very tenuous by the late 1960s. According to McKenzie, attendances at Labour Party branch meetings are estimated to range from 1 to 5 per cent of the paper membership[40] and other reviews of the available evidence confirm that very low attendances are *normal.* Likewise most students of the subject testify to the dominance of 'business items' on the agendas of such meetings and to the presence of an ethos which is inimical to strictly political and ideological activity. Hindess concludes that 'the entrist position is thus, in a sense, self destructive for unless those who support it can muster massive support within the party, their numbers are likely to decline as a result of expulsion or of voluntary movement to the Right or Left'.[41] The history of entrism between 1944 and 1970 appears to uphold this assessment. By the end of this period all the main revolutionary organizations except the Militant Tendency had left the Labour Party.

THE ORGANIZATIONAL STATUS OF MILITANT

We have established the entrist origins of the Militant Tendency which can be traced back to Ted Grant's Revolutionary Socialist League. However, whereas the latter consisted of a small group of conscious entrists — cohesive and conspiratorial — it is unlikely that this description applies to the Militant Tendency which evolved from it. For as the RSL evolved and grew numerically, a larger proportion of its supporters — that is those subscribing to the politics of the *Militant* journal — played no part in the organization's internal life. By 1975 an internal bulletin referred to '. . . the problem outlined in previous bulletins, *that the tendency consists of a layer of cadres, a layer of half-formed cadres and a layer of raw new comrades'* [my emphasis]. Such a division is possible in any organization: but in the case of the Militant Tendency it is probable that the largest category is the last one mentioned and that it consists merely of regular readers of its publications among Labour activitists — people, also, who vote for Tendency positions in the Party. These Labour activists do not necessarily play any part in shaping Militant policy or even participate in Militant discussions.

That the Tendency has its own organizational life is indisputable. The documents circulated by Reg Underhill are full of references to 'readers' meetings', caucuses for youth, trade unionists and immigrants, and make mention of 'central committee' meetings. In the case of the Labour Party Young Socialists, which Militant controls, it is easy to see how participation by the rank and file is identical with participation in (at the minimum) voting on Militant-inspired resolutions. The same is true of the National Organization of Labour Students (NOLS) where, likewise, the Militant presence is strong. But in the Labour Party, Militant supporters are a tiny percentage even of the rank-and-file activists. Thus, attendance at a ward or branch meeting is not synonymous with activity *within* the Militant Tendency. To participate in the latter it is necessary to attend the group's parallel organizations. However, it is precisely at this point that the bulk of Militant sympathizers are excluded, for only those entrusted with *selling* the newspaper, the group's cadre, attend its own meetings.

The Militant's mode of operation is a concomitant of its 'unofficial', quasi-clandestine status. Contacts are made via newspaper sales: only when the contact proves himself reliable is he introduced to the Militant organization proper. We have already noted the tendencies to centralism in far left organizations: it seems probable that Militant's entrist existence has reinforced such tendencies in its own case. As with other far left organizations, the Militant group's leadership echelon is remarkably stable. These figures — Ted Grant, Peter Taaffe, Lynn Walsh, Keith Dickinson, Clare Doyle, Roger Silverman, Brian Ingham etc — have between

13 and 27 years' activity as Trotskyists in the Labour Party. These are the names which appear in the list of twenty-five shareholders in Workers International Review Publications Ltd, the owners of Militant publications. This group of full timers represents the longest serving, inner core of the group's decision-making centre — which as recently as 1975 was only 22 strong (the group now claims 60-plus full timers). The recurrence of these names in the group's theoretical journal — *Militant International Review* over the last twelve years is evidence of their centrality in shaping Militant politics.

But it is unclear what the contribution of the ordinary supporter can be. For a perusal of the group's internal documents — Students Bulletins, Perspectives Documents etc. — reveals that these consist of unsigned articles carrying instructions, reports and, in general, attempts to co-ordinate or in some way organize the membership. There is no evidence of discussion and debate or of the involvement of the rank and file. It is clear, too, that the conditions in which Militant operates must make it more difficult to convene regional aggregates, national conferences and the like, which actually determine the group's policies. Fear of furnishing proof of the group's 'party within a party' status might be sufficient to deter this. The national meetings which Militant *does* hold appear to be organized more like rallies than conferences with the audience playing a relatively passive role. (On this see P. Wintour's (1980, 1981) reports in *New Statesman,* 18 January, and 24 April.) The difficulties of 'horizontal' political activity in any democratic centralist organization are particularly problematic for an entrist group and the dispersal of Militant supporters would seem to make the chances of forming tendencies or factions, to pursue platforms different than those of the leadership echelon, very slim indeed. This is perhaps why I have found no written evidence whatever of such fissures in the group's long history and it is this which explains the absence of internal discussions in our account of the group's politics, to which I now return.

1970-81

It is difficult to be sure of Militant's current strength because of the very nature of the organization as a secret faction. Tom Forester's estimate is that the group have around 2,000 members, plus the 3,500 strong LPYS and about 40 per cent of the National Organization of Labour Students (NOLS). The print order for *Militant* is over 9,000 and the group employs around 63 full timers. Its growth in the 1970s has been in the context of '. . . a general increase in Labour Party activity . . . even during the difficult years of the 1974-9 government.[42] The context in which Militant operates has not simply been one of rising political activity; it is a much more left-wing grass roots base that the Trotskyists work in today. The Trotskyists were also favoured by the abolition of the list of proscribed organizations in 1973 and the mainly successful resistance against its re-introduction since then (notwithstanding the expulsion of Militant leaders in 1983). Since 1971 the PLP itself adopted a rhetoric and programmes which represented a shift to the left as big as any since 1931. Indeed since the onset of the Party's constitutional battles, from 1979, it is argued that '. . . the strength of the Trotskyist position in the Labour Party stems primarily from the widespread acceptance of the worldview it implies'.[43] While this is doubtless an enormous exaggeration, there is no doubting the real increase in Militant's strength. By January 1982 seven members of the Tendency had been adopted by their CLPs as prospective parliamentary candidates. It has been alleged that they have effective control of Liverpool City Labour Group and Liverpool district Labour Party.

Since 1970, Militant has retained a majority on the National Committee of the LPYS and since 1972 has always had one representative on the NEC in consequence of this majority. An indication of the Militant Tendency's hegemony in the LPYS is the voting figure for the national committee of the latter in 1979: Militant received 200 votes while the rest were divided equally between two other Trotskyist groups — Workers' Action and Clause 4 — which received 20 votes each. Militant supporters are prominent in the Rank and File Mobilizing Committee for Labour Party Democracy and the Socialist Campaign for a Labour Victory which also includes the small Trotskyist 'groupuscules' 'Workers' Action' and the 'Chartists'. Since 1979 when the Tribunite *Briefing* merged with the SCLV's broadsheet, Militant has had a voice in this organ which is distributed at national and regional Labour Party conferences. According to Webster the block vote of 50-60,000 in the constituency section of the NEC '. . . can be clearly identified as Trotskyist controlled'.[44] Another indicator of Militant's strength is the survey conducted by Paul Whiteley and Ian Gordan at the Labour Party's annual conference in 1979 which discovered the tendency commanded 'the single largest faction among conference delegates, outstripping even the Tribunites' by 36 per cent of the delegates to 24 per cent.[45]

However, controversy surrounds many of these figures — the latter for failing to make clear to delegates whether it referred to 'militants' or 'Militant'. A more reliable guide to the group's strength, though unfortunately fragmentary, is its own internal bulletins, which we will briefly consider before examining the reasons for its relative rise.

By 1975 Militant drew the following account of its strength in the Labour Party:

The Marxist tendency has not yet an important, let alone dominating influence in even a fifth of [the CLPs] . . . two thousand cadres by the end of next year leading to 10,000 as rapidly as possible must be our aim in the next few years.

In the same year the organization referred to the founding conference of the entrist International which was attended by 46 people. This revealed that there were '. . . still only four established national sections in Britain, Ireland, Sweden and Germany'. Of these the Militant Tendency was described as 'by far the strongest section . . . with a membership of over 600 . . . and 22 full-time workers'. Of the 22 full timers it transpires that nine are 'political workers at the centre', four are print workers, eight are described as regional field workers and one specializes in 'international work'. The documents compiled by Underhill also refer to Militant's industrial strength. In the mid-seventies it had trade union caucuses comprising ten members in engineering, eleven in the EEPTU, twelve in ASTMS, fourteen in railways, twenty-one in NALGO and an unspecified number among teachers. A *NALGO Conference Report* published by the relevant caucus in an internal bulletin of 1976 refers to Militant's presence, which was confined to 'three comrades, one full-timer and one close contact' at this event. Similar reports are given for the TASS, NUAAW, and AUEW conferences.

But the impression gained from these documents is of Militant's optimism and confidence concerning its rate of growth and immediate future. A document printed at the end of 1978 bears this out. Observing that in 1972, Militant had had just two groups in the Midlands (six members in Birmingham and eight in Coventry) the document goes on to claim 15 cells for the same region by 1978 including groups in Birmingham, Wolverhampton, Stafford, Telford, Coventry East, Coventry West, Banbury, Oxford City and Oxford County. The Leicester branch is specified as having thirty members, consisting of ten workers, seven white-collar employees, five teachers, two school students and five students. The same bulletin announces, 'we control 22 youth branches in the area and influence 3 others'. Of course Militant's strength is unevenly distributed within the Labour Party. By 1978 the Merseyside group, for example, is described as being 'well entrenched' with a social composition which is mainly white-collar and craft workers. This group boasts of supporters in the Fire Brigade Union, four trade union caucuses and the district secretary of one of the print unions. It also managed to send seven delegates to the Labour Party annual conference of 1977. In fact Militant claims that its impact at the annual conference is out of all proportion to its strength in the CLPs. Thus it argues that in 1975 '. . . three quarters of the CLPs voted for resolutions putting the Marxist position'. In 1976, according to Militant Tendency, about one third of all speeches at the annual conference were 'from the Marxists' although 'there were only about forty Marxist delegates, though the press thought it was much more, such was their impact'.

Of course this indicates the real point about Militant's strength: it has been not so much a numerical matter as a question of unequalled activism in the context of Labour politics. The Militant Tendency occasionally reveals its awareness of the actual basis of its influence in the CLPs. Ted Grant refers to the 'organisational incapacity and formlessness' together with the 'conspicuous absence of *Tribune*' at the local level. This, he explains, is why 'in many important parties the struggle is between the "Neanderthal" wing, entrenched for decades in positions of control and the Marxist current'. Two years later, in 1977, the absence of an active, organized tendency in ideological contest with Militant enabled the latter to refer derisively to

. . . the Neanderthal MPs and councillors [who] retain a semblance of influence only in the worst rotten boroughs, wards and GMCs that have an almost completely dead membership and a virtually complete lack of outside activity.

Drucker makes the same point in explanation of the rise of Militant: 'By the 1970s the Labour organisations in the inner cities had begun to look like rotten boroughs', and this was the context in which alternatives to official Labour emerged.[46] That Militant was a beneficiary of this process may well have something to do with the 'doctrineless' state of official Labour which, the same author notes, had forsaken its traditional two-pronged commitment to equality and planning. Perhaps Militant has understood Labour's grass roots ethos well enough to stress these very issues in its own propaganda.

Certainly the group represents a strident economism which echoes the traditional preoccupations of labourism quite accurately. Likewise its stress on programme and leadership are not alien priorities for official Labour. Militant's belief in an Enabling Act with which to usher in socialism[47] approximates the Bevanite faith in the efficacy of Parliament, though it is worth noting that the Tribunite belief in the unique importance of Westminster socialism has itself taken many knocks in the last decade (for example, over the EEC, devolution, the influence of the IMF, the drift to corporatism, over NATO and the power of multinationals and so on). In other words in ideological terms Militant and a substantial part of the Labour left may have converged producing a much more congenial atmosphere for the former than has ever been the case before.

The campaign for democratization of the Labour Party accords well with the traditional Trotskyist interest in this and related issues such as workers' control, opposition to usurping trade union and political bureaucracies together with generalized Marxist opposition to the EEC. Both Trotskyism and 'ultra democracy' are connected in another way too: the resurgence of anti-bureaucratism and the growth of the new left originate in the late 1960s and have overlapping personnel. The participatory thrust of Bennism appeals to the activist and vanguardist ethos of Trotskyism. Benn's invitation to Trotskyists to join the Labour Party has latterly been taken up with enthusiasm precisely because of his advocacy of participatory democracy. An article in *International,* the IMG's theoretical journal, cites three reasons for regarding Benn as an associate of the revolutionary tradition:

(1) in bringing socialism's democratic heritage out front where it belongs;
(2) in arguing for a socialist strategy based on a fight for the control and administration of the economy by workers in industry;
(3) and in his endorsement of direct popular action for political ends.[48]

It will be seen that Benn's advocacy of rank-and-file political initiatives is what appeals to IMG, since it opens the door to extra-parliamentary strategies for socialism.[49] Yet, while this may explain the IMG's conversion back to entrism, it seems at odds with the emphasis on leadership which has caused some to dub Militant substitutionist. However, in reality there is no contradiction, since Militant imagine that a change in leadership will precisely be hastened by the constitutional changes championed by Benn. At the same time there is no evidence of Militant changing its strategic goal which remains the adoption of its demands by the parliamentary leadership of the Labour Party. The wider educative and con-sciousness-raising aspects of greater participation do not concern it.

In the first half of the seventies Militant probably benefited indirectly by the drift to the left of the Labour Party as indicated by a number of factors which can be traced back to the late 1960s. Among the most significant of these must stand the rejection of *In Place of Strife* and the Industrial Relations Act and the rise of shop stewards, industrial militancy and the issue of industrial democracy. The change in leadership in the TGWU and AEU from 1967 symbolized and reflected such processes as did the adoption of Labour's programme of 1973 — the most radical of Labour's post-war programmes. When the pendulum began to swing against the left after 1975 the Militant Tendency was in a position to explain this in terms of class betrayal and sell-outs by unaccountable MPs. Its explanation of the crisis — which stressed the *necessity* for cuts in living standards and the dismantling of trade union power via a return to mass unemployment — seemed vindicated by the facts as first Labour and then Conservative governments pursued monetarist goals in an effort to restore the profitability of private enterprise in Britain.

Indeed it may be that the most important economic and political developments in Britain over the last decade or so have been seen to vindicate Militant's *general* perspectives, which have stayed remarkably constant since the late 1960s. In 1968 Grant envisaged that a new economic crisis would lead to a leftward swing in the unions and the Labour Party and that the parliamentary wing of social democracy would split, with the right wing joining the Tories.[50] Throughout the period since 1968, Militant have returned to the perspective of a national government or an alliance of conservatism and right social democracy designed to exclude a socialist Labour Party from power. 'This "National" coalition would merely be a label for a ferocious capitalist government prepared to take the offensive against the Labour Movement and the working class in all fields'. By 1982 leading Labour politicians had begun to predict an SDP-Tory coalition along these lines. Likewise the Militant Tendency has been able to make political capital out of the defections of Prentice and Jenkins, the split within the Tribunites and its own successes in various reselection battles — all of which it has been predicting since the mid-1970s. To its young audience — particularly within the LPYS — and, after 1975, to a growing number of disillusioned Labour Party activists, Militant may have come to resemble an authentic voice of Labour speaking for this tradition against usurping, middle-class betrayers of socialism. But Militant's growth is also connected with problems persistently encountered by official Labour in the latter's youth wing and it is to the LPYS that I now turn.

THE LABOUR PARTY YOUNG SOCIALISTS

To account for Militant's rise it is necessary to account for its success among Labour's youth, since that is where the bulk of its support lies. The historical record of relations between the Labour Party and its youth section, however, shows these to be so bad that we are, at least in part, forced to discuss the failings of official Labour in order to explain Militant's hegemony within the LPYS.[51] In the first place official Labour has always left a vacuum in its youth work in the sense that having been slow to recognize the need for a youth movement it greatly circumscribed the latter's terms of reference once it obtained one. Paradoxically Labour denied a political role to its original youth league for fear that such a role would encourage Marxist activity within the youth organization. In the event the dominance of Marxism within the youth section has been aided by official Labour's patronizing and, at times, repressive attitude towards its own youth. For the most part Labour required a youth section in so far as this fulfilled an instrumental role as recruitment agency, and regarded this section as a nuisance to the extent that it generated a critical spirit. In fact the high points of youth recruitment to Labour coincide with high points in the youth section's political activism; in both respects upturns in the youth's fortunes correlate closely with its shifts to the left. Thus in 1935-9, 1948-51 and 1960-5 the youth section strongly supported left-wing policies opposed by official Labour and grew in numbers and activity. In 1939, 1955 and 1964-5 the youth section either fell to pieces or was dismantled by the repressive action of the Labour leadership as the latter responded to the increasing militancy of its youth.

The Labour Party Young Socialists dates from 1965 when its forerunner was restructured following 'administrative' action against the Trotskyist infiltrators of the SLL. Yet within three years of its creation, the LPYS elected a majority to its national committee which supported Militant. During the 1970s the Militant Tendency retained its hegemony within the LPYS and faced serious opposition only from other groups of Marxists. How can this be explained?

The idealism of youth inclines them to place loyalty to doctrine above loyalty to party. This places them in spirit closer to Trotskyism than to official Labour. The routinism of the latter and its 'responsibilities of office' serve to estrange youth just as the greater campaigning zeal and elan of the Marxists leads to empathy. If we add to this the record of repression, alternating with condescension, which characterizes relations between the youth wing and its parent, the *general* disposition of Labour youth to support the Marxists within their ranks is understood. If Labour's *peculiar* failure to attract youth is considered, then it is perhaps necessary to note Labour's especial disregard for socialist doctrine even within the camp of European social democracy, for this often entails an obvious disregard for principles and ideals. As Tawney observed, Labour's 'gravest weakness' is its poverty of creed. While this latter is sufficient to attract some youth into the party, it is normally left to the Trotskyists to elaborate on Clause Four and sustain the idealism of the young recruit.

On the basis of our characterization of the Militant Tendency's brand of Marxism, it might seem difficult to reconcile its noted workerism and economism with its relative success among youth. But this is to forget other factors of a contingent nature which have favoured the entrists in the 1970s and early 1980s. Official Labour's poverty of socialist vision was highlighted during lengthy spells of office which weakened support among activists for the leadership. At the grass roots level this may have been hastened by processes of deindustrialization and urban renewal which — together with political complacency — led to the atrophy of Labour's machine in the traditional centres of its strength. This not only discredited the Labour establishment — both local and national — but called forth a reaction in the shape of younger, more militant elements who took over the new rotten boroughs. The process which led to the selection of Peter Tatchell in Bob Mellish's fiefdom of Bermondsey was hardly necessary in the LPYS, where official Labour was already weak, but undoubtedly boosted the prestige and influence of Militant among Labour's youth. (I cite the Tatchell affair as an example precisely because the latter is not a member of Militant and in order to emphasize the more general radicalization which has benefited the Trotskyists.) Recent speculation suggests that in the 1970s the new Labour recruit was increasingly likely to belong to that age cohort influenced by the radicalization for which '1968' is emblematic.[52] If so, such recruitment contributed to the development of a political milieu favourable to the growth of Trotskyism in the Labour Party. Unhindered by competition from its main Trotskyist rivals, Militant was able to exploit these developments. By the mid-1970s it could point to the stagnation or impasse reached by the sects and contrast this with its own advances. The wave of strikes between 1970 and 1974 seemed to confirm Militant's doctrinal priorities, as did the decline of student militancy in the same period. Grant and his co-thinkers may also have learned that youth is repelled by ceaseless doctrinal disputes between rival groups and that it is not attracted by abstruse theoreticism. Certainly the Militant Tendency is far less concerned than its rivals with internecine polemics, doctrinal hair-splitting, and esoteric debates. Likewise Militant refrains from the ultra-activism of WRP-SWP vintage. By focusing the energies of its supporters on the campaigns officially sanctioned by the party and/or the trade unions, Militant incidentally avoids overstretching its organizational and human resources. Finally, unlike official Labour, Militant has a high regard for youth as a political force:

The youth will always be, if not the backbone, then one of the mainstays of the Tendency. It is the principal reservoir of the Movement. Nor could it be different . . . the youth have the necessary idealism, stamina, elan and enthusiasm. They are not burdened . . . with the cares of family life, and theoretically armed, can resist the subtle and deep pressures of capitalism.

CONCLUSIONS

The Militant Tendency adheres to a brand of Marxism which we have termed economism-workerism. This is characterized by the tendency to reduce all problems of politics to the struggle of the organized, industrial working class and especially its political wing (the Labour Party) in a context of worsening economic crisis, which is expected directly to radicalize these elements. Struggles by other sections of society which identify with the working class and socialist movement are regularly dismissed as petty bourgeois distractions by the Militant Tendency as long as these campaigns refuse to accept its methods and priorities. Thus the Militant Tendency believes that the Anti-Nazi League, the women's movement and CND obstruct, rather than aid, the socialist cause. At its 1981 conference the LPYS voted in favour of affiliation to CND. Militant had belatedly recognized the importance of the peace movement without in any way disowning its earlier statements concerning CND's insignificance. Likewise Militant regards the rest of the Marxist left as a sectarian and reactionary force. Indeed, Militant regards itself as uniquely endowed with the requisite theoretical-strategic armoury to lead the socialist revolution in Britain. Militant's arrogance in this respect is augmented by its inordinate confidence in the centrality of political leadership as the key to socialist advance in Britain. It is this tendency to regard all other relevant issues as already 'solved' or 'rotten-ripe for revolution' which inclines Militant to place a substitutionist stress on its tactical and strategic propaganda. Thus the pages of its organs constantly repeat the need for a clear socialist programme and a change of leadership in the Labour Party and the trade unions as if these measures would suffice for political advance. But the substitutionist emphasis of Militant reaches its apogee in its repeated call for an Enabling Act to usher in socialism in the best tradition of Sidney Webb, Stafford Cripps, Clement Attlee and others of this bureaucratic-paternalist vintage. But all these matters are just one side of Militant's political naivete.

Militant's economic reductionism prevents it from developing any account of the relative autonomy of political factors. Its adherence to the theory of state monopoly capitalism (see the Appendix to this chapter) — according to which the state has fused with the hegemonic fraction of the bourgeoisie (finance capital) — may help to explain Militant's crude economic determinism. The reader searches Militant publications in vain for any attempt at an analysis of political and ideological crises, the ways in which these unfold, the extent to which Britain currently experiences such problems and their relationship to economic crises. Rather one finds instead the assumption that economic crises result in crises of the political system 'which shake the very foundations of the state'. To the extent that Militant explains the current economic crisis as a consequence of distributional struggles over relative shares of national income, its neglect of the state's role in these issues is compounded. I examine Militant's analysis of the economic crisis in the Appendix to this chapter: here I merely note that it forwards no explanation of the state's role in the restructuring of production or of the causes and limitations of such state interventions. Instead it suggests that wage and public expenditure cuts are sufficient to resolve the economic crisis.

Because Militant employs an economic determinism which regards political factors, for the most part, as epiphenomena it is forced to resort to the language of conspiracy theories whenever it wishes to account for the independent impact of such non-economic forces. The following passage exemplifies this procedure:

The attitude of the bourgeoisie seems to be that if they are to be saddled
with a Tory government, then it needs to be one with a sizeable majority.
This is the only explanation for the lifting of reporting restrictions and the
savaging of the Liberals by the press and the media in relation to the
'Thorpe Affair'. They are determined to cut down the support for the
Liberals and to ensure the swinging back to the Tories of those who voted
Liberal in protest in the last two general elections.[53]

In this way, relatively trivial matters (the lifting of reporting
restrictions on the Thorpe case), which could easily be accounted for
if the relative autonomy of political factors was acknowledged, must
perforce be exaggerated into matters of class conspiracy by those,
like Militant, who reduce all political issues direct to economic class
forces. Likewise the larger issues of state power and parliamentary
democracy, the durability of reformism and the stability of the social
system are dealt with in the same simplistic way. Indeed it is a
testimony to Militant's neglect of political factors that it continues to
regard Lenin's theory of imperialism as the last word on all of these
matters.

The organizational advances made by Militant in the 1970s may
owe something to the coincidence in that decade of Militant's
preoccupations with those of the conjuncture. Perhaps Militant's
economism gained credibility in certain circles when the context was
one of increasing industrial militancy as in 1970-4. It is more than
likely that the apparent confirmation of its prognoses (such as the
defections from Labour, the failure of the Labour government, the
worsening economic crisis etc.) in the latter part of the 1970s brought
Militant some kudos particularly as its rivals, the sects, were
simultaneously experiencing disappointment and stagnation in their
own projects. However Militant's growth is mainly attributable to
the radicalization of Labour's grass roots which began in the early
1970s and was greatly accelerated with the onset of the campaign for
internal constitutional changes led by Tony Benn. Throughout this
period Militant has indirectly benefited from internal campaigns
which it did nothing to initiate. Even the most sensational accounts
cannot name a single cause or issue championed by Labour's left
which depended on Militant for its advance. In all probability the
situation within the Labour Party in 1982 is that the conspiratorial
entrism represented by the Militant Tendency is one of the least
important factors contributing to the left-wing composition of the
CLPs. Indeed since the spontaneous influx of Marxists after 1979

together with the rediscovery of entrism by groups such as IMG, Militant's forces may well represent a diminishing proportion of the revolutionaries within the CLPs but they remain, so far, the most publicized and the best organized. Given the narrowness of Militant's strategic-theoretical vision and its insularity, however, it is not likely to hold its favoured position for very long. For once a range of ideological alternatives appears among Labour's grass roots and engenders real debate and contestation, Militant is likely to be exposed in all its weaknesses as indicated here.

APPENDIX: MILITANT'S ANALYSIS OF THE ECONOMIC CRISIS

The current economic crisis was predicted by Ted Grant in a pamphlet which was first published in 1961.[1] The 'timeless' nature of Grant's analysis is illustrated by the re-publication of this essay in 1978 and by the generalizations it employs. According to Grant 'a period of catastrophic downswing' is 'absolutely certain' in consequence of a fall in the rate of profit occasioned by an increase in the amount of constant capital in proportion to variable capital, 'whatever the exact date'. Grant uses similarly broad sweeps of his brush when depicting the relationship between state and economy. For him it has been satisfactorily shown (by Lenin and Trotsky) that 'there was a fusion of monopoly capital with the state which acted as the direct agent of Big Business' such that in Britain '. . . the real role of the State [is] as the tool of the banks and the trusts'. The merging of state and finance capital has come about, according to this analysis, because of the weakness of capitalism as a system. Thus the paradox that, 'the state in the modern period has become a monstrous incubus and parasitic burden on production. What the state gains on the swings capitalists lose on the roundabouts'. Keynesian deficit financing can only lead to an inflation of the currency, so for Grant pump-priming is no long-term solution either.

Yet alongside this argument, Militant also maintain that it is precisely 'the capitalist apologists [who] try to say that government spending is used to featherbed the welfare state at the expense of profits. On the contrary, the increase in government spending is used to prop up the system increasingly at the expense of the worker'.[2] The state is seemingly both 'a parasitic burden on production' and a source of expenditures which 'prop up the system' at the expense of the worker. Likewise state parasitism is, in

Militant's analysis, often replaced by '. . . the increasing parasitism of Big Business and its reliance on the state as a crutch'.[3]

Of course the state can be both a parasite and a prop in its relations with corporate capital depending on which areas of its activity we consider; but Militant's analyses do not specify these different areas and prefer broad generalizations that are ultimately contradictory. The analyses it proffers are not detailed enough in relation to the British state and economy for them to show how these contradictions can be reconciled, if at all. And while adumbrations of the overloaded government thesis (and of corporatist theories and of theories of fiscal crisis) can be found in Militant documents these remain the merest hints. The only theory of the state which is at all developed is that of state monopoly capitalism. This complements exactly Militant's economic reductionism and expresses also its theoretical conservatism. As we have already indicated in other respects, Militant has no conception of the relative autonomy of the political unless (as in the case of Bonapartism) this has already been given detailed exposition in relation to a particular problem in one of the Marxist classics. Indeed Militant establishes the class character of the British state in terms of the social backgrounds of its leading personnel and thus advances a particularly simplistic, positivist version of economic reductionism.

All the commanding positions in society are placed in the hands of people whom the bourgeoisie can trust. That is the reason the state machine is a tool in the hands of the bourgeoisie which cannot be used by the proletariat and must be smashed by them.[4]

In contrast to Militant's one-dimensional view of the state its analysis of the current economic crisis is multi-causal to the point of eclecticism. Ted Grant regards the stability of the post-war period in the capitalist economies as stemming from the assertion of American economic and political hegemony which enforced GATT, the dollar exchange, and the extension of the world market. It was this expansion of world trade which permitted the 'enormous development of production to an unparalleled extent' in the post-war boom. Keynesian techniques of demand management contributed to this growth and stability, according to Grant, but only at the cost of 'an explosion of inflation internationally and especially in Britain'.

Militant's explanation of Britain's particular economic ills invokes most of the factors commonly cited in such discussions. Thus:

. . . it has been the failure of the bosses over the years to reinvest their profits in manufacturing industry which has led to the particular crisis of British capitalism.[5]

Discussing this alleged failure to invest in British industry Grant discovers several causes: '. . . the role of the City and finance capital and the Empire, the parasitism of finance and the high concentration in monopolies'.[6] According to Militant (in 1977) those like the Tribunites who explain the lack of investment in terms of a shortage of investment funds are quite simply wrong:

. . . in the post-war period British industry has generally had a higher rate of profit than her rivals abroad. *And because of higher profits (especially for the monopolies) the capitalists have had no incentive to invest.*[7]

Yet it is also a *central* contention of Militant's that another cause of the world economic crisis is precisely that

Every capitalist power, to a greater or lesser extent was affected by the tendency of the rate of profit to fall.[8]

In the British instance this has recently been cited as the basic cause of rising UK unemployment by Militant. Thus Andrew Glyn refers to '. . . the catastrophic fall in the rate of profit sustained by British capitalism — from 13.5 per cent in 1960 to 3.5 per cent in 1975.'[9] Despite Militant's insistence on this falling rate of profit (which I investigate further below), contradictory explanations are to be found in both its internal documents and public discussion papers. Again considering the low level of investment in British manufacturing Militant argues that,

The low wages . . . of the British workers gave no incentive to the capitalists to invest. More profitable overseas investment, property investment, speculation and the monopolisation by giant firms, which made super profits, gave no spur to the modernisation of industry.[10]

However it is a special feature of one of Militant's versions of the theory of the tendency of the rate of profit to fall that it stresses the rising share of wages in national income (rather than the increasing proportion of constant capital) as the basic cause of this tendency.

Each year the Militant Tendency compiles a long *Perspectives* document and each year this sets about the task of analysing economic trends and political developments in Britain and abroad. Each year the list of factors invoked to explain the economic slump is slightly different. In addition to the causes already discussed, Militant attributes a role to the following: the attempt by British industry to keep up dividends which in amount and proportion are higher than in West Germany. Credit expansion, the role of the dollar and its over-valuation, growing state expenditures and the nostrums of Keynesianism — all account for the current financial instability. More recently Militant has discovered in the specially heavy arms expenditure of Britain another cause of low investment. But this is not to omit the decline in industry's ability to finance its own investment: high interest charges are proving 'prohibitive' now whereas in the 1950s British industry was 80 per cent self-financing. To this must be added the fact that 'like the former Empire of Spain, the loss of Empire has meant decline and downfall'. Even the decline of the Protestant work ethic has played its part in Militant accounts of Britain's economic demise which speak of its replacement by the 'parasitic drones and the coupon clippers'.

It is not the number of explanations proffered by Militant on this issue which is surprising; after all the complexity of the problem is all too obvious. It is the fact that Militant's accounts of British capitalism's economic problems do not attempt to structure the arguments it uses according to causal significance. Nor do they situate these arguments in historical time. The result is an imprecise and eclectic list of timeless arguments and contradictory explanations. Of course this does not prevent Militant from deducing a political stance on these issues and differentiating its 'product' from rivals such as *Tribune*. But this results from a metaphysical faith in Britain's 'irreversible decline' and the idea that 'there are no capitalist solutions to the problems of world capitalism, let alone to the acute difficulties facing the British capitalists'.[11]

In Militant's view the capitalists can forward only two roads to recovery but both of these — Keynesian and monetarist — will result in 'exacerbating the slump': 'They are faced with . . . mass unemployment of 2 or 3 million . . . or running inflation. Either would shake the capitalist state to its foundations'.[12] The Communist-Tribunite policy of import controls would simply provoke retaliation and stimulate chauvinism. More generally,

only the Tribunites and the so-called Communist Party continue to mouth yesterday's delusions of the bourgeois economists and advocate a capitalist solution of the crisis based on raising living standards and increasing state expenditure (i.e. deficit financing . . . one of the main causes of inflation).[13]

In Militant's view the Alternative Economic Strategy (AES) is not transitional to socialism '. . . but is transitional to a tremendous disaster'. Holland's notion of selective nationalizations designed to stimulate competition in the meso-economic layer (i.e. among oligopolists) overlooks the fact that these firms cannot withstand *current* rates of competition. Compulsory planning agreements are simply a contradiction in terms and will fail. Price controls could not be sustained without exacerbating the decline of profits and further diminishing manufacturing investment. In almost every respect Militant finds the AES incapable of moving Britain towards socialism but sufficiently damaging to capitalism to provoke a violent reaction. Against this, as we have seen, Militant proposes transitional demands such as the call for a 35-hour week, a sliding scale of wages, a minimum wage of £70 per week, a programme of public works and the demand for workers' inspections of capitalists' books and financial records. Ultimately Militant regards nothing short of the nationalization of at least 200 monopolies, including the financial institutions, as appropriate for the salvation of the British economy.

To some extent this programme of demands stems from Militant's analysis of the nature of British capitalism's specific decline. But this is not to overlook that these demands also emanate from Trotsky's Transitional Programme and the general analysis of imperialism contained therein which are key features of the intellectual legacy of Militant. On the question of Militant's specifically British analysis, some confusion has already been noticed. Grant asserts that the falling rate of profit is attributable to a rise in the constant composition of capital (the orthodox view) while Glyn regards it as a function of the rising share of wages in national income after 1960-4[14] combined with the growing intensity of international competition which allegedly prevents monopoly mark-up (the neo-Ricardian view). The fact that Grant has also asserted low wages as a prime cause of low investment in Britain, further reinforces the suspicion that Militant has no coherent analysis of capitalism's economic malaise. In so far as one can abstract a coherent analysis of this problem from the publications of Militant supporters, it consists largely of Andrew Glyn's writings. A brief outline of Glyn's neo-Ricardian views will demonstrate the extent to which they deviate from and complement different aspects of the Militant position and the politics it gives rise to.

The analysis of Britain's economic crisis outlined in Glyn's and Sutcliffe's study of 1972[15] argued that

. . . British capitalism has suffered such a dramatic decline in profitability
that it is now literally fighting for survival. This crisis has developed
because mounting demands from the working class for a faster growth in
living standards has coincided with growing competition between capitalist
countries.

According to this analysis the halving of the rate of profit between
1964 and 1970 is directly attributable to wage increases since 1950
and led to a situation where '. . . profitability . . . can only be
[restored] at the expense of the living standards and political strength
of the working class'.

Glyn and Sutcliffe thus found themselves reinforcing the
conventional wisdom of the early 1970s in blaming the working class
for the capitalist crisis. But their thesis, if taken seriously, could also
provide a rationale for economism since the logic of their analysis
also suggested that bigger and bigger wage increases would
undermine the capitalist system itself: '. . . capital and labour are
bargaining not only about wages, nor even the division of the
national income, but about the survival of the capitalist system'. This
argument also envisaged the trade unions becoming 'instruments of
the revolutionary movement of the proletariat',[16] a view which, as
we have seen, also underpinned the IS-SWP's rank-and-file
strategy.[17] Such conclusions follow from the neo-Ricardian analysis
of capitalist crisis because it regards the real source of falls in the rate
of profit to be determined by economic class struggles fought over
the distribution of incomes. To this extent it may serve as a rationale
for the economism of Militant's 'transitional demands'.

However, as we have noticed, Ted Grant (somewhat confusingly)
also urged that low wages were a cause of Britain's low investment
in manufacturing industry. This underconsumptionist explanation of
the crisis can also serve as a rationale for a reformist strategy for
recovery such as that proposed by Tribune and the TUC which
imagine a recovery based on investment aid and re-flated demand.
Likewise Grant's multi-causal analysis of Britain's peculiar
difficulties — low investment, heavy arms burden, the City,
speculation, mismanagement, etc. — implies a solution based on a
radical reformist programme which would deal with each of these
problems. Yet Militant retain the rhetoric of catastrophism and
occasional references to the rise in the organic composition of capital
also appear in its bulletins (thus suggesting an analysis of capitalist
crisis which locates it at the point of production, in the accumulation
of capital). Thus Militant's eclecticism spans the whole gamut of

possibilities ranging from reformist economism to a strategy based on the irreversible demise of capitalism; or from the crisis seen as accidental and contingent (the neo-Ricardian view)[18] to a vision of crisis as the inevitable outcome of iminent laws of capitalist development. The only constant factor in all of this is Militant's dogged persistence in demanding that the Labour Party adopt its list of economic demands: these too range from reform to revolution and are sometimes regarded as 'transitional' by Militant. In fact they merely reflect the syncretic explanation of capitalist crisis which emerges from a close inspection of Militant documents.[19]

Conclusion

Trotskyist organizations remain on the margins of British politics to the extent that so far none of them has been able to surpass the tiny Communist Party in membership or trade union influence or in terms of working-class implantation. Against these criteria revolutionary socialism as interpreted by the far left has to be judged a failure. However, since the 1960s Marrxism has experienced a definite renaissance in Britain and Trotskyist groups have played a significant part in generating single cause campaigns outside the traditional mass organizations of Labour. The role of the far left — especially organizations like the SWP and IMG — as a catalyst in such radical movements is far more important than the undoubted growth of Trotskyist organizations which remain very small. Indeed, it is no exaggeration to say that the growth of radical politics in Britain is among the most significant developments of the domestic scene over the last twenty years.

Undoubtedly this is connected with the decay of Labourist ideology and the breakdown of the post-war party consensus. By the mid-sixties the social and political settlement for which 1945 is emblematic was in process of disintegration. British social democracy was one of the first victims of these developments as it became increasingly obvious during the first two Wilson governments that its traditional formulae were unequal to the problems afflicting the domestic economy. It was during this period, 1964-70, that the Labour Party lost tens of thousands of members while to the left of the Party radical movements and campaigns began to proliferate. At first the initiatives taken outside the Labour organizations could be classified as single-issue, pressure group campaigns. Vietnamese Solidarity and the early feminist campaigns were perceived in this way. But it has now become apparent that movements begun on the extremist fringe have grown to embrace more and larger interconnected issues that represent a major challenge to labourism and its traditional preoccupations. Opinion poll evidence indicates mass support for the objectives of the peace campaigns and the women's movement while Labour's ideological stock — nationalization, incomes policies and similar variations on the corporatist theme — command a dwindling support.

Thus looked at in this way — that is from the simultaneous decay of labourism and the growing popularity of radical alternatives — the situation is uniquely favourable to Marxist politics. But while there is clear evidence of ideological ferment of a type which presents opportunities for socialist advance it is equally obvious that this is still very far from being translated into organizational terms. In other words none of the organizations of the left have yet been able to draw together the many radical fragments that can separately mobilize mass support. This suggests, among other things, that quite apart from labourism, the socialist politics currently on offer are cast in irrelevant and archaic moulds.

This, at any rate, is the conclusion that can be inferred from what we have already discussed in our analysis of Trotskyist politics. Organizations like the SWP and IMG have championed causes which might otherwise have been completely neglected — certainly if the Labour Party had anything to do with it. The Troops Out movement and the Anti-Nazi League are cases in point. They have also played a part disproportionate to their numerical strength in CND, the Right to Work campaign, the women's movement, the Bennite left and within the trade unions. Yet it cannot be said that the Marxist groups have succeeded in persuading many activists to join them. Nor are they any more successful in holding on to the militants they do recruit. Both failures are connected with certain aspects of Trotskyist politics.

Of course it would be simplistic to argue that this was the only explanation for the failure to establish a major socialist organization to the left of Labour. The fact that the Labour Party never fought for socialist politics is a principal reason for the absence of even a minority vanguard layer within the British working class armed with a thorough-going socialist consciousness. But a contributory factor to this state of affairs has to do with the 'artificial' character of

apparent alternatives to labourism of which the early Communist
Party is the most pertinent example. Since the formation of the CP,
organized Marxism in Britain '. . . did not look as if it was a natural
growth springing from the experiences of the British working class.
Instead it appeared to be under Russian domination'.[1]

The significance of this verdict for an assessment of contemporary
Trotskyism lies on the ideological plane. Both the early CP and
contemporary Trotskyist groups exhibit an inordinate and
conservative attachment to Bolshevik doctrine. In the case of the
young Communist Party the character of this dependency was
illustrated by the 'blind loyalty' which inspired its support for the
Comintern's 'Theses, Statutes, Resolutions and Conditions' without
the majority of its delegates having even read them. Stuart McIntyre
has described in detail how this spirit led by 1922 to the assimilation
of 'both a particular interpretation of Marxist theory and a particular
doctrine of politics' such that the CP 'looked on further debate as a
waste of limited resources'.[2] Likewise, we have shown that
Trotskyism rarely departs from the stock of theoretical, strategic and
tactical conceptions enshrined in the first four congresses of
Comintern. Yet the question of how this legacy relates to
contemporary Britain has not greatly preoccupied this tradition,
even though Lenin himself viewed the attempt to export Bolshevism
with some disquiet.[3]

A review of the central theoretical assumptions and practices of the
early Comintern will illustrate the deficiencies of the British far left.
Its characterization of the imperialist epoch remains a basic
Trotskyist assumption. Lenin's talk of 'moribund' capitalism,
repeated by Trotsky in the late 1930s, continues to underpin the
immediate political perspectives of groups like the WRP and the
Militant Tendency just as it did for the RCP in the 1940s. Reformism
— depicted as a spent force in consequence of chronic capitalist decay
— merits no further analysis: its persistent grip on mass allegiances is
merely the result of the treacherous role of a labour bureaucracy
resting on the ultimately shaky foundations of a labour aristocracy.
In the SWP variant of this analysis, reformism is bankrupt during
economic recession, superfluous during a boom. In either case it can
be simply ignored since the dominant schema among Trotskyists
reduces politics to an epiphenomenum of economic forces.

We have seen that the Trotskyists have invariably connected the
advance of socialism in Britain to perspectives of economic collapse.
A slump of current proportions was always held to be the sufficient
cause of an explosion of proletarian class consciousness. One reason

for this conviction — aside, that is, from the fact that the early Comintern occasionally spoke in this way — is that the Trotskyist tradition has always assumed that parliamentary democracy is a mere sham. Thus, during a major economic crisis there is nothing to prevent the proletariat from overthrowing it. Today the SWP position is precisely that parliament is irrelevant and the job of socialists is to prepare a revolution to overthrow it. Of course, this is exactly what Trotsky and Lenin implied on dozens of occasions. What else is to be understood by Trotsky's remark that bourgeois democracy is merely the 'hypocritical form of the domination of the financial oligarchy' or Lenin's that it 'is no more than a machine for the suppression of the working class'?

All such formulations completely ignore the fact that it was class struggle waged by the proletariat which wrested democratic concessions from a reluctant ruling class. When this is realized it has to be acknowledged that the working class has a stake in such institutions and it is not the helpless victim of illusions promoted by the bourgeoisie. This becomes particularly apparent under present circumstances when democratic institutions are under attack. But Marxists accustomed to seeing these institutional arrangements as mere camouflage for the rule of capital are not the best qualified to lead the defence of working-class democratic rights.

The energies of the Trotskyists are instead typically consumed in the struggle to perfect the instrument which will deliver the working class from capitalism: the revolutionary party. Enough has been said on this subject already to indicate that the Trotskyist practice follows that of the early Comintern in so far as this effort is largely directed at maintaining the doctrinal purity of the organization. The appearance of quasi-Stalinist practices in Trotskyist groups is associated with this labour of Sisyphus. Proceeding on the assumption that the finished revolutionary theory is ready to hand in the classic texts, the job of the Marxist cadre is to interpret, assimilate and apply the canon properly. Problems arise when a plurality of interpretations attempt to coexist because they each believe in the singular nature of the vanguard party, its monopoly of Marxist science. This usually leads the rival interpretations to condemn each other as heretics. Such is particularly likely where the groups are habitually disposed to regard ideas as expressions of alien class interests. Thus a recent Internal Information Bulletin of the Socialist League (dated March 1983) informs us that 'we take as our starting point the positions put forward by Trotsky in relation to the fight in the American SWP in the mid-1930s. At that time Trotsky explained, "any serious factional struggle in the party is always in the final analysis a reflection of the class struggle".' From this 'starting point' the author concludes that the majority of the Socialist League 'has been swayed by petit bourgeois public opinion in relation to the positions it developed on the Iranian revolution and the actions of the PLO in the Lebanon'.

While the particular debate cited here is of no interest to us, the method of debate is a familiar one which we have noted also in the case of the SLL–WRP, the RCP and the Militant Tendency. It consists of heaping odium on political opponents instead of rebutting arguments. The fact that adepts in this field regularly invoke the authority of Lenin and Trotsky merely serves to remind us that epigones are wont to celebrate each and every facet of the master's political practices. One of the dubious results of this is that the far left does not permit mistakes and errors. Anyone or any group guilty of 'deviation' is denounced in the harshest language and driven out of the fold. If leaders make mistakes the practice in the SLL–WRP and Militant Tendency is to pretend it has not happened or invent an explanation which blames somebody or something else. In either case learning from mistakes does not happen, the educative potential of internal debates is frequently nullified and collaboration between Trotskyist groups is impossible.

Not only, then, does each group go its own way; the separate paths are continually being retraced because of the refusal to learn from past experience; and the enormous membership turnover ensures that only a fraction of the ranks can remember the debates of the previous year.

Previous chapters will have made clear that the full force of these criticisms does not apply to all of the groups equally. The IMG-Socialist League and the SWP do not indulge in the excesses associated with the Healy organization. But neither of these organizations has emancipated itself from the economism and vanguardist traditions here under attack. Apart from the fact that their politics are of little appeal to the activists in the new radical movements — and these are, after all, the most likely source of future socialists militants — the Trotskyists have yet to fashion an orientation appropriate to British conditions.

While it would be the purest idealism to expect such small forces to perfect a finished strategy for socialism, some indicators of what this might look like can be construed. As the International Socialists never tired of pointing out, for Marx the emancipation of the working class will be the act of the working class. This eminently democratic starting point — which has nothing to do with the bureaucratic paternalism of other socialist traditions such as Fabianism — is a prerequisite for Marxists precisely because they are alive to the paradoxes and contradictions of the elitist alternatives which Marx summarized in the question, 'Who will educate the educator?' These problems are solved if social change comes about in such a way that it involves an educative and self-changing dimension. Since the socialist goal is a self-governing society of the associated producers it must be prefigured in the socialist politics of the present. Socialist organizations which do not even allow the widest possible democratic rights for their own members do not seem to understand this in even a minimalist sense.

But in fact this commitment to democracy has to be taken much further. As Rosenberg pointed out, '[an] extreme form of democracy is . . . for Marx the preliminary condition for socialism inasmuch as socialism can only be realised in a world enjoying the highest possible measure of individual freedom'.[4] Such conditions cannot be said to prevail in modern Britain where the extremely limited forms of democracy which ·do exist are, once again, under attack. The working class and its radical allies have been, in Britain as elsewhere, the historic champions of democratic reforms and responsible for such erosion of oligarchy as has already taken place. It was only in the second half of the nineteenth century that the language of democracy was usurped by the defenders of the capitalist *status quo*. That they were so easily enabled to do this owes something to the profound pessimism and fatalism concerning the survival of democratic rights which infected the Comintern's analysis of the imperialist powers after 1914-18. Of course, there were good conjunctural reasons for this pessimism throughout the inter-war period but it should be clear from our history of post-war Trotskyism that this became a fatalist metaphysic. The conviction that laws of economic development in the imperialist epoch ensured the passing of bourgeois democracy into forms of blatant authoritarianism seems not to have encouraged a militant struggle for the extension of democratic rights short of the full socialist revolution. But the point is that a socialist revolution will not take place unless socialists engage in such a struggle. As Lenin said

. . . just as socialism cannot be victorious unless it introduces complete democracy so the proletariat will be unable to prepare for victory over the bourgeoisie unless it wages a many-sided, consistent and revolutionary struggle for democracy.[5]

Unfortunately, as we have seen, there is much in the pronouncements of Lenin's Comintern which served to obscure this fact and encourage a strategy for socialism based essentially on catastrophist perspectives. The argument that parliamentary democracy is a mere sham is not the least offender in this respect. It can be said to be logically related to the ludicrous and suicidal belief which gripped the Stalinist Comintern that fascism in blowing away the democratic illusion actually aided the socialist revolution. Once, however, it is recognized that far from being a ruling-class charade liberal democracy involves a permanent tension between the liberalist logic that denies the logic of democracy and a democratic potential which can challenge the dynamic of capital accumulation, it is incumbent on socialists to be the best defenders of existing democratic gains and champions of their extension. The reality is somewhat different not least because of the spectacle of 'actually existing socialism' and the fact that Stalinist authoritarianism is the best propaganda in the arsenal of anti-socialists. The Trotskyists start out with the best chances for defeating the logic which equates Marxism with authoritarianism because their movement has always championed workers' rights in the Stalinist dictatorships. But this opportunity is ruined if their own practices are anything short of fully democratic.

This is not simply a matter of developing internally democratic organizations such as the IMG, important though this is. It also consists in acting on the recognition, as Rosa Luxemburg put it, that the specificity of the struggle for socialism lies in its dependency on the enlightenment of the masses, their self-emancipatory struggles, and in permitting the forces for socialism to learn from their own mistakes. If such is to be the case it is hard to defend practices such as conspiratorial entrism, which necessarily involve duplicity, or the manipulation of autonomous movements. Still less is it compatible with the belief that a single revolutionary party contains within itself all the vision and strategic wisdom to orchestrate the whole working class. This is neither possible nor desirable. The socialist revolution must be based on a plurality of organizations and movements.

The case for a socialism which takes democracy seriously does not rest simply on epistemological grounds. In Britain since the mid-sixties we have the sociological fact that increasing numbers of radical movements and campaigns have taken up the demand for an extension of democratic rights. It seems likely that the call for various types of participatory democracy is connected with the growing realization that labourism is founded on the illusions of state capitalism. For it is surely no coincidence that as the paternalist and bureaucratic practices of successive Labour governments revealed a growing authoritarian dimension, a growing chorus could be heard to the left of the party demanding more participation, decentralization and more community control. Among the first manifestations of this radical democracy were the Institute for Workers' Control — which began a debate on forms of decentralization in 1968 — and a number of campaigns which implied a democratic critique of the welfare state such as the claimants' unions, the squatters' movements and the groups involved in community politics, during the late sixties and early seventies. The same themes were also evident in the shop stewards' movement, in tenants' associations and the revival of workers' co-operatives, as well as the campaigns for Scots and Welsh devolution. The feminist, environmentalist, and peace movements have all extended the range and depth of this incipient critique of corporate capitalism.

Of course such developments eventually caught up with the Labour Party. As early as 1968 the local election results helped to weaken the big city paternalist political machines in London, Liverpool and Birmingham. So corrupt and decayed had the inner-city Labour organizations become that a younger, more radical left was able to step in to the vacuum and, in some cases, take over despite the small scale of the new forces. Indeed this fact only serves to emphasize that the Labour Party played virtually no part in the genesis of the new movements. The fact needs especially to be borne in mind now that the focus of attention is on the Bennite left inside the party. The failure of any socialist group outside the Labour Party to champion these forces must be regarded as a factor in determining the trajectory of these radicals after 1979 when they rallied behind the campaign for constitutional changes. But unless, in opposition to all the historical evidence, it is believed that these radicals will obtain political satisfaction by transforming the Labour Party, independent socialists must expect that they will once again seek a genuine socialist alternative. Certainly the proliferation of issues commanding mass attention and support for which labourism has no answers must be expected to continue, for it would seem that deep structural causes are at work which the present slump has recently accelerated.[6]

If the new radical forces have helped to revitalize 'one of the oldest, yet most revolutionary ideas in the labour movement: that democracy demands socialism and socialism demands democracy',[7] it is necessary for Marxists to prove that Marxism represents the best recognition of this fact. For the Trotskyist groups this means above all a rejection of those aspects of their theoretical legacy and tradition which obstruct that recognition.

Appendix 1

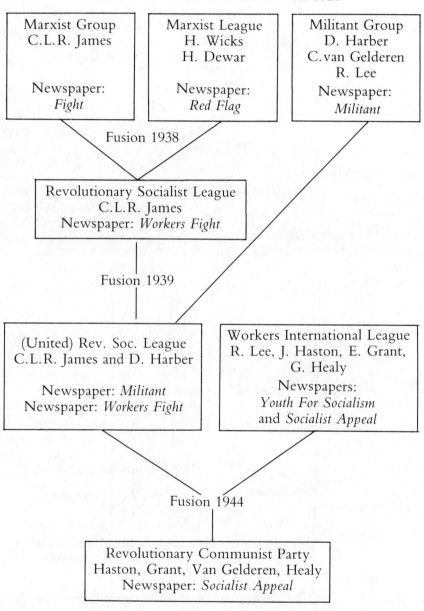

Marxist Group
C.L.R. James

Newspaper:
Fight

Marxist League
H. Wicks
H. Dewar

Newspaper:
Red Flag

Militant Group
D. Harber
C. van Gelderen
R. Lee
Newspaper:
Militant

Fusion 1938

Revolutionary Socialist League
C.L.R. James
Newspaper: *Workers Fight*

Fusion 1939

(United) Rev. Soc. League
C.L.R. James and D. Harber

Newspaper: *Militant*
Newspaper: *Workers Fight*

Workers International League
R. Lee, J. Haston, E. Grant,
G. Healy
Newspapers:
Youth For Socialism
and *Socialist Appeal*

Fusion 1944

Revolutionary Communist Party
Haston, Grant, Van Gelderen, Healy
Newspaper: *Socialist Appeal*

Appendix 2

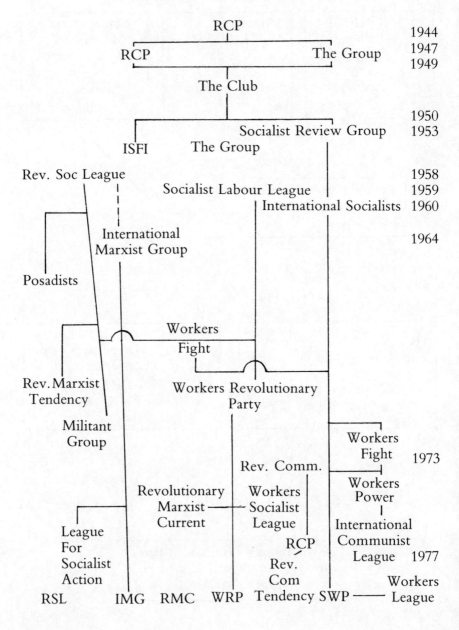

RCP	1944
RCP — The Group	1947 / 1949
The Club	
	1950
Socialist Review Group	1953
ISFI — The Group	
Rev. Soc League	1958
Socialist Labour League	1959
International Socialists	1960
International Marxist Group	1964
Posadists	
Workers Fight	
Rev. Marxist Tendency	
Workers Revolutionary Party	
Militant Group	
Workers Fight	1973
Rev. Comm.	
Workers Power	
Revolutionary Marxist Current — Workers Socialist League	
League For Socialist Action	International Communist League	1977
RCP	
Rev. Com Tendency	
RSL IMG RMC WRP Tendency SWP — Workers League	

Appendix 3

MAJOR INTERNATIONAL DIVISIONS IN TROTSKYISM

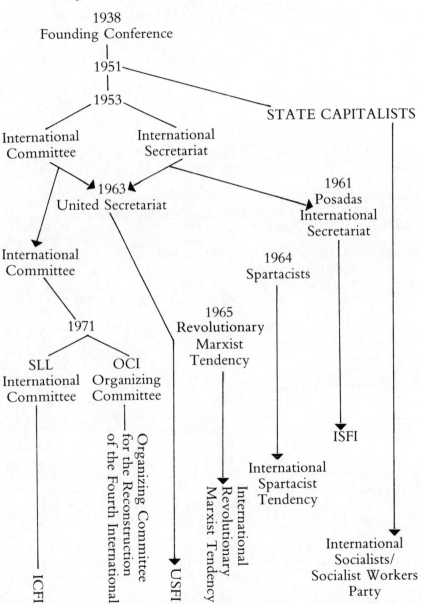

Notes and References

INTRODUCTION

Most references to documentary material have been deleted for the sake of brevity. Readers interested in full citations should consult my PhD thesis, University of Manchester, 1982.

1. Jean Van Heijenoort (1973) 'How the Fourth International was conceived', in *Towards a History of the Fourth International'* Education for Socialists, New York: Pathfinder, November.
2. L. Trotsky (1977) *The Writings of Leon Trotsky 1935-6*, New York: Pathfinder, New York, p.4.
3. A recent example of this is afforded by Kostas Mavrakis (1976) *On Trotskyism*, London: Routledge & Kegan Paul.
4. R. Groves (1974) *The Balham Group: How British Trotskyism Began*, London: Pluto Press.
5. See Appendix I for a geneaology of the pre-war groups.
6. I. Deutscher (1970) *The Prophet Outcast*, Oxford University Press, p.514.
7. A recent example of the same usage is contained in A. Brewer (1980) *Marxist Theories of Imperialism*, London: Routledge & Kegan Paul.
8. See Blake Baker (1981) *The Far Left: An Exposé of the Extreme Left in Britain*, London: Weidenfeld & Nicholson; John Tomlinson (1981) *Left, Right: The March of Political Extremism in Britain*, London: Calder; and P. McCormick (1979) *Enemies of Democracy*, London: Temple-Smith.
9. Blake Baker (1981) makes this analogy on p.viii.
10. D. Webster (1981) *The Labour Party and the New Left*, Fabian Tract 477, October.
11. This period was approximately from 1914, the time of social democracy's 'great betrayal', to 1924 and the death of Lenin.
12. L. Trotsky (1973) *The Transitional Programme For Socialist Revolution*, New York: Pathfinder.
13. Shirley Williams reiterated this accusation (1977), see her article

'Trotskyism and Democracy' in *The Guardian*, 22 January. See G. Hodgson (1977) *Socialism and Parliamentary Democracy*, Nottingham: Spokesman, for a discussion of this issue.

14. See, for example, Martin Linton (1981) in *The Guardian*, December 14, p.2 reporting on the Militant Tendency.

15. S. Rowbotham et al. (1979) *Beyond The Fragments*, London: Merlin Press.

16. N. Geras (1973) 'Proletarian self-emancipation', in *Radical Philosophy*, No. 6, Winter.

17. Perry Anderson (1976) *Considerations On Western Marxism*, London: New Left Books, pp.100-1.

18. Anderson, 1976.

19. See Peter Jenkins (n.d.) *Where Trotskyism Got Lost: The Restoration of European Democracy after the Second World War*, Spokesman Pamphlet no. 49.

CHAPTER 1

1. Jane Degras (ed.) (1965) *Documents of the Communist International*, vol. 1, Oxford University Press, p.1.

2. Quoted in Joseph Hansen's introduction to L. Trotsky (1973) *The Transitional Programme for Socialist Revolution*, New York: Pathfinder, p.19.

3. Denise Avenas (1976) 'Trotsky's Marxism' in *International*, vol. 3, no. 2, Winter, p.29.

4. See V. Lenin(1960-70), 'Report on the international situation', *Collected Works*, vol. 31, pp.215-34.

5. G. Lukacs (1971) *History and Class Consciousness*, London: Merlin Press, p.306.

7. For example in the essay 'Marxism in our time' Trotsky (1970) argues '. . . but now . . . human progress is stuck in a blind alley. Nothwithstanding the latest triumphs of technical thought the material productive forces are no longer growing', New York: Pathfinder, p.25. *The Transitional Programme* (1973) also argues that 'mankind's productive forces stagnate . . . the bourgeoisie itself sees no way out' (p.72).

8. E. Mandel (1979) *Trotsky: A Study in the Dynamic of his Thought*, London: New Left Books. Mandel points out that 'in his [Trotsky's] more thorough going historical analyses, especially his report to the Third Congress of Comintern in 1921, and his critique of the Comintern Programme of 1928, Trotsky states his position in a more rounded and correct way', pp.37-8 and p.39.

9. See chapter 2.

10. For example G. Hodgson (1975) *Trotsky And Fatalistic Marxism*, Nottingham: Spokesman. Hodgson's basic contention is that Trotsky's major error was to '. . . insist that the soul of revolutionary Marxism must depend upon the prognosis of the ultimate stagnation of the system, as an automatic consequence of its own inbuilt laws of development' (p.35).

Since the 'conception of the epoch' is held to be the root of this error, it is surprising that Hodgson should single out Trotsky for special criticism as this conception was also held by the entire leadership of the Third International. Furthermore, the view that capitalism would collapse as a result of its own inherent tendencies was first put forward by Marx.

11. For example Trotsky erred in his account of the significance of the New Deal: 'The New Deal policy with its fictitious achievements and its very real increase in the national debt, leads unavoidably to ferocious capitalist reaction and a devastating explosion of imperialism. In other words it is directed into the same channels as the policy of fascism.' L. Trotsky, 'Marxism in our time', p.25. With the *caveat* that socialist revolution could save the day, Trotsky was also pessimistic, if not fatalistic, about the survival of the USSR in the war and the future of fascism as the 'normal' government type of the capitalist social formations.

12. L. Trotsky (1975) 'Germany: what next?' in *The Struggle Against Facism in Germany*, Harmondsworth: Penguin Book.

13. L. Trotsky (1974) *Writings 1938-9*, New York: Pathfinder, p.340.

14. L. Trotsky (1971) *Writings 1933-4*, New York: Pathfinder, p.22.

15. L. Trotsky (1977) *Writings 1935-6*, New York: Pathfinder, p.51.

16. Trotsky said that '. . . after the miserable collapse of the Third International it is much harder to move them to bestow their confidence upon a new revolutionary organisation. That's just where the crisis of proletarian leadership lies' (*Writings 1935-6* p.31; and also p.46 for an identical sentiment). See p.32 where he envisages '. . . an extremely prolonged process' before overcoming these difficulties.

17. L. Trotsky *The Transitional Programme* p.72.

18. According to Trotsky: 'If not liquidated in time by socialist revolution, fascism will inevitably conquer in France, England and the USA with or without the aid of Hitler and Mussolini'. L. Trotsky *Writings 1938-9* p.234.

19. In his polemics against the Comintern's ultra leftism during the so-called Third Period, Trotsky constantly reiterated the need for united front action against fascism. But after 1933, and as war approached, Trotsky was concerned to expose the opportunism in the Popular Front movement announced as the new tactic by Dimitrov at the seventh congress of Comintern in 1934. (Trotsky had predicted 'a period of opportunist experiments like the Anglo-Russian Committee and the workers and peasants Kuomintang' as early as 1930. See L. Trotsky's *Writings 1930* pp.61-62). The emphasis of his argument became concerned with the necessity of socialist revolution as the *only* antidote to the fascist and war menace.

20. L. Trotsky *Writings 1938-9*, p.234.

21. L. Trotsky (1973) in *Documents of the Fourth International 1933-40*, New York: Pathfinder.

22. L. Trotsky *The Transitional Programme*, p.72 and p.94.

23. L. Trotsky *Writings 1933-34*, p.235.

24. L. Trotsky (1969) *The Revolution Betrayed*, London: New Park, p.94.

25. In *The Transitional Programme* he said 'the workers and peasants themselves by their own free vote will indicate what parties they recognise as soviet parties' p.105.

26. Trotsky acknowledged that Stalin '. . . profoundly believed that the task of creating socialism was national and administrative in nature' (*The Revolution Betrayed*, p.97).

27. L. Trotsky (1973) *In Defence of Marxism*, New York: Pathfinder, p.4.

28. L. Trotsky *Writings 1938-39*, p.32.

29. L. Trotsky *Writings 1933-34*, p.329.

30. L. Trotsky *Writings 1938-39*, p.342.

31. Trotsky said, in the very act of launching the Fourth International: 'The Fourth International has already arisen out of great events: the greatest defeats of the proletariat in history', *Documents of the Fourth International 1933-40*, p.219.

32. Isaac Deutscher *The Prophet Outcast*, pp.425-6.

33. The 'Statutes of the Fourth International' provided for the following structure:

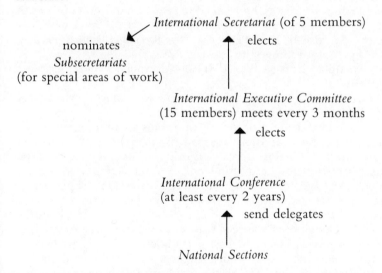

The International Conference was made the policy-making body with the International Executive Committee (IEC) forming the elected leadership. A smaller International Secretariat was responsible for day-to-day political work, administration and liaison with the national sections. It was also charged with responsibility for publishing a monthly bulletin. See *Documents of the Fourth International 1933-40*, pp. 177-9.

34. He referred to its Seventh Congress as the 'liquidation congress' (*Writings 1935-36* p.84) and there is some evidence that Stalin only delayed his decision to disband Comintern for fear that the Trotskyists would capitalize on it (F. Claudin, 1975, *The Communist Movement,*

Harmondsworth, Penguin Books, p.124). In 1938 Trotsky wrote: 'It is not only possible but probable, almost sure, that the Comintern will end its career as a vigorous movement before the definite fall of the Kremlin clique in the Soviet Union.' L. Trotsky *Writings 1937-38,* p.305.

35. P. Frank (1972) *Intercontinental Press,* vol. 10, p.370.

36. Thus Ralph Miliband argues that 'democratic centralism . . . has always served as a convenient device for authoritarian party structures'. R. Miliband (1977) 'The future of socialism in England', in *Socialist Register 1977,* London: Merlin Press, p.50. Another notable member of the 'Old new left', Edward Thompson, who regards Trotskyism as a variant of Stalinism, sees in both '. . . the same religious cast of thought, in which Marxism is proposed as an ultimate system of truth: that is, a theology'. This theology is, for Thompson, Leninism converted into 'universalist axioms'. See E. P. Thompson (1978) *The Poverty of Theory,* London: Merlin Press, p.375.

37. According to Ernest Mandel '. . . Trotsky fully adopted Lenin's theory of organisation and until his death stubbornly defended them against all sceptics and arch-pessimists (who claimed to see in them the "embryo" of Stalinism)'. E. Mandel (n.d.) *The Leninist Theory of Organisation,* IMG Pamphlet, p.7. See also B. Knei-Paz (1978) *The Social and Political Thought of Leon Trotsky'* Oxford University Press, p.228.

38. See for example, Scott Meikle (1981)*Has Marxism a Future?,* Critique no. 13, Glasgow.

39. Guy Lewis and Paul Thompson (1977) *The Revolution Unfinished: A Critique of Trotskyism,* Big Flame Pamphlet p.30.

40. At the minimum, democratic centralism entails a commitment to full and open discussion *before* decisions are made by the party's members and complete unanimity in action once a majority opinion is reached. The Trotskyists insist that the right to form tendencies and factions is implicit in this formula for the decision-making process to be truly democratic: access to the party's press is also seen as a prerequisite for inner-party democracy by groups in this tradition. However, if one consults points 12 to 19 of the Comintern's '21 Conditions', it is seen that the above formula also involves giving draconian powers to the highest party bodies. The precise balance between the democratic and centralist features is, therefore, ultimately determined by the leadership. The absence of 'horizontal' communications and collaboration between party cells can also facilitate the dominance of the centre. See F. Claudin *The Communist Movement* and A. Rosenberg (1934) *A History of Bolshevism,* London: pp.146-9.

41. E. Mandel *The Leninist Theory of Organisation* and G. Lukacs (1970) *Lenin,* London: New Left Books, are authoritative accounts of this question by advocates of Leninism. V. I. Lenin (1977) *Collected Works,* vol. 13, pp.106-8, Preface to the Collection *Twelve Years,* (fifth printing) Moscow.

42. Leninists are agreed on the centrality of this assumption. Thus Lukacs says that '. . . the Leninist form of organisation is indissolubly linked with the ability to foresee the approaching revolution', G. Lukacs *Lenin* p.26.

Liebman narrows this argument to the quintessential proposition that 'it is impossible to understand anything about Leninism if one ignores the fact that it accords *primordial* importance to the idea of armed, organised, insurrection as an indispensable, decisive form of political struggle — its highest form'. M. Liebman, p.103.

43. V. I. Lenin (1970) *Imperialism, The Highest Stage of Capitalism'* Peking.

44. See A. Brewer (1980) *Marxist Theories of Imperialism,* London: Routledge & Kegan Paul.

45. V. I. Lenin *Collected Works,* vol. 23, p.43. *passim.*

46. See F. Claudin *The Communist Movement.*

47. L. Trotsky (1973) *Documents of the Fourth International 1933-40,* New York: Pathfinder, p.349.

48. No doubt passages in Marx can be seen as supportive of this catastrophism, but these were obviously not intended as part of a systematic characterisation of the modern epoch, while the catastrophism of Comintern was.

49. While it is true that the Third Congress of Comintern spoke of 'the epoch of imperialism . . . [as a] . . . protracted epoch of social revolution' the tenor of its pronouncements display none of this verbal caution. Capitalism is still referred to as being 'moribund', and immediate perspectives include civil wars and world war. See B. Hessel (ed.) (1980) *Theses, Resolutions and Manifestos of the First Four Congresses of the Third International,* London: Ink Links, pp.274-99.

50. As Claudin observes, Comintern made clear that '. . . any other tendency in the working–class movement, however radical, could accompany the Communists along only part of the road leading to "the complete dictatorship of the proletariat" and must in the end give place to exclusive leadership by the Communist Party'. F. Claudin *The Communist Movement,* p.147. See also B. Hessel *Theses, Resolutions and Manifestos of the Communist International,* p.93 and p.134.

51. B. Hessel, ibid, p.27.

42. Ibid, 'On tactics', Third Congress p.275.

53. Ibid, p.98, 'The Communist Party and parliament', Second Congress.

54. Ibid p.389, 'Theses on Comintern tactics', Fourth Congress.

55. See, for example, Lenin, 'Thesis and report on bourgeois democracy', *Collected Works,* vol. 28, pp.460-7.

56. This is especially apparent in *The Transitional Programme* and 'Marxism in our time' and characteristic of other writings *immediately* concerned with setting up the Fourth International or produced by Trotsky shortly before his death. In other words, this catastrophism was a salient feature of his theoretical and literary bequest to his followers.

57. See E. Mandel (1965) *A Socialist Strategy For Western Europe,* Nottingham: Spokesman. Influenced by the Belgian general strike of the early 1960s Mandel evolved to a new position which stressed a programme of 'structural reforms' as the best route to socialism in the advanced capitalist countries. Dramatic economic collapses were specifically ruled out

as a serious trigger of socialist advance.

58. M. Liebman, *Leninism under Lenin,* pp.60-1.
59. See L. Trotsky (1973) *In Defence of Marxism,* New York: Pathfinder.
60. Thus T. Cliff (1976) *Lenin: Building the Party,* vol. 1, London: Pluto Press, expresses his readiness to change the organizational structure of the party 'at every new development of the class struggle'. The Schumpeter version of democracy as a mere political method is what emerges here rather than any awareness of its educative dimension (see pp.67-8).
61. N. Geras (1981) 'Marxism and Pluralism', *New Left Review,* no. 125, January-February.
62. G. Healy (1949) *Internal Bulletin,* no.9, p.9, Revolutionary Communist Party.

CHAPTER 2

1. R. Stephenson (1976) 'The Fourth International and our attitude towards it', *Fourth International Series* no. 1, Chartist Publications, p.5. 'Documents of The Fourth International' p.270. Stephenson, maintains that this was due to a 'tactical manoeuvre' accomplished by J.P. Cannon, leader of the American Socialist Workers Party.
2. Howell (1976) *British Social Democracy* (London: Croom Helm) p.128.
3. During 1942 *Socialist Appeal* devoted considerable space in its pages to disputes involving miners, the Belfast strike, and ICL's women workers. *Socialist Appeal* replaced *Youth For Socialism* in 1941.
4. This was retrospectively described by a former members as being 'almost laughable in [its] arrogant wrong headedness'. (J. Higgins [1963] in *International Socialism Journal,* no.14, Autumn, p.28.)
5. P. Addison (1977) *The Road to 1945,* London: Quartet, p.15.
6. 'Fusion has assured the Trotskyists in Britain of a single unified and compact organisation. The RCP has 400-500 members and a sale of *Socialist Appeal* claimed to be as high as 20,000, also a theoretical monthly, *Workers International News*. In an inflammatory situation the RCP with its leftist and socialist demagogic phrases is capable of great actual and potential danger to the working class, viz. the Barrow dispute and the Albion strike. There is no doubt that this consolidation has considerably strengthened them and that great vigilance is necessary in order to isolate and expose these pernicious elements.' Betty Reid (1944) *Trotskyist Organisations in Britain,* CPGB Internal Document.
7. P. Addison *The Road To 1945* (n.d.) pp.103-4.
8. M. Foot (1975) *Aneurin Bevan,* vol. 1, London: Paladin, pp.506-7.
9. R. Miliband ,The future of socialism in England', Cambridge U.P., p.42.
10. D. Coates (1975) *The Labour Party And The Struggle For Socialism,* Cambridge: Cambridge University Press, p.42.
11. P. Addison *The Road to 1945,* p.142.

12. P. Addison, ibid, p.143 and p.163.
13. The terms are those of K. Middlemas (1979) *Politics in Industrial Society*, London: Andre Deutsch, p.284.
14. Jock Haston, Roy Tearse, Heaton Lee and Ann Keene were arrested under the Trades Dispute Act in connection with the Tyne apprentices strike of April 1944. See *Socialist Appeal* (1944) vol.5, no.21, April.
15. *Perspectives in Britain*, 6 June 1945, pp.1-6.
16. M. Foot *Aneurin Bevan*, vol.2, p.13.
17. *The New Imperialist Peace and the Building of the Parties of the Fourth International*.
18. G. Healy (1947) *Against The Politics Of Stagnation*, July.
19. E. Germain (Mandel) (1947) *From the ABC to Current Reading: Boom, Revival, or Crisis?*, September.
20. See *Internal Bulletin*, no. 9, June 1945.
21. G. Healy (1945) *British Labour and the Tasks of the Fourth International*, December, p.1.
22. G. Healy (1946) *The Marxist Method versus Eclecticism and Empiricism*, January, p.9.
23. *The Crisis in the RCP*, August, 1047.
24. *Statement from the National Conference of the Minority Supporters*, June 14/15, 1947.
25. E. Upward (1969) *The Rotten Elements*, London: Heinemann, gives an account of these years from the vantage point of a participant who, though troubled by CP policy, has no sympathy for Trotskyism.
26. *Labour Party Faction Report*, August/September, 1946.
27. *The Party Organiser*, vol. 1, no. 2, p.6.
28. *Organisational Report*, December, 1947.
29. 'IS. To The Political Bureau of the RCP' 8 February 1949. The RCP leaders did correspond with Felix Morrow and Albert Goldman (both of whom were expelled from the FI for alleged heresies) and exchanged views on policy and personalities. Morrow attempted, at the October 1943 Plenum of the FI, to amend a resolution which insisted that the bourgeois-democratic governments were impossible in Europe after the war — and failed. Goldman complained of 'the haughty and bureaucratic attitude of the top (American) SWP leadership. Of course none of this could justify Pablo's allegations. In his 'Reply To Comrade Haston', written in the month following the ISFI's authoritarian decision to split from the RCP, he refers to 'the spirit of mistrust, contempt, and hostility, which characterised the relations of the WIL towards the International since the former's foundation until the unifications in 1944 and which is not dead in its ranks. Just the opposite'. The RCP Majority is accused of becoming 'a centre for regrouping all the malcontents opposed to the main tendency which we represent in our International'. No evidence is cited by Pablo to support these accusations and none can be found in either the Tarbuck or Haston documents which we have used.
30. *Main Resolutions at RCP Conference 1945* p.10.

31. *The World Situation and the Tasks of the Fourth International* November 1974.
32. *The New Imperialist Peace and the Building of the Parties of the Fourth International* adopted April 1946, p.8.
33. *On the Coming European Revolution,* April, 1945.
34. *The New Imperialist Peace,* ibid, p.25.
35. See on this M.R. Upham (1980) unpublished PHD Thesis, University of Hull.
36. *The Emergence of Russia From World War II,* p.6.
37. *RCP Conference Documents,* August, 1946, pp.7-13.
38. Ibid, p.14.
39. A.W. Atkinson (1947) *On The Russian Question,* July, p.6.
40. Thus he forced the ISFI to allege that they were 'cryptic state capitalists'. The furthest Haston would go was in arguing that 'it seems theoretically correct to assume that there is no reason why a new capitalist class in Russia cannot arise and dominate the economic life of the country without destroying the state property as such' (*The Dual Character of the USSR* p.32). For Trotsky, of course, this was theoretically *incorrect* and constituted 'the film of reformism run backwards'.
41. E. Grant (1949) *Against the Theory of State Capitalism,* August, p.8. Grant's views on this subject have been republished in an amended form, in T. Grant (1980) *The Marxist Theory of the State,* Militant Pamphlet, August.
42. Ibid, p.16. Of course, in either case, the Soviet economy operates according to capitalist principles of the competitive quest for profit via the production of exchange values. But Grant's confusion merely reflects the ISFI's *Draft Theses* of 1947 which claimed that the law of value applies to '. . . all pre- and post-capitalist societies which, like the Soviet Union, produce commodities' (see *Fourth International* November/December, 1947, p.29). What this forgets, of course, is that in the age of capitalism, regulation of the law of value ceases to be determined by the movement of commodities. For it is now the movement of capital which determines the regulation of the law of value and since the free movement of capital does not exist in the USSR, neither does the law of value.
43. *Main Resolution RCP Conference 1945,* p.4.
44. *Draft Theses of the ISFI,* p.15.
45. Ibid, p.16.
46. L. Trotsky 'Stalin after the Finnish experience' in *Writings 1939-40* pp.160-4. Trotsky called this a 'shameful war' started by a 'senseless invasion' but concluded that once begun it should proceed '. . . to the sovietisation of Finland', p.164.
47. Quoted by W. Hunter (1949) *The IS and Eastern Europe,* May. See also *Fourth International,* 1948.
48. *The Evolution of the Buffer Zones,* resolution of the 7th Plenum of the IEC, April, 1949, p.5.
49. 'Amendments of the RCP to draft theses', *The Fourth International and Stalinism.* This also observes the absurdity of making the abolition of

frontiers into a litmus test of structural transformation.

50. M. Pablo (1949) 'The evolution of Yugoslav centrism', in *Fourth International,* November, p.292.

51. G. Clarke (1950) 'Leon Trotsky — a new vidication' in *Fourth International,* July/August.

52. G. Bloch (1950) 'The test of Yugoslavia' in *Fourth International* July/August.

53. Ted Grant's (1949) *Reply To James,* February.

54. L. Trotsky (1973) *In Defence of Marxism,* New York: Pathfinder, p.19.

55. *Statement on the Perspectives of the RCP,* December 1948.

CHAPTER 3

1. M. Pablo (1974) 'Where are we going?' reprinted in *Education for Socialists,* Part 4, vol.2, New York: Pathfinder, March, p.5.

2. Ibid, p.6. In saying this, Pablo demonstrates that the FI did not yet realize (in 1951) that imperialism could operate *without* colonies, as Marxists now maintain.

3. *Trotskyism versus Revisionism: A Documentary History* (1974) vol.1, London: New Park, p.50.

4. Ibid, p.78.

5. The significance, and irony, of this lies in the fact that the SWP later split from the FI because of the latter's Pabloism which it characterized in much the same way as the PCI had done.

6. *Trotskyism versus Revisionism* pp.93-3 and p.94.

7. M. Pablo (1958) 'On the duration and nature of the transition from capitalism to socialism' in *Fourth International,* Winter, no. 1.

8. E. Mandel (1951) 'What should be modified and what should be maintained in the theses of the Second World Congress of the Fourth International on the questions of Stalinism?' January, reprinted in *Fourth International,* Winter 1958.

9. Ibid, p.23.

10. Mandel says that it is 'extremely improbable in Western Europe' for the CPs to display revolutionary potential.

11. 'Theses on orientation and perspectives', resolution adopted by the Third World Congress in *Fourth International* (1958) Winter, no.1, p.27.

12. Reprinted in *Fourth International* (1958) Winter, no.1.

13. *Trotskyism versus Revisionism,* p.118.

14. Ibid p.131.

15. See F. Richards (1975) 'The question of the International' in *Revolutionary Communist,* no.2, May, pp.20-41, and Martin Cook (1975) 'The myth of "Orthodox" Trotskyism', *Fourth International,* series no.2, May, Chartist Publication. These authors are members of the new Revolutionary Communist Party and the Chartist group respectively.

16. See the correspondence between J.P. Cannon and G. Healy in chapter 4

of *Trotskyism versus Revisionism,* vol.1.

17. M. Pablo (1958) 'The rise and decline of Stalinism' reprinted in *Fourth International,* Winter, no.1. The first draft of this article was, in fact, written by E. Mandel, though this was little known at the time. See *Trotskyism versus Revisionism,* vol.2, p.4.

18. I. Deutscher (1953) *Russia After Stalin,* London: Hamish Hamilton.

19. M. Pablo *The rise and decline of Stalinism,* p.34.

20. Ibid, p.37.

21. Pablo's analyses of 1951-53 are very similar, in the essential explanations of the Cold War that they offer, to the arguments of Gabriel Kolko (1972) *The Limits Of Power,* Harper & Row: New York, and also (1970) *The Politics Of War,* New York: Vintage. See also D. Horowitz (1969) *Imperialism And Revolution,* Harmandsworth: Penguin Books, and D. Horowitz (ed.) (1967) *Containment And Revolution,* London: Blond. This 'alternative' theory of the origins of the Cold War locates it in (a) the USA's undisputed post-war hegemony over the capitalist world combined with (b) the rise in insurgency in the Third World which the Americans attributed to Soviet expansionist ambitions.

22. Any similarities between Pablo and Deutscher end here. Deutscher's exaggeration of the scope of the Malenkov reforms was titanic, arguing that they were 'precisely the limited revolution envisaged by Trotsky'. I. Deutscher *Russia After Stalin* p.164. Their analyses, though, converged at several points. Deutscher also argued that 'the crumbling of Stalinist orthodoxy is sure to be followed by an intense ferment of ideas which may eventually transform the outlook of the Communist parties everywhere' (p.154). Both emphasized that objective processes initiated by Stalin would eliminate Stalinism, thus Deutscher said that 'Stalinism has persistently and ruthlessly destroyed the soil in which it had grown, that primitive, semi-Asiatic society on whose sap it fed, (p.54). Industrializations and 'modernization', therefore, would create the preconditions and the agency for socialist advance in the USSR.

23. *Trotskyism versus Revisionism,* vol.1, p.324.

24. Ibid, p.329.

25. Attributed to him by the ISFI in Ibid, p.330.

26. The 'Pabloite', Fred Emmett, was removed from the editorial board of *Labour Weekly.*

27. *Trotskyism versus Revisionism,* vol.2, p.92. For Farrell Dobbs, also '. . . the problem is not one of unification . . . our task is to consolidate the forces that have broken with Pablo and carry the split deeper into the Pabloite ranks', Ibid, p.167.28. Ibid, vol.1, p.221.

29. Ibid, p.227.

30. 'What form will it (liquidation of the Soviet bureaucracy) then take? Will it be that of an acute crisis and of violent inter-bureaucratic struggles between the elements who will fight for the *status quo,* if not for turning back, and the more numerous elements drawn by the powerful pressure of the masses?' M. Pablo quoted in Ibid, vol.1, p.221.

31. Ibid, p.268.
32. Ibid, p.267.
33. See, for example, Ibid, p.253.
34. Ibid, p.251.
35. As an example of Pablo's 'Stalinist' organizational methods the open letter cites the former's suspension of the French majority which is described in terms equally applicable to the ISFI's intervention in the RCP which Pablo's erstwhile critics condoned. Thus, 'by fiat of the International Secretariat the elected majority of the French section was forbidden to exercise its rights to lead the political and propaganda work of the party', Ibid, p.311.
36. Ibid, p.302.
37. Ibid, p.312.
38. See R. Stephenson (1976) 'The Fourth International: and our attitude towards it', *Fourth International,* Series no.1, Chartist publication, December, pp.12-13.
39. See Ibid; and F. Richards and Martin Cook.

CHAPTER 4

1. This is revealed by headlines in *Socialist Outlook* of which the following are instances: 'Bevan gives the lead that workers want', 3 October 1952; 'Bevan and Morrison: it is a difference of principle', says Gerry Healy, 14 May 1954; 'The Tories must resign: let's have a petition to get 'em out!', 27 November 1953.
2. Some members of the RCP Majority formed the 'open party faction' but this merely gave birth to a number of ephemeral splinter groups such as Eric Heffer's Socialist Workers Federation.
3. Jock Haston was among the first to resign (June 1950). It is of significance that when one 'JD' (Jimmy Deane) asked that Haston be given the chance to produce a written statement in his defence, before the vote of expulsion was taken, he not only failed but was told that '. . . it is necessary that you indicate in writing political support for the EC resolution condemning Haston without any reservations *immediately* (JDH 15B/110 May 1950). JD's 'cryptic sympathy' for Haston led to his own expulsion soon afterwards.
4. John Walters (1969-70) 'Some Notes on British Trotskyist history' in *Marxist Studies,* vol.2, no.1, Winter, p.46. According to Walters, who participated in these discussions, Cliff explained The Club's silence on Stalinism as the result of the workers' state thesis.
5. In the event it was Cliff and his supporters who benefited from the ideological confusion of The Club and from 1950 formed their own Socialist Review Group around the newspaper *Socialist Review.*
6. G. Healy (n.d.) *The Way To Socialism in Britain'* (pamphlet) pp.40-1.
7. Michael Foot says of the 1951 elections that they showed that 'given a

quarter of a chance the Party was going Bevanite'. M. Foot, *Aneurin Bevan 1945-1960,* p.349. See also M. Jenkins (1979) *Bevanism: Labour's High Tide,* Nottingham: Spokesman, and D. Howell (n.d.) 'The Rise and Fall of Bevanism', Labour Party Discussion Series no.5.

8. Bevan declared his conviction that socialists 'must never carry doctrinaire differences to the point of schism' and refused contact with the Labour left while a minister. Like his worshipper, Michael Foot, Bevan zealously guarded the parliamentary conventions even when they imprisoned him. See M. Foot, Ibid, p.348.

9. According to Lewis Minkin 'to a far greater extent than was the case for the trade unions, the CLPs were subject to organised attempts to instigate and mobilise resolutions and amendments for the Annual Conference'. But the success of the national factions of the left in doing this was 'very limited'. In the case of the Bevanite 'second eleven' '. . . they never sought any mass circulation for their resolution suggestions'. L. Minkin (1978) *The Labour Party Conference,* London: Allen Lane, pp.41-3.

10. Bevan, to be fair, held that the Annual Conference was subordinate to the PLP in that the latter must '. . . interpret [its] policies in the light of the Parliamentary situation'. Quoted in R.T. McKenzie (1963) *British Political Parties,* London: Heinermann, p.516.

11. D. Coates (1975) *The Labour Party and the Struggle for Socialism,* Cambridge University Press, p.194.

12. P. Foot (1968) *The Politics of Harold Wilson,* Harmondsworth: Penguin Books, p.110.

13. M. Pablo, *The Rise and Decline of Stalinism,* p.6.

14. G. Healy (1957) *Revolution and Counter-Revolution in Hungary,* pamphlet 1957, p.59.

15. Quoted in D. Widgery (ed.) (1976) *The Left in Britain,* London: Peregrine, p.59.

16. This socialist humanism produced obscure slogans such as 'Stalinism is Leninism turned to stone' which did nothing to advance a non–Stalinist Marxism. See E.P. Thompson (1956) 'Through the smoke of Budapest', in *The Reasoner,* November.

17. Brian Behan, Peter Fryer, Peter Cadogan, Alastair Macintyre, Ken Coates, Cliff Slaughter, Chris Pallis and Bob Pennington were among those won to The Club during this period.

18. *The Newsletter* 10 May 1957.

19. In 1957 Annual Conference supported a unilateralist motion seconded by Viv Mendelson, a SLL supporter from South Norwood CLP which was led by Trotskyists until Transport House 'reorganised' it.

20. Internal Document: 'The Newsletter Conference: National Industrial Rank and File Conference', 16 November 1958.

21. A Charter of Workers Demands, p.8.

22. This reply and the pamphlet itself, said Healy, '. . . constitutes a policy statement which the editorial board of *The Newsletter* submits to all trade unionists as a basis for the launching of a socialist organisation inside the

trade unions'. See G. Healy (1959) 'Our answer to the witch hunt and our policy for labour', January. First published in *The Newsletter* 6 December 1958.

23. Ibid, p.8.

24. In fact Healy seems to have been wedded to the view that the short-term choice in Britain was between socialism and fascism. See Tom Forrester 'The Labour Party's militant moles' in *New Society* 10 January 1980 p.53. The Militant Tendency allege that Healy reiterated this view from 1945 onwards. See 'Entrism', Militant internal document, November 1973, p.4.

25. Between 1957 and 1959 *Labour Review* claimed that it '. . . is *not* a sectional Trotskyist journal. We wish to make it the main journal for conducting the principled discussion of every aspect of revolutionary theory. Our columns are open to all who wish to put a point of view on how Marxist science is to be evolved', *Labour Review,* March-April.

This attitude was adhered to for the first two years of the journal's existence during which time independent Marxists such as Isaac Deutscher contributed essays and The Club's theoreticians, like Cliff Slaughter, wrote useful critical appreciations of non-Trotskyist thinkers such as Gramsci and Lukacs. But this period, 1957-9, was dominated by the Club's efforts to recruit dissident Communists. From the launching of the SLL in 1959 *Labour Review* and its successors became increasingly concerned with 'Pabloism' and other internecine quarrels of diminishing relevance.

26. 'Draft Constitution of the Socialist Labour League', 1959.

27. Editorial *Labour Review,* April-May, 1959.

28. Among other points raised by Behan, in this connection, was Healy's joint ownership (with Mike Banda) of the SLL's printshop and his monopoly of the power positions in the organization; general secretary of the SLL, editor of *The Newsletter,* secretary of the International Committee and treasurer of the SLL plus manager of the printshop. See Internal Bulletin no.3, April 1960.

29. B. Behan, Internal Document January 1960 p.5.

30. Internal Bulletin No.4 May 1960 p.14.

31. For example, Tony Whelan *The credibility gap: the politics of the SLL* (IMG phamphlet); and E. Mandel 'Marxism versus ultraleftism' in *Marxism versus Ultraleftism,* Education For Socialists, New York: Pathfinder.

32. Quoted by Alan Jones (1976) in 'Battle of ideas no.1' in *Red Weekly* October.

33. N. Young (1977) *An Infantile Disorder? The Crisis and Decline of the New Left,* London: Routledge & Kegan Paul, p.154.

34. See below, ch.7.

35. J. Castle (1965) 'Cuba: Marxism and the revolution' in *Fourth International* theoretical journal of the ICFI, August, vol.2, no.2. (This journal replaced *Labour Review* in 1965.) The SLL's invocation of criteria such as 'the structures of workers' democracy' and the Leninist party in order to disqualify Cuba as a workers' state seems completely arbitrary in

view of the fact that it simultaneously regarded North Korea, China etc. as *bona fide,* though 'deformed', members of this club.

36. In 1961 the SLL had arrived at the conclusion that 'the greatest danger confronting the revolutionary movement is liquidationism, flowing from a capitulation either to the strength of imperialism or of the bureaucratic apparatuses in the Labour movement, or both. Pabloism represents, even more clearly now than in 1953 this liquidationist tendency in the international Marxist movement'. See 'Draft Resolution on International Perspectives' 28/29 January 1961 p.25 (Purdie Papers). On these assumptions the struggle to 'build the party' and to combat the evil represented by Pabloism could be achieved by announcing the formation of an independent organization: or such, at any rate, was the temptation ultimately succumbed to.

37. Quoted from a letter to Bob Purdie (Purdie Papers) 8 July 1968.

38. Tariq Ali recounts the way in which the SLL admitted young people into discotheques such that they became members of the organization on payment of the entry fee. See *The Coming British Revolution* p.127.

39. In February 1974 *Workers Press* declared: 'Four days to military dictatorship'. A. Thornett (1976) *The Battle For Trotskyism: Documents of the 1974 Opposition,* Oxford: Frampton, p.2.

40. This was, apparently, taken to the extent of physical attacks on 'Pabloites'. See J. Hansen *Marxism versus Ultraleftism,* p.108. According to Lewis Sinclair, Healy was found 'guilty' of the attack on Ernie Tate at an enquiry chaired by the late Isaac Deutscher. More recently Healy has alleged that Joseph Hansen of the SWP was a KGB agent at the same time when he acted as one of Trotsky's secretaries in Mexico. The rest of the Trotskyist left dismiss this as a slander which betrays Healy's unscrupulousness and paranoia.

41. For the WRP's views on VSC see Cliff Slaughter (1969) *A Balance Sheet of Revisionism,* London: Plough Press, February.

42. E. Mandel in *Marxism versus Ultraleftism* argues that 'the historical origin of the Healy tendency . . . arose within the Workers International League, a split-off from the Communist Party which never really broke with Third Period politics, simply turning away from Stalinism when the CP leadership shifted from its ultra left Third Period tactics to ultra-opportunist 'People's Frontism' in 1935', p.63.

T. Ali believes Healyism to be largely a legacy of the undemocratic practices of the RCP. T. Ali *The Coming British Revolution,* p.124.

43. G. Healy (1949) 'Internal Bulletin', no.9, p.9, Tarbuck Papers.

44. G. Healy (1946) quoted by Paul Dixon in Tarbuck Papers p.3, February.

45. Quoted by G. Thayer (1965) *The British Political Fringe,* London, p.134.

46. *The Battle for Trotskyism,* p.85 and p.89.

47. Ibid, p.94.

48. Such explanations figure prominently in the arguments proffered by T. Ali, *The Coming British Revolution;* T. Whelan, *The Credibility Gap;* A. Jones

Red Weekly, and E. Mandel *Marxism versus Ultraleftism.*

49. See the Workers Revolutionary Party (1982) *Defeat British Imperialism: the enemy is at home,* pamphlet, London.

50. M. Banda (1975) *Whither Thornett?* London: WRP, pp.1-2.

51. C. Slaughter (1970) *The Class Nature of the 'International Socialism' Group,* Workers Press pamphlet, February, p.5.

52. Ibid, p.5.

53. C. Slaughter (1971) *Who Are The International Socialists?,* Workers Press pamphlet, April, p.3.

54. See, for example, P. Jeffries (1974) 'Falsifiers of Lenin', Workers Revolutionary Party Pocket Library No. 9, London, May; 'A Marxist Analysis of the Crisis' (n.d.) Socialist Labour League pamphlet; C. Slaughter (1969) 'A Balance Sheet of Revisionism', Newsletter pamphlet, February; C. Slaughter (1970) 'Reform or Revolution?', Workers Press pamphlet, October.

CHAPTER 5

1. See I.H. Birchall (1975) 'History of the International Socialists', Part 1, in *Interntional Socialism* no.76, March.

2. *Socialist Challenge,* no.126, December 1979.

3. T. Cliff 'Revolutionary traditions' in D. Widgery (ed.) *The Left in Britain,* p.93.

4. *Origins of the International Socialists* (1971) London: Pluto Press, p.3.

5. Mensheviks, Austro-Marxists, and centrists (such as Kautsky) were the early proponents of the theory of state capitalism. These were succeeded by renegades from the Third International such as Bordiga and Urbahns followed by sympathizers of Trotsky like Bruno Rizzi and Grandizo Munis. More recently, Maoists such at Paul Sweezy and Charles Bettleheim have reconstructed the theory. See Erich Farl (1973) 'The genealogy of state capitalism' in *International,* vol.2, no.1, Spring.

6. L. Trotsky, *The Revolution Betrayed,* p.245.

7. I. H. Birchall (1973) *Workers Against The Monolith,* London: Pluto Press, p.234.

8. T. Cliff 'On the class nature of the people's democracies' in *Origins of the International Socialists,* p.36.

9. T. Cliff interviewed (1979) in *The Leveller,* no.30, September, pp.20-21.

10. According to Hallas, Trotsky's account '. . . had been a realistic (if provisional) attempt at a Marxist analysis of the course of development in the USSR' until the late 1920s. D. Hallas (1979) *Trotsky's Marxism,* London: Pluto Press, p.38.

11. T. Cliff (1974) *Russia: A Marxist Analysis,* London: Pluto Press, p.153.

12. D. Hallas, *Trotsky's Marxism,* p.40.

13. 'The fact that the bureaucracy fulfils the tasks of the Capitalist class, and

by doing so transforms itself into a class, makes it the purest personification of this class'. T. Cliff, *Russia: A Marxist Analysis,* pp.169-70.

14. D. Hallas, *Trotsky's Marxism,* p.107. And yet the International Socialists persistently refer to Western capitalism as the 'old' and state capitalism as the 'new' types of capitalism. See, for example, (1976) 'Mao and the Chinese Revolution', in *International Socialism Journal (ISJ),* no.92, October.

15. T. Cliff, *Russia: A Marxist Analysis,* p.162. This is similar to a statement of Bukharin's: '. . . the dictatorship of the proletariat . . . will be state capitalism turned upside-down, its dialectical reversal of poles into its own opposite'. N. Bukharin (1971) *Economics of the Transformation Period,* London: Pluto Press, p.71. Inspired by the Western war economies of 1914–18, Bukharin considered the *hypothetical,* but theoretically interesting, possibility of a single state capitalist trust dominating a national economy. This, he conceived, would plan its domestic affairs, but compete internationally with the state capitalist trusts of other nations. The anarchy of capitalist production would, therefore, merely shift to the interntional level and, from there, dictate the pattern of national development.

16. T. Cliff, *Russia: A Marxist Analysis,* p.210. Here, again, the parallels with Bukharin's argument are striking. He also observed that if competition betweeen firms became exclusively competition between states 'the state power must . . . grow tremendously' leading to an '. . . immensely growing state budget (devoting) an even larger share to "defence purposes" as militarism is euphemistically termed'. N. Bukharin (1972) *Imperialism and World Economy,* London: Merlin Press, pp.124-5.

17. See Chris Harman's (1969-70) defence of the state capitalist theory in 'The Inconsistencies of Ernest Mandel' in *ISJ* no.41, December/January, p.38.

18. M. Kidron (1968) *Western Capitalism Since the War,* Harmondsworth: Penguin Books, p.49.

19. See R. Luxemburg and N. Bukharin (1972) *Imperialism and the Accumulation of Capital,* Harmondsworth: Penguin Books.

20. M. Kidron, *Western Capitalism Since the War,* p.56. Kidron sharply criticised Mandel's (1968) *Marxist Economic Theory,* London: Merlin, for, among other things, asserting that the rate of profit had fallen since 1945. Kidron argued that 'there [has] been no long-term slide in profit rates [and] . . . since nothing beyond the forties could sustain Mandel's thesis, the facts are suspended then'. See M. Kidron (1974) *Capitalism and Theory,* London: Pluto Press, p.84. Yet, one year after this publication, Cliff wrote that 'in the last 25 years pre-tax profits for large companies have almost halved'. Indeed, says Cliff, this decline '. . . has been particularly steep since the mid-fifties'. See T. Cliff (1975) *The Crisis,* London: Pluto Press, p.16. Since the permanent arms economy thesis depends on a falling rate of profit (if it is to explain the post-war boom), Cliff's latter statement (which Kidron did no contradict) explodes its claims to scientificity.

21. M. Kidron, *Capitalism and Theory,* p.160.

22. Ibid, p.163.

23. See V. Karalasingham 'The War in Korea' in *The Origins of the International Socialists*, p.78.

24. I.H. Burchall *Workers Against the Monolith*, pp.59–60.

25. T. Cliff, *Russia: A Marxist Analysis*, p.162, p.183; *ISJ* (1976) no.12, no.92; *Socialist Review* (1955) March; *New Politics* (1962) Winter, pp.51–65.

26. T. Cliff, *The Crisis*, p.29. Since the election of Reagan this pattern is, presumably, in reverse: i.e. towards greater arms expenditure.

27. Kidron has now disowned this theory. See 'Two valid insights don't make a theory' in *ISJ* (1977) no.100, July.

28. For example, D. Purdy (1973) in *The Bulletin of Socialist Economists*, Spring; G. Hodgson (1973) in *International*, January; B. Warren (1972) in *New Left Review*, no.72, March–April; and by E. Mandel (1975) *Late Capitalism*, London: New Left Books. While Mandel acknowledges the permanent arms economy as 'one of the hallmarks of late capitalism' he rejects the claim that it can stablize the system by arresting the tendency for the rate of profit to fall. Since, as we have mentioned, Cliff admits of a falling rate of profit in the 1950s and 1960s (the very period of stability which his theory purports to explain) Mandel is on safe ground in observing the contradiction. See chapter 9 of *Late Capitalism*.

29. I. Birchall *History of the International Socialists*, p.17.

30. T. Cliff (1959) *Rosa Luxemburg*, London: p.43.

31. Ibid, p.54.

32. I. Birchall, *History of the International Socialists*, p.20.

33. D. Howell, *British Social Democracy*, pp.214–17.

34. 'It does not follow that the last words in organisational wisdom is to be found in the Bolshevik model. In the very different conditions of the late twentieth century capitalism, arguments for or against Lenin's position of 1903 are not so much right or wrong as irrelevant'. D. Hallas in T. Cliff and D. Hallas et al. *Party and Class*, London: Pluto Press, p.15 and p.17.

35. D. Hallas, *Party and Class*, pp.17–18. Hallas argues that the wider, though related, problem of class consciousness is not settled by reference to the recurring antimonies of party and spontaneity. This debate, says Hallas, 'has absolutely no relevance to modern conditions': it is a 'hoary red herring'. See Ibid, p.20.

36. Ibid, p.42. Cliff's (1960) essay, reprinted in *Party and Class*, first appeared as 'Trotsky on substitutionism' in *International Socialism*, no.2, August.

37. M. Shaw (1978) 'The making of a party' in R. Miliband and J. Saville (eds.) *The Socialist Register*, p.109.

38. *Rank-and-File Teacher* reached a peak circulation of about 9,000 in 1974. IS's other publications geared to its industrial work had circulations which ranged from 1,000 to 10,000 each. These included *Case-Con* (since 1973 for NALGO Social Workers), *Journalists Charter*, *NALGO Action News*, *Carworker*, *Collier*, *Hospital Worker*, *Textile Worker*, *Redder Tape* (for members of the CPSA), *Scots Rank-and-File*, *Technical Teacher*, *Dockworkers*,

GEC Rank-and-File, Building Workers, Electrician Special. The IS also produced *Women's Voice,* which had a print order of 10,000, and an Urdu publication called *Chingari* (since 1973) which sold around 5,000 copies. *Socialist Worker,* itself reached a peak circulation of 60,000 in 1972. All these journals declined in sales from the mid-seventies as we point out in detail below. See P. Shipley (1976) *Revolutionaries in Modern Britain* London: Bodley Head, pp.140-1. According to B. Baker, *The Far Left,* the paid sales figure for *Socialist Worker* declined from 18,250 in November 1974 to 13,550 in 1978.

39. Yaffe's group became the Revolutionary Communist Group.
40. T. Cliff, *The Crisis,* p.182.
41. M. Shaw, 'The making of a party', p.136.
42. R. Rosewall (n.d.) *The Struggle for Workers Power,* IS pamphlet, p.27.
43. D. Hallas, *Trotsky's Marxism,* p.84.
44. T. Cliff (1975) *Lenin: Building the Party,* vol.2, London: Pluto Press, pp.67-8.
45. This was reported by *The Guardian* under the headline 'Trotsky's heirs and Stalinist disgraces'.
46. T. Cliff interviewed in *The Leveller.*
47. R. Kline (n.d.), 'Can Socialism Come Through Parliament?', IS pamphlet.
48. T. Cliff, *The Crisis,* p.172.
49. D. Hallas (1977) 'How can we move on?' in *Socialist Register,* London: Merlin Press, pp.3-4.
50. R. Hyman (1973) 'Industrial conflict and the political economy: trends of the sixties and prospects for the seventies' in *Socialist Register,* London: Merlin Press, p.107.
51. T. Cliff, *The Crisis,* pp.154-5.
52. See K. Middlemas *Politics in Industrial Society,* p.432.
53. R. Hyman, pp.108-9.
54. T. Cliff (1970) *The Employers Offensive,* London: Pluto Press, p.201.
55. The IS was not alone in stressing the significance of the antimony of 'rank-and-file' versus trade union bureaucracy'. See for example R. Blackburn and A. Cockburn (eds.) (1967) *The Incompatibles,* Harmondsworth: Penguin Books, and the essay by P. Anderson in particular. More recently Leo Panitch has observed that as the recession got underway the state attempted '. . . to integrate lower levels of the (trade union) movement — right down to the shop floor — more effectively'. L. Panitch (1980) 'Trade unions and the capitalist state' in *New Left Review* no.125, January-February, p.37. The significance of this strategy is that it obviates the need for coercive measures which might risk political instability and over-reliance on the trade union leadership to discipline and the rank and file. To the extent that it succeeds, this strategy avoids risking the very alienation of the rank and file from national trade union leaderships which the IS-SWP hoped to exploit.
56. See T. Cliff, *The Crisis,* p.182.

57. S. Jeffreys (1975) 'The challenge of the rank-and-file' in *International Socialism Journal,* March, p.7.

58. R. Hyman, pp.107-9.

59. For example Steve Jeffreys writes that '. . . untrammelled by a reformist bureaucracy they [the trade unions] will also be capable of challenging capitalism itself'. See Ibid, p.7.

60. See J. Hinton (1973) *The First Shop Stewards Movement,* London: Allen & Unwin; and Bob Holton (1976) *British Syndicalism 1900-1914,* London: Pluto Press.

61. See *International Socialism Journal* (1974) February, pp.12-13, and (1975) November, p.15.

62. *In Defence of Marxism: Platform of the Left Opposition of IS* (1974), internal document, September. Elsewhere Cliff made his personal role in the development of the IS strategy very clear. Thus:

I don't believe it would be intellectually honest for me to say to you that our ideas developed systematically, that I saw all the connections between Rank-and-Filism, the theory of state capitalism, the permanent arms economy, and all the rest of it . . . originally it was really me — resenting the idea that you can have a workers' state without a workers' revolution and workers' activity and workers' consciousness and a revolutionary party.

T. Cliff interviewed in *The Leveller,* p.21.

63. T. Cliff refers to this 'insidious trend' in N. Harris and J. Palmer (eds.) (1971) *World Crisis,* London: Hutchinson, p.235.

64. S. J.T. Murphy (1972) *The Workers' Committee: An Outline of its Principles and Structure,* London: pamphlet, Pluto Press. The explanation forwarded by Murphy (that is the embourgeoisiement of union officials) on p.6, is cited approvingly by Cliff in *The Crisis,* p.121.

65. T. Cliff *The Crisis,* p.121.

66. R. Hyman in *Socialist Register 1973,* p.122.

67. T. Cliff, *The Employer's Offensive,* p.231. Here Cliff is basing himself on L. Trotsy's (1972) 'Trade unions in the epoch of imperialist decay' in *Marxism and the Trade Unions,* New Park pamphlet.

68. Rosewall's pamphlet, *The Struggle for Workers Power,* is described as the organization's 'programme for the overthrow of capitalism' and, as such, may be presumed an authoritative IS statement. In this it is argued that the alternative to integration consists of

. . . a national rank-and-file organisation that can surmount the barriers of industry and union and unite trade unionists around a programme . . . central [to which] . . . is the question of democratic control by the rank-and-file at all levels of factory and union organisation . . . [to] . . . *convert them into organisations of real revolutionary struggle under a marxist leadership. We believe in trade unionism because of its vital role in the class structure to overthrow capitalism.* [p.13, my emphasis]

The Leninist strategy is to build a revolutionary party. Only when this project is well under way can the trade unions be converted along Rosewall's lines. To put the process in reverse is to take a syndicalist stance on this question.

69. R. Hyman (1971) *Marxism and the Sociology of Trade Unionism,* pamphlet, London: Pluto Press, p.37.

70. T. Cliff, *The Crisis,* p.11.

71. The table is reproduced from the SWP *Internal Bulletin* (1982) June, p.8.

72. This is further revealed in the group's 1982 composition 'one third of our members are manual workers, one third white collar trade unionist, the rest students, unemployed, at school etc'. Ibid, p.8. This shows little change from the situation in 1974 when the NRFM was launched.

73. An indication of IS's theoretical stagnation in the 1970s was the decision to transform the theoretical journal *International Socialism* into a monthly review in 1975. It was after this that the IS lost much of its intellectual support and when the theoretical journal was reconstituted in 1978 it was with seriously reduced intellectual forces.

74. See E.J. Hobsbawm (1979) 'Syndicalism and the working class' in *New Society,* 5 April, vol.48, no.861, pp.8-10.

75. By celebrating each and every strike the IS-SWP even came close to the syndicalist strategy in this respect too. But as Giovanni Arrighi has pointed out 'neither the strength exhibited by the workers' movement during the struggles of the second half of the sixties . . . nor the capacity of resistance to the blackmail of unemployment . . . can easily be ascribed to factors of *political* consciousness and organisation'. G. Arrighi, 'Towards a theory of capitalist crisis', in *New Left Review,* no.111, September/October 1978, p.23. The IS-SWP strategy assumed the opposite.

76. The SWP's electoral failures in the seventies were a more accurate reflection of the real state of political consciousness which its economism tried hard to deny. 'In Newcastle and Walsall in November 1976 the party gained only 184 (1.8 per cent) and 574 (1.5 per cent) votes respectively. In Stetchford in March 1977 it won only 377 (1.1 per cent) votes and in Ladywood the following August it won only 152 (1.1 per cent)'. The figures are cited by Peter Mair, 'The Marxist left' in H.M. Drucker (ed.) (1979) *Multi-Party Britain,* London: Macmillan, p.167. Despite this poor showing the SWP fielded candidates of its own even when the opportunity arose for joint campaigns with the International Marxist Group. The SWP's sectarianism resulted in election campaigns at Hull and Newham in which the National Front candidate polled more votes than either the Socialist Unity or the SWP candidate. In the Ladywood by-election of 1977, the first Socialist Unity candidate polled almost four times the vote gained by the SWP — yet the latter continued to field its own candidates in subsequent campaigns.

77. Hyman, Sedgewick, Shaw, Protz, Higgins, Palmer and Nagliatti all left the IS after the internal changes of 1974-75. An attempt by these to salvage something of the IS tradition failed to materialize and Shaw — the

instigator of the attempt — is himself now, inevitably, a member of the Labour Party.

78. An International Socialism group was formed in the USA in 1969. Like its British counterpart, the American IS was not initially organized along democratic lines and was only ambiguously Leninist in its ideology at the time of its founding conference. It also made no claim at being a party and placed party building in the distant future. However the American IS, like the SWP, soon after attempted to transform 'an almost entirely campus-derived organization into an instrument of working class power'. Its orientation was towards oppositional caucuses organized nationally within unions. See J. O'Brien (1977-8) 'American Leninism in the 1970s', *Radical America,* Winter. There are no organized links between these 'fraternal' organizations.

79. 'This readiness to bend the stick too far in one direction and then to go into reverse and bend it too far in the opposite direction was a characteristic that he (Lenin) retained throughout his life.' T. Cliff, *Lenin,* vol.1, pp.66-7. Elsewhere in this book Cliff makes much of Lenin's 'very keen intuitive sense' (p.263), his 'daring improvisation' and ability to 'sense the mood of the masses' (p.258). Marxism, says Cliff, is not just a science but, as a guide to action it must also be an art' (p.254). The trouble with these emphases is that they overplay the gifts of leadership and, in the context of a leadership-dominated organization like the current SWP, can be used to justify the practical exclusion of the membershp in the group's internal life.

80. References to 'The republican faction' in the SWP *Internal Bulletin* (1972) June, suggest this relaxation of internal discipline.

CHAPTER 6

1. See 'The 20th congress of the CPSU' (1978) in *The Struggle To Re-unify the Fourth International (1954-63)* vol.3; *De-Stalinisation, the Hungarian Revolution and the World Trotskyism,* documents 1955-7; *Education For Socialists,* February, New York: pp.53-4.

2. Ibid, p.60. This report was given to the Seventh plenum of the IEC in May 1956.

3. See E. Mandel (1970) 'Prospects and dynamics of the political revolution against the bureaucracy' in *The Development and Disintegration of World Stalinism,* New York: Education For Socialists, March.

4. See 'The Hungarian revolution and the crisis of Stalinism' (resolution adopted by the SWP National Committee in January 1957) in *The Struggle to Re-unify the Fourth International* (1954-63) vol.3, pp.33-9 and G. Healy (1957) *Revolution and Counter-Revolution in Hungary,* pamphlet.

5. *Trotskyism versus Revisionism* (1974) vol.3, London: New Park, pp.37-8.

6. Quoted by Frank Richards (1975) in 'The question of the International' in *Revolutionary Communist* no.2, May, p.32.

7. The new 'colonialist' emphasis was pursued with especial zeal in the case

of Michel Pablo, the ISFI's secretary, who became involved in the Algerian revolution in a personal capacity after having set-up an Algerian Bureau under the auspices of the ISFI. Pablo and his supporters eventually broke with the ISFI on this issue in 1964. In Britain a tiny 'Revolutionary Marxist Tendency' of Pabloites existed until 1968: their removal from the ISFI did not lessen Healy's attacks on that organization for 'Pabloite liquidationism' — indeed such attacks increased!

8. See 'Draft resolution on international perspectives' (1961) adopted by SLL National Executive Committee 28/29 January, p.27.

9. The Re-unification Congress of June 1963 said of Castroism that it '. . . will more and more play a genuinely international role . . . It is at this stage . . . the most advanced political leadership by far of all the workers' states'. See 'The Sino-Soviet conflict' (1970) in *The Development and Disintegration of World Stalinism*, New York: Education For Socialists, March, p.67.

10. *Trotskyism versus Revisionism*, vol.3, p.259.

11. For the SLL argument see *Trotskyism versus Revisionism*, vol.4, p.XIII.

12. In the absence of documents produced by this group the rest of this account of the origins of the IMG relies heavily on the accounts of Pat Jordan and Tariq Ali. Jordan was a founder member of the IMG and Ali was its best known spokesman. See 'Aspects of the history of the IMG' (1975) by Peter Peterson (alias Pat Jordan), IMG Pre-Conference document no.6, January, and T. Ali's *The Coming British Revolution*, pp.137-40.

13. The programme of *Young Guard* — which united several left-wing groups outside of *Keep Left* — included unilateral nuclear disarmament, withdrawal from NATO, a programme of nationalization under workers' control and comprehensive education. In 1962 its supporters won four seats on the Young Socialists national committee while *Keep Left* obtained three amid accusations of violence and intimidation. See Zig Layton-Henry (1976) 'Labour's lost youth' in the *Journal of Contemporary History*, vol.11, July, pp.275-308.

14. Since 1960, and CND's Committee of 100, Russell had become organizationally dependent on Ralph Schoenman and politically influenced by him. See Bertrand Russell (1975) *The autobiography of Bertrand Russell*, London: Unwin, p.603. According to Tariq Ali it was Schoenman who conceived the Vietnamese Solidarity Campaign. See *Red Mole*, vol.1, no.9, September, p.8. When the International War Crimes Tribunal was set up in the summer of 1966 IMG members such as Ali became involved in its international fact-finding missions. Indeed the IMG began to build a London branch in 1966 because Jordan had to move there to work full time for the VSC.

15. In 1961 the sixth world congress of the ISFI had claimed that '. . . special attention must be paid to the situation in Great Britain where . . . the strongest left-wing tendency in Western Europe is developing under extremely favourably conditions for a decisive intervention of revoltuionary Marxists' inside the Labour Party. See *Fourth International*

(1960) no.12, Winter. There is no doubt that the FI was as unrealistic as the Labour left in its hopes for the socialism of Harold Wilson (see chapter 7) and that the 'intense secrecy' under which the IMG laboured in the early sixties (see Tariq Ali *The Coming British Revolution,* pp.139-40) was justified in terms of an expected strengthening of the Labour left. Even when this hope was shown to be illusory the IMG persisted with entrism until 1969.
16. See Lewis Minkin (1978) *The Labour Party Conference,* London: Allen Lane, p.44.
17. Ken Coates has a rather different version of the events which caused the split between him and Jordan. According to his account the breach in relations between them was caused by 'Jordan '. . . unilaterally changing the basis of our working relationship. Our association had always been based upon an agreement that we were *not* establishing a classic Leninist type of organisation, but on the contrary, a novel kind of catalyst. Indeed Pat had declared himself to be quite as rigorously "revisionist" as any of us. All of a sudden, he was converted to an extreme form of organisational piety, not to say dogmatism'. (from a letter to the author).
18. Recorded by Nigel Young (1977) *An Infantile Disorder? The Crisis and Decline of the New Left,* London: Routledge. See also his typology of old and new lefts on p.310.
19. This estimate is made by Martin Thomas (1976) in 'The logic of scenario politics: The IMG 1972-6' in 'The ICL and the Fourth International', *International Communist Special,* no.1, theoretical journal of the International Communist League, p.33.
20. N. Young, p.144 and p147.
21. *International* (1968) July, p.13.
22. Adrian Mitchell resigned from the *Black Dwarf* editorial board over IMG's criticism of the African National Council.
23. E. Mandel (1965) *A Socialist Strategy For Western Europe,* Nottingham: Institute for Workers' Control, Spokesman pamphlet, p.1. This analysis appeared also in *International* (1968) September.
24. See E. Mandel (1971) *The Lessons of May 1968,* IMG pamphlet. Yet, paradoxically, the May events rekindled faith in perspectives of insurrectionary roads to socialism, 'explosions' of consciousness, and economic collapses.
25. Mandel cites the following theses of the FI in particular:
(a) Lenin's conception of the epoch as one of wars, civil wars, and revolutions
(b) the crisis of proletarian leadership
(c) the necessity of a vanguard organization
(d) the revolutionary role of the proletariat
(e) the centrality of the demand for workers' control of industry in the transition from capitalism to socialism. See E. Mandel, Ibid, pp.16-22.
26. E. Mandel (1971) *The Revolutionary Student Movement: Theory and Practice,* New York: Pathfinder pamphlet, p.36. A similar analysis is presented by Gareth Steadman-Jones (1969) in *Student Power,*

Harmondsworth: Penguin Books; by IS in Susan Buddle et al. (1972) *Students and the Struggle For Socialism,* International Socialist Pamphlet, and the Communist Party of Great Britain in D. Cook (n.d.) *Students,* CP Pamphlet, and D. Cook (1974) 'Students, left unity and the Communist Party, *Marxism Today,* October.

27. *International* (1968) December, p.7.
28. *International* (1969) January.
29. *Red Mole* (1970) vol.1, no.1, March, p.2
30. *Red Mole* (1970) vol.1, no.3, 15 April. The title of Blackburn's essay is itself of interest since it was taken from a Rolling Stones LP and symbolizes the youth-oriented nature of the IMG. The notoriety achieved by Blackburn (through his expulsion from the LSE) accounts for *Red Mole's* public announcement of his subsequent recruitment to IMG: such 'news' was presumably of interest to the student left — though perhaps a little mystifying to anyone else who happened to read it.
31. See 'Battle of ideas', monthly supplement to *Red Weekly* (1976) no.3, December, 'Proletarian and bourgeois democracy: a reply to Geoff Roberts' by Tariq Ali and Robin Blackburn.
32. See, for example, 'Documents of the 1965 world congress of the Fourth International' in *International Socialist Review* (1966) Spring.
33. For more detail on this see R.J. Alexander (1973) *Trotskyism in Latin America,* Stanford: Stanford University Press.
34. *Intercontinental Press* (1969) July, p.720.
35. Ibid, vol.X, no.1, p.49.
36. *International* (1973) vol.2, no.1, p.40. See also Geoff Roberts (1976) 'The politics of the IMG', in *Marxism Today,* February, and the self-criticism of Tariq Ali and Robin Blackburn in 'The battle of ideas', supplement to *Red Weekly,* entitled 'Proletarian revolution and bourgeois democracy' (1976) *Red Weekly,* no.3, December.
37. *International* (1969) May, p.4.
38. Much of this emphasized Connolly's Marxism and the significance of the Easter Rising of 1916. See *International,* nos.1,3,5 and 8 for examples.
39. *International* (1970) July, p.39.
40. *International* (1971) January-February, vol.1, no.3; *Red Mole,* vol.1, no.12.
41. *International* (1971) vol.1, no.6, September/October.
42. *Red Mole* (1970) vol.1, no.3, 15 April.
43. In 1971 the IMG briefly canvassed for Saor Eire — an ephemeral grouping based in the Republic which somewhat tentatively avowed that it '. . . could be called an urban guerilla group'. See *Red Mole* (1971) vol.2, no.1, January.
44. This was stressed in 'Ireland: the acid test for British Socialists' in *Red Mole* (1971) September.
45. *Red Mole* (1971) vol.2, no.6, April. As if to underline the IMG's ignorance of the republican movement in 1971 an article in which it declared its support for the latter's military campaign consisted of an interview with

three Officials who condemned the 'catholic nationalist' project of the Provisionals. At this time the IMG supported both wings of the IRA. See *International* (1971) vol.1, no.6, September–October.

46. *Workers Press* (1971) 4 September, objected that '. . . no socialist can tolerate or defend the indiscriminate bombings of the IRA'. Bob Purdie, for IMG, denounced this statement as 'slanderous'. See *Red Mole* (1971) no.28, September.

47. *Red Mole* (1971) 15 November.

48. *Red Mole* (1972) 16 October.

49. *Red Mole* (1972) 27 November.

50. *Notes to Organisers* (1973) New Series, vol.1, no.13, 28 August. In this the following resolution was put before the IMG Political Committee meeting of 26 August 1973.

The FI is opposed to individual terrorism. The IMG holds that the present bombings — for which both the Official and the Provision IRA deny responsibility — obstruct the struggle against capitalism.

This was unanimously defeated (7 votes against, none for). The members who put forward this resolution constituted themselves 'the Tendency' and declared unequivocal opposition to terrorism, noting that '. . . not one of Trotsky's statements on this question has ever appeared in the pages of *Red Weekly* (successor to *Red Mole*) or its predecessor — *not one*. See 'Internal discussion bulletin. (1973) vol.2, no.8, November. In fact, despite the emphasis to the contrary, *Red Mole* did, as we have noted, print Trotsky's article on Grynszpan (but the substance of the Tendency's objections is sound).

51. *International Socialism Journal* (1974) no.70, mid-June, p.13.

52. This point was made by the Militant Tendency. See P. Taaffe (n.d.) *Marxism Opposes Individual Terrorism,* Militant Pamphlet, p.10. Militant also recognized that the partition of Ireland no longer had any economic significance for British capitalism and have always regarded the defeat of the IRA as 'inevitable'. See, for example, Ted Grant (1973) 'British perspectives and prospects', in *Militant International Review* (MIR), no.6, January, p.8.

53. The majority of the IMG National Committee decided in May 1973 that 'the issue of the repressive role of the army in Ireland is the key issue'. See Liam Sykes (1973) 'Ireland: a review and some perspectives', IMG Pre-Conference Discussion Bulletin, vol.2, no.22, p.8.

54. *Red Weekly* (1973) no.15, 24 August.

55. *Red Weekly* (1974) no.52, 16 May.

56. See *Red Weekly* (1974) no.79, 5 December, for both IS and IMG statements on the Birmingham pub bombing.

57. The Militant Tendency's position on Northern Ireland amounts to a restatement of its arguments concerning the advance of socialism in Britain (see chapter 7). This involved support for the still-born Northern Ireland Labour Party and the election of an 'independent' Labour Party in the south together with a call for the adoption of Militant's economic demands.

Today Militant also calls for the establishment of a non-sectarian Trade Union Defence Force to act as a militia in defence of workers against terrorism after the army has been withdrawn. Militant now calls for the creation of a trade union-backed Labour Party in the North to implement its economic programme. See P. Hadden (1980) *Divide and Rule: Labour and the Partition of Ireland*, Militant Pamphlet, August, and his (1980) *Northern Ireland: Tory Cuts, Common Misery, Common Struggle*, Militant Pamphlet, March, reprinted January 1981.

58. See the International Socialist — Socialist Workers Party pamphlet (1980) *Troops Out of Ireland*, September, and Geoff Bell's (1979) *British Labour and Ireland: 1969-1979*, IMG Pamphlet, August, for the most recent statements of the two organizations.

59. See the publication *Hands Off Ireland* (1978) quarterly bulletin of the Revolutionary Communist Group, no.4, May, pp.11-14.

60. S. Rowbotham et al. (1979) *Beyond The Fragments: Feminism and the Making of Socialism*, London: Merlin Press, p.95.

61. On several occasions in the early 1970s the intervention of the ISFI was a moderating and calming influence on tendencies within IMG engaged in prolonged dispute. There is no doubt that only the authority and prestige of the International leadership prevented splits in the IMG. See United Secretariat thesis, 'The Situation in Britain and the tasks of the IMG' in *International* (1973) vol.2, no.2, Summer, pp.7-14 and United Secretariat theses 'The British Crisis' in *International* (1976) vol.3, no.1, Spring, pp.9-23.

62. J. Mitchell (1971) *Women's Estate*, Harmondsworth: Penguin Books, p.54.

63. Kathy Ennis (1974) 'Women's consciousness' in *International Socialism Journal*, April, no.68, pp.27-8.

64. J. Ross (1977) 'Capitalism, politics and personal life' in *Socialist Woman: A Journal of the IMG*, vol.6, no.2, Summer.

65. S. Rowbotham (1977) 'Leninism in the lurch' in *Red Rag*, no.12, Spring.

66. S. Rowbotham et al. *Beyond the Fragments*, pp.21-50.

67. *Fourth International, Women's Liberation and the Socialist Revolution* (1979) Sydney: Pathfinder, p.15.

68. Ibid, p.69.

69. Ibid, p.75-7.

70. V. Beechey (1977) 'Female wage labour in capitalist production', in *Capital and Class*, no.3, p.61.

71. *Fourth International*, p.21.

72. Ibid, p.21.

73. See as an instance of this Marxist functionalism the Revolutionary Communist Group's argument in O. Adamson et al. (1976) 'Women's oppression under capitalism', *Revolutionary Communist*, no.5.

74. M. Barrett (1980) *Women's Oppression Today*, London: verso, p.85.

75. M. Coulson et al. (1975) 'The housewife and her labour under

capitalism — a critique', *New Left Review* 89, January–February, p.61.

76. H. Hartmann (1981) 'The unhappy marriage of Marxism and feminism', in L. Sargent (ed.) *Women and Revolution,* London: Pluto Press, p.7.

77. The most influential of these is J. Mitchell (1975) *Psychoanalysis and Feminism,* Harmondsworth: Penguin Books. See also R. Coward (1982) 'Sexual politics and psychoanalysis' in R. Brunt and C. Rowan (eds.) *Feminism, Culture and Politics,* London: Lawrence and Wishart.

78. J. Mitchell, ibid, p.415.

79. See W. Seccombe (1983) 'Marxism and demography', *New Left Review,* 137, January–February, p.28-9.

80. *Big Flame* started as a local Socialist newspaper in Liverpool in 1970 and developed into a Merseyside-based revolutionary group. By 1981 the group had established branches in most of the large town in England. See J. Howell (1981) 'Big Flame: resituating Socialist strategy and organisation', *Socialist Register.*

81. The Marxist Workers Group consisted of a dozen splitters from Workers Fight (itself a breakaway from the International Socialists-SWP) based in the Bolton and Leigh districts of Lancashire.

82. The so-called Communist faction consisted of only a handful of IMG members who were (unwittingly) led by members of the Spartacist Tendency intent on disrupting the IMG organization. The Spartacist Tendency is a tiny group of fundamentalists whose *raison d'être* is the disruption of political meetings and organizations of the Marxist left. The point appears to be a caricatured version of the splitting tactics endorsed by the Bolshevik Comintern and, later, by Trotskyist entrists, in the mass working-class organizations.

83. The attitude of IS to student politics switched dramatically from one which envisaged 'the mass of students against the system' to a position which relegated their role to a politically equivocal force that is useful in so far as it is linked to working-class struggles off campus. The change in position had its casualties as can be seen by comparing M. Shaw (1973) 'Which way for student revolutionaries?' in *International Socialism Journal,* March, and the pamphlet by S. Buddle et al. (1972) *Students and the Struggle For Socialism.*

84. A. Jones and R. Thompson (1972) *After the Miners' Strike — What Next?* pamphlet.

85. R. Miliband (1982) *Capitalist Democracy in Britain,* Oxford: Oxford University Press, p.152.

86. IMG Pre-Conference Bulletin (1975) no.5, January, p.8.

87. E. Mandel (1975) *Late Capitalism,* London: New Left Books.

88. See note 36.

89. See 'International internal discussion bulletin' (1983) vol.10, no.1, January; no.7, June; no.20, October; no.21, November, for the terms of the dispute.

90. See Pre-Conference Bulletin (1978) no.13, 'Tactics for building a

unified revolutionary organisation'.

CHAPTER 7

1. Ken Coates (1973) 'Socialists in the Labour Party' in *Socialist Register 1973,* London: Merlin Press, p.155.
2. L. Trotsky *Writings 1935-36,* p.382.
3. 'Entrism' (1973) Militant Internal Pamphlet, November p.8.
4. 'History of the Labour Party' (n.d.) articles reprinted from *Militant,* West London Militant Supporters, p.10 and p.18.
5. *Programme of the International* (1970) Publication of the International Bureau for the Fourth International, London, May, p.20.
6. *CWI International Bulletin* (1975) no.2, January.
7. 'British perspectives 1977' (1977) Internal Document, September, p.29.
8. British Perspectives 1977, p.15.
9. *CWI International Bulletin,* no.1, p.21. This was quoted by Reg Underhill's (1980) report on 'Entryist activities of the Militant Tendency', March.
10. 'British perspectives and tasks 1975', Internal Document, p.25.
11. T. Forrester (1980) 'The Labour Party's militant moles', in *New Society,* 10 January.
12. T. Grant (1982) *Falklands Crisis: A Socialist Answer,* Militant Pamphlet.
13. Pete Duncan (1980) *The Politics of Militant'* Clause 4 Pamphlet, London, p.25.
14. Lynn Walsh (1980) '40 years since Leon Trotsky's assassination', *Militant International Review,* Summer, no.20, p.11.
15. *Programme of the International,* p.19.
16. P. Hadden (1980) *Northern Ireland: Tory Cuts, Common Misery, Common Struggle,* Militant Pamphlet March, reprint January 1981, p.9. See also T. Grant (1972) 'British perspectives' in *Militant International Review,* no.12, February, where he specifies that 'the cycle of boom and slump will run from two to six years instead of the ten years or so', p.4.
17. A Woods (1980) 'Britain's crisis: are import controls the answer?' in *Militant International Review* no.20, Summer, pp.8-9.
18. See, for example, T. Grant (1973) 'British perspectives and prospects' in *Militant International Review* no.6, January. According to Grant 'every capitalist power, to a greater or lesser extent, was affected by the tendency of the rate of profit to fall', p.3.
19. A. Woods (1980) 'The crisis of Thatcherism', in *Militant International Review,* no.19, Spring, p.6.
20. P. Hadden, *Northern Ireland,* p.15.
21. British perspectives in 1977' (1977) Internal Document, September, p.10 and p.12.
22. P. Taaffe (1978) 'British Communist Party in crisis' in *Militant International Review,* no.15, Autumn, p.28.

23. 'British perspectives 1977', p.29.

24. *Student Bulletin* (1978) June, p.4.

25. 'British perspectives 1977', p.11.

26. P. Taaffe, 'British Communist Party in Crisis', p.24 and p.27.

27. *Programme of the International*, pp.15-16.

28. B. Ingham (n.d.) *The 35-Hour Week: The Fight Against Unemployment*, Militant Pamphlet, p.21 and p.28 respectively.

29. See Patrick Wintour (1980) *New Statesman*, 18 January, and Tom Forrester, *New Society*,

30. W. Wyatt (1977) *What's Left of the Labour Party?* London: Sidgwick and Jackson, p.177, and S. Haseler (1976) *The Death of British Democracy*, London: Elek, p.219.

31. D. Webster (1981) *The Labour Party and the New Left*, Fabian Tract 477, October, p.4.

32. B. Baker (1981) *The Far Left: An Expose of the Extreme Left in Britain*, London: Weidenfeld and Nicolson, p.5.

33. Z. Bauman (1972) *Between Class and Elite*, Manchester: Manchester University Press, p.286. P. Foot (1968) *The Politics of Harold Wilson*, Harmondsworth: Penguin Books, p.146.

34. See I. Budge et. al. (1976) *Party Identification and Beyond*, London: John Wiley, p.39.

35. See H. Himmelweit et al. (1981) *How Voters Decide*, London: Academic Press, and I. Crewe (1982) 'The Labour Party and the electorate' in D. Kavanagh (ed.) *The Politics of the Labour Party*, London: Allen & Unwin.

36. See I. Crewe, B. Sarlvick and J. Alt, 'Partisan dealignment in Britain 1964-1974' in *British Journal of Political Science*, vol.7, p.187.

37. See T. Forester (1976) *The British Labour Party and the Working Class*, New York: Holmes and Meier, who says '. . . evidence showing the amount of campaigning actually being done suggests that there has, indeed, been a marked decline in recent years', p.104.

38. See L. Minkin (1978) *The Labour Party conference*, London: Allen Lane, p.276, who quotes Crosland to this effect.

39. Ibid, p.87.

40. R.T. McKenzie (1983) *British Political Parties*, London: Heineman, p.547.

41. T. Forrester *The British Labour Party and the Working Class*, p.82 and B. Hindess (1971) *The Decline of Working Class Politics*, London: Paladin, p.126.

42. G. Hodgson (1981) *Labour at the Crossroads*, Oxford: Martin Robertson, p.58.

43. D. Webster, *The Labour Party and the New Left*, p.32.

44. Ibid, p.22.

45. See *New Statesman* (1980) 11 January, p.41.

46. H.M. Drucker (1979) *Doctrine and Ethos in the Labour Party*, London: Allen & Unwin, p.109.

47. See *Militant International Review* (1976) no.10, March, editorial.

48. A. Freeman (1981) 'Benn and British Socialism' in *International*,

September, vol.6, no.3, p.24.

49. See T. Ali (1981) *The Guardian,* Friday, 20 November.

50. Ted Grant (1970) 'Perspectives for Britain' in *Militant International Review* no.2, Spring/Summer, first published in October 1968.

51. My remarks are based on Zig Layton-Henry's account, 'Labour's lost youth', *Journal of Contemporary History,* vol.11, pp.275-308.

52. See D. Webster, *The Labour Party and the New Left.* Also Tony Benn (1980) in *Marxism Today,* October, and K. Livingstone (1981) in *Marxism Today,* November, p.18.

53. Editorial 'Decisive turn in Britain', in *MIR* (1979) Winter, p.7.

APPENDIX CHAPTER 7

1. Ted Grant (1978) *Will There Be A Slump?,* Militant Pamphlet 1978 and 1961.

2. West London Militant Supporters (WLMS) (1977) *Inflation and the Financial System,* Militant Pamphlet, July.

3. Ted Grant (1973) 'British perspectives and prospects' in *Militant International Review,* no.6, January, p.4.

4. Ted Grant (1980) *The Marxist Theory of the State,* Militant Pamphlet, August, p.39.

5. P. Hadden (1981) *Northern Ireland: Tory Cuts, Common Misery, Common Struggle,* Militant Pamphlet, reprinted January, p.11.

6. T. Grant (1977) 'British perspectives' in *MIR,* no.12, February, p.10.

7. Ibid, p.11.

8. T. Grant (1973) 'British Perspectives and Prospects', *MIR,* no.6, January, p.3.

9. A. Glyn (1980) *Capitalist Crisis: Tribune's 'Alternative Strategy' or 'Socialist Plan',* Militant Pamphlet, p.12.

10. 'British Perspectives and Tasks 1975', Internal Document, p.4.

11. P. Hadden, *Northern Ireland,* p.15.

12. A. Woods (1980) 'Britain's crisis: are import controls the answer?' in *MIR,* no.20, Summer, p.7.

13. Editorial in *MIR* (1976) no.10, March, p.3.

14. A. Glyn (1979) 'Profits — catastrophic drop', in *MIR,* Autumn, p.22.

15. A. Glyn and B. Sutcliffe (1972) *British Capitalism, Workers and the Profits Squeeze,,* Harmondsworth: Penguin Books.

16. Ibid, p.215.

17. The IS-SWP also held that 'of course, high wages are part of the explanation for high prices'. See *Socialist Worker* (1975) 5 April, p.3.

18. Since the Militant Tendency has never repudiated Glyn's views — indeed it publishes them alongside its other arguments — his most recent exposition on the neo-Ricardian view (*The British Economic Disaster* (1980) A. Glyn and J. Harrison, London: Pluto Press) must also be considered a statement of the group's position. While sticking to the 'profits squeeze'

thesis, Glyn now contends that the fall in profits post-1964 was due to the internal dynamics of the accumulation process rather than action of the part of trade unions. By modifying his earlier position Glyn seeks to reconcile the neo-Ricardian theory of crises with the view that capitalist crises are inevitable features of the accumulation process. This is achieved by attributing the 'profits squeeze' to over-accumulation in relation to the supply of labour which is allegedly the cause of wage bidding and the rise in real wages at the expense of profits after 1964.

19. I do not wish to imply either that a 'finished' theory of the economic crisis can be found within the corpus of Marxist writings on this subject or that the other far left groups are free of problems of coherence (or lack of it) in their own analyses. For useful surveys of the literature, see B. Fine and L. Harris (1976) 'Controversial issues in Marxist economic theory' in *Socialist Register*, London: Merlin Press, and P. Bullock and D. Yaffe (1975) 'Inflation, the crisis and the post-war boom' in *Revolutionary Communist*, no.3/4, November. To demonstrate the second point one only has to consider E. Mandel (1980) *Long Waves of Capitalist Development*, Cambridge: Cambridge University Press. Mandel tries to reconcile his belief in long waves of capitalist development with the conception of the imperialist epoch: that is, between a belief in the recurring possibility of long booms such as that between 1940 and 1968 and a belief in the permanent long-term characteristics of capitalist decline since 1914. His argument by analogy is singularly unconvincing and metaphorical. But the special point about the Militant Tendency is that it sets inordinate store by its analyses of capitalist economic development and the self-proclaimed scientificity of these 'Perspectives' documents. It accordingly deserves special attention in our study.

CONCLUSION

1. R. Challinor (1977) *The Origins of British Bolshevism*, London: Croom Helm, p.221. See also W. Kendall (1969) *The Revolutionary Movement in Britain 1900-21*, London: Weidenfeld and Nicolson, p.xii.
2. S. McIntyre (1980) *A Proletarian Science: Marxism in Britain 1917-33*, Cambridge: Cambridge University Press, pp.81-2.
3. See H. Dewar (1976) *Communist Politics in Britain: the CPGB from its Origins to the Second World War*, London: Pluto Press, pp.21-2.
4. A. Rosenberg (1934) *A History of Bolshevism*, London, p.88.
5. V. Lenin, *Collected Works*, vol.21, p.408.
6. See D. Massey and R. Meegan, *The Geography of Industrial Reorganisation, Progress in Planning*, vol.10, no.3.
7. A. Freeman (1982) *The Benn Heresy*, London: Pluto Press, p.33.

Bibliography

MANUSCRIPTS

Harber Papers (MSS 151), Brynmoor Jones Library, University of Hull.
Jock Haston Papers Ibid.
Purdie Papers Ibid.
Tarbuck Papers (MSS 151) Modern Records Centre, University of Warwick.

OTHER DOCUMENTS

Degras, J. (ed.) (1965) *Documents of the Communist International*, Vol. 1, Oxford.
Class, Party, and State and the Eastern European Revolution (1969) Education For Socialists, New York: Pathfinder.
The Development and Disintegration of World Stalinism (1970) Education For Socialists, New York: Pathfinder, March.
Origins of the International Socialists (1971), London: Pluto Press.
Reisner, W. (ed.) (1973) *Documents of the Fourth International 1933-40*, New York: Pathfinder.
Hansen, J. (ed.) (1974) *Marxism versus Ultraleftism*, Education for Socialists, New York: Pathfinder, January.
Towards A History of the Fourth International (1974) 4 vols, Education for Socialists, New York: Pathfinder.
Trotskyism versus Revisionism: A Documentary History (1974) 6 vols, London: New Park.
Thornett, A. (ed.) (1976) *The Battle For Trotskyism: Documents of the 1974 Opposition*, Oxford: Frampton.

The Struggle to Re-unify the Fourth International (1954-63) (1978) 12 vols,
 Education For Socialists, New York: Pathfinder.
Bertil Hessel Theses (1980) *Resolutions and Manifestos of the First Four
 Congresses of the Third International,* Ink Links.

LEON TROTSKY

The Revolution Betrayed (1967) New Park.
The Permanent Revolution (1969) New York: Pathfinder.
Marxism In Our Time (1970) New York: Pathfinder.
The Third International After Lenin (1970) New York: Pathfinder.
The Writings of Leon Trotsky 1928-40 (1970) 12 vols, New York: Pathfinder.
Marxism and the Trade Unions (1972) New Park.
In Defence of Marxism (1973) New York: Pathfinder.
The First Five Years of the Communist International (1973) 2 vols, New York:
 Pathfinder.
The Transitional Programme (1973) New York, Pathfinder.
Trotsky's Writings On Britain (1974) 3 vols, New Park.
Whither France? (1974) New Park.
The Struggle Against Fascism in Germany (1975) Harmondsworth: Penguin
 Books.

THEORETICAL JOURNALS

Fourth International
Inprecorr. *Inprecorr*
        Hands off Ireland
Intercontinental Press
International
International Communist
International Socialism Journal
Labour Review
Marxism Today
Militant International Review
New Left Review
Red Rag
Revolutionary Communist
Socialist Review
Socialist Woman
Women's Voice
Workers International Review

NEWSPAPERS

Black Dwarf

Keep Left
Militant
The Newsletter
The Newsline
Red Mole
Red Weekly
Socialist Appeal
Socialist Challenge
Socialist Outlook
Workers Press
Young Guard

BOOKS

(unless otherwise stated the place of publication is London)

Addison, P. (1977) *The Road to 1945*, Quartet Books.
Alexander, R.J. (1973) *Trotskyism in Latin America*, Stanford.
Ali, T. (1972) *The Coming British Revolution*, Jonathan Cape.
Anderson, P. (1976) *Considerations on Western Marxism*, New Left Books.
Anderson, P. (1965) (ed.) *Towards Socialism*, Fontana.

Baker, B. (1981) *The Far Left*, Weidenfield & Nicolson.
Bauman, Z. (1972) *Between Class and Elite*, Manchester.
Beer, S.H. (1965) *Modern British Politics*, Faber.
Beetham, D. (1974) *Max Weber and the Theory of Modern Politics*, Allen & Unwin.
Benn, T. (1973) *Arguments For Socialism*, Jonathan Cape.
Berry, D. (1970) *The Sociology of Grass Roots Politics*, Macmillan.
Birchall, I. (1973) *Workers Against the Monolith*, Pluto Press.
Blackburn, R. and Cockburn, A. (1967) *The Incompatibles*, Penguin Books.
Brewer, A. (1980) *Marxist Theories of Imperialism*, Routledge & Kegan Paul.
Budge, I. et al. (1976) *Party Identification and Beyond*, John Wiley.
Bukharin, N. (1971) *Economics of the Transformation Period*, Pluto Press.
Bukharin, N. (1972) *Imperialism & World Economy*, Merlin Press.

Calder, A. (1969) *The People's War*, Jonathan Capes.
Castells, M. (1978) *City, Class & Power*, Macmillan.
Challinor, R. (1977) *The Origins of British Bolshevism*, Croom Helm.
Claudin, F. (1975) *The Communist Movement*, Harmondsworth: Penguin Books.
Cliff, T. (1959) *Rosa Luxemburg*, London.
Cliff, T. (1970) *The Employers' Offensive*, Pluto Press.
Cliff, T. (1974) *Russia: A Marxist Analysis*, Pluto Press.

Cliff, T. (1975) *The Crisis,* Pluto Press.
Cliff, T. (1975) *Lenin,* 4 vols, Pluto Press.
Cliff, T. (1971) et al. *Party & Class,* Pluto Press.
Coates, D. (1975) *The Labour Party and the Struggle for Socialism,* Cambridge.
Coates, D. (1980) *Labour in Power?* Longman.
Coates, K. (1971) *The Crisis of British Socialism,* Nottingham: Spokesman.
Coates, K. (1979) *What Went Wrong?* Nottingham: Spokesman.
Colletti, L. (1972) *From Rousseau To Lenin,* New Left Books.
Crouch, C. (1977) (ed.) *The British Political Sociology Yearbook Vol. 3: Participation in Politics,* Croom Helm.

Deutscher, I. (1953) *Russia After Stalin,* Hamish Hamilton.
Deutscher, I. (1970) *The Prophet Outcast.* Oxford.
Dewar, H. (1976) *Communist Politics in Britain,* Pluto Press.
Drucker, H.M. (1979) *Doctrine and Ethos in the Labour Party,* Allen & Unwin.
Drucker, H.M. (1979) (ed.) *Multi-Party Britain,* Macmillan.

Foot, M. (1975) *Aneurin Bevan,* 2 vols, London: Paladin.
Foot, P. (1968) *The Politics of Harold Wilson,* Harmondsworth: Penguin Books.
Footman, D. (ed.) (1960) *St. Anthony's Papers: Number IX,* Chatto & Windus.
Forester, T. (1976) *The British Labour Party and the Working Class,* New York: Holmes and Meier.

Gerth, H.H. and Mills, C.W. (1970) *From Max Weber,* Routledge.
Glynn, A. and Harrison, J. (1980) *The British Economic Disaster,* Pluto Press.
Glynn, A. and Sutcliffe, B. (1972) *British Capitalism, Workers and the Profits Squeeze,* Harmondsworth: Penguin Books.
Goldethorpe, J. (1981) *Social Mobility and Class Structure in Modern Britain,* Oxford: Oxford University Press.
Gough, I. (1979) *The Political Economy of the Welfare State,* Macmillan.
Gouldner, A. (1980) *The Two Marxisms,* Macmillan.
Groves, R. (1974) *The Balham Group,* Pluto Press.

Habermas, J. (1976) *Legitimation Crisis,* Heinemann.
Hallas, D. (1979) *Trotsky's Marxism,* Pluto Press.
Harris, N. and Palmer, J. (eds.) (1971) *World Crisis,* Hutchinson.
Haseler, S. (1976) *The Death of British Democracy,* Elek.
Hatfield, M. (1978) *The House the Left Built,* Garden City Press.
Himmelweit, H. et al. (1981) *How Voters Decide,* Academic Press.
Hindess, B. (1971) *The Decline of Working Class Politics,* Paladin.
Hinton, J. and Hyman, R. (1975) *Trade Unions & Revolution: The Industrial Politics of the Early Communist Party,* Pluto Press.
Hinton, J. (1973) *The First Shop Stewards Movement,* Pluto Press.

Hodgson, G. (1975) *Trotsky and Fatalistic Marxism,* Nottingham: Spokesman.
Hodgson, G. (1977) *Socialism and Parliamentary Democracy,* Nottingham: Spokesman.
Hodgson, G. (1981) *Labour at the Crossroads,* Oxford: Martin Robertson.
Holton, B. (1976) *British Syndicalism 1900-14,* Pluto Press.
Horowitz, D. (1969) *Imperialism and Revolution,* Harmondsworth: Penguin Books.
Horowitz, D. (ed.) (1967) *Containment and Revolution,* Blond.
Howell, D. (1976) *British Social Democracy,* Croom Helm.

Jacoby, R. (1981) *Dialectic of Defeat,* New York: Cambridge.

Kendall, W. (1969) *The Revolutionary Movement in Britain 1900-21,* Weidenfeld.
Kidron, M. (1968) *Western Capitalism Since the War,* Harmondsworth: Penguin Books.
Kidron, M. (1974) *Capitalism and Theory,* Pluto Press.
Knei-Paz, B. (1978) *The Social and Political Thought of Leon Trotsky,* Oxford 1978.
Kolakowski, L. (1981) *Main Currents of Marxism,* 3 vols, Oxford.
Kolko, G. (1970) *The Politics of War,* New York: Wintage.
Kornhauser, W. (1972) *The Politics of Mass Society,* Routledge.

Lenin, V.I. (1960-70) *Collected Works,* Moscow.
Liebman, M. (1975) *Leninism Under Lenin,* Jonathan Capes.
Lindberg, L. et al. (eds.) (1975) *Stress and Contradiction in Modern Capitalism,* Lexington: D.C. Heath.
Lukacs, G. (1970) *Lenin,* New Left Books.
Lukacs, G. (1971) *History and Class Consciousness,* Merlin Press.
Luxemburg, R. and Bukharin, N. (1972) *Imperialism and the Accumulation of Capital,* Harmondsworth: Penguin Books.

McCormack, P. (1979) *Enemies of Democracy,* Temple-Smith.
McKenzie, R.T. (1963) *British Political Parties,* Heinemann.
McKenzie, R.T. and Silver, A. (1968) *Angels in Marble,* London.
Mandel, E. (1968) *Marxist Economic Theory,* Merlin Press.
Mandel, E. (1975) *Late Capitalism,* New Left Books.
Mandel, E. (1979) *Trotsky: A Study in the Unity of his Thought,* New Left Books.
Mandel, E. (1980) *Long Waves of Capitalist Development,* Cambridge.
Mann, M. (1973) *Consciousnes and Action in the Western Working Class,* Macmillan.
Mavrakas, K. (1976) *On Trotskyism,* Routledge.
Michels, R. (1968) *Political Parties,* New York: Free Press.
Middlemas, K. (1979) *Politics in Industrial Society,* André Deutsch.

Miliband, R. (1973) *Parliamentary Socialism*, Merlin Press.
Minkin, L. (1978) *The Labour Party Conference*, Allen Lane.
Mitchell, J. (1971) *Women's Estate*, Harmondsworth; Penguin Books.

Nettl, J.P. (1967) *Political Mobilisations*, Faber & Faber.
Newton, K. (1968) *The Sociology of British Communism*, Allen & Lane.
Nordlinger, E. (1967) *Working Class Tories*, London.

O'Connor, J. (1973) *The Fiscal Crisis of the State*, New York: St James Press.

Parry, G. (1969) *Political Elites*, Allen & Unwin.
Pollard, S. (1979) *The Development of the British Economy 1914-67*, Edward Arnold.

Rosenberg, A. (1934) *A History of Bolshevism*, London.
Rowbotham, S. et al. (1979) *Beyond the Fragments*, Merlin Press.
Russell, B. (1975) *The Autobiography of Bertrand Russell*, Unwin.

Schumpeter, J. (1952) *Capitalism, Socialism and Democracy*, Unwin.
Shipley, P. (1976) *Revolutionaries in Modern Britain*, Bodley Head.

Thompson, E.P. (1978) *The Poverty of Theory*, Merlin Press.
Tomlinson, J. (1981) *Left, Right: The March of Political Extremism in Britain*, Calder.

Upward, E. (1969) *The Rotten Elements*, Heinemann.

Warren, G. (1980) *Imperialism: Pioneer of Capitalism*, Verso.
Weber, M. (1964) *The Theory of Social and Economic Organisation*, Macmillan.
Widgery, D. (ed.) (1976) *The Left in Britain*, Peregrine.
Williams, R. (ed.) (1968) *The May Day Manifesto 1968*, Harmondsworth: Penguin Books.
Wolfe, A. (1977) *The Limits of Legitimacy*, New York: Free Press.
Wyatt, W. (1977) *What's Left of the Labour Party?*, Sidgwick & Jackson.

Young, N. (1977) *An Infantile Disorder?: Crisis and Decline of the New Left*, Routledge.

PAMPHLETS

Banda M. (1975) *Whither Thornett?*, WRP.
Bell, G. (1979) *British Labour and Ireland 1969-79*, IMG, August.
Buddle, S. et al. (1972) *Students and the Struggle for Socialism*, IS.

Cook, D. (n.d.) *Students,* CPGB.
Cook, M. (1975) *The Myth of Orthodox Trotskyism,* Chartist.

Duncan, P. (1980) *The Politics of Militant,* Clause 4, London.

Grant, T. (1961, 1978) *Will There Be A Slump?,* Militant.
Grant, T. (1982) *Falklands Crisis: a socialist answer,* Militant.
Grant, T. (1980) *The Marxist Theory of the State,* Militant.
Glyn, A. (n.d.) *Tribunes' Alternative Strategy,* Militant.

Hadden, P. (1980) *Northern Ireland,* Militant, March.
Hadden, P. (1980) *Divide and Rule,* Militant, August.
Healy, G. (n.d.) *The Way To Socialism in Britain,* London.
Healy, G. (1957) *Revolution and Counter-Revolution in Hungary,* London.

Ingham, B. (n.d.) *The 35-hour Week,* Militant.

Jenkins, P. (n.d.) *Where Trotksyism Got Lost,* Nottingham: Spokesman, no.59.
Jeffries, P. (n.d.) *Falsifiers of Lenin,* WRP Pocket Library No.9, May 1974.
Jones, A. and Thompson, R. (1972) *After the Miners Strike — What Next?,* IMG.

Kline, R. (n.d.) *Can Socialism Come Through Paliament?,* International Socialism.

Lewis, G. and Thompson, P. (1977) *The Revolution Unfinished,* Big Flame.

Mandel, E. (1971) *The Revolutionary Student Movement,* New York: Pathfinder.
Mandel, E. (1971) *The Lessons of May 1968,* IMG.
Mandel, E. (n.d.) *The Leninist Theory of Organisation,* IMG.
Mandel, E., *A Socialist Strategy For Western Europe,* Nottingham: Spokesman No.65.
Mandel, E. (n.d.) *Marxism Versus Ultra-Leftism,* IMG.
Murphy, J.T. (1972) *The Workers Committee,* Pluto Press.

Rosewall, R. (n.d.) *The Struggle For Workers' Power,* International Socialism.

Slaughter, C. (1969) *A Balance Sheet of Revisionism,* Plough Press, February.
Slaughter, C. (1970) *The Class Nature of the IS Group,* Workers Press, February.
Slaughter, C. (1970) *Reform or Revolution?,* Workers Press, October.
Slaughter, C. (1971) *Who Are the IS?,* Workers Press, April.
Socialist Labour League (n.d.) *A Marxist Analysis of the Crisis,* SLL.

Socialist Workers Party (1980) *Troops Out of Ireland,* SWP, September.
Stephenson, R. (1976) *The Fourth International and our Attitude Towards It,* Chartist.
Sussex Socialist Club (n.d.) *World Perspectives.*

Taaffe, P. (n.d.) *Marxism Opposes Individual Terrorism,* Militant.
Thomas, M. (1976) *The Logic of Scenario Politics,* International Communist.
Trotsky, L. (1981) *Marxism and the Trade Unions,* New Park.

Webster, D. (1981) *The Labour Party and the New Left,* Fabian Tract 477, October.
West London Militant Supporters Group (n.d.) *History of the Labour Party,* Militant.
West London Militant Supporters Group (1977) *Inflation and the Financial System,* Militant.
Whelan, T. (n.d.) *The Credibility Gap: Politics of the SLL,* IMG.
Workers' Revolutionary Party (1982) *Defeat British Imperialism,* WRP.

ARTICLES

Ali, T. (1978) 'Revolutionary Politics: ten years after 1968" *Socialist Register.*
Ali, T. and Blackburn, R. (1976) 'Proletarian revolution and bourgeois democracy', *Socialist Challenge,* no.3, December.
Anderson, P. (1964) 'Origins of the present crisis', *New Left Review,* 23, January-February.
Anderson, P. (1965) 'The left in the fifties', *New Left Review,* 29.
Anderson, P. (1968) 'Components of the National Culture', *New Left Review,* 50, July-August.
Arrighi, G. (1978) 'Towards a theory of capitalist crisis', *New Left Review,* 111.
Avenas, D. (1976) 'Trotsky's Marxism', *International,* vol.3, no.2, Winter.

Benn, T. (1980) 'Interview', *Marxism Today,* October.
Birchall, I., 'History of the International Socialists', *International Socialism,* 76 & 77.
Bullock, P. and Yaffe, D. (1975) 'Inflation, the crisis and the post-war boom', *Revolutionary Communist,* no.3/4, November.

Cliff, T. (1960) 'Trotsky on substitutionism', *International Socialism,* 2.
Cliff, T. (1962) 'Permanent revolution', *International Socialism,* 12.
Cliff, T. (1979) 'Interview', *The Leveller,* no.30, September.
Coates, K. (1973) 'Socialists and the Labour Party', *Socialist Register.*
Coates, K. (1976) 'How not to reappraise the new left', *Socialist Register.*
Challinor, R. (1969) 'Origins of IS', *International,* December.
Clarke, G. (1950) 'Leon Trotsky — a new vindication, *Fourth International,*

July-August.

Cook, D. (1974) 'Students, left unity and the Communist Party', *Marxism Today,* October.

Crewe, I. (1982) 'The Labour Party and the electorate', in D. Kavanagh (ed.) *The Politics of the Labour Party,* Allen & Unwin.

Crewe, I. (1976) et al., 'Partisan dealignment in Britain 1964-1974', *British Journal of Political Science,* vol.7.

Ennis, K. (1974) 'Women's consciousness', *International Socialism,* 68, April.

Farl, E. (1973) 'The genealogy of state capitalism', *International,* vol.2, no.1.

Field, J. (1978-9) 'British historians and the concept of the Labour aristocracy', *Radical History Review,* vol.19.

Fine, B. and Harris, L. (1976) 'Controversial issues in Marxist economic theory', *Socialist Register.*

Forester, T. (1980) 'The Labour Party's militant moles', *New Society,* 10 January.

Frank, P. (1972) 'History of the Fourth International', *Intercontinental Press,* no.10-22.

Freeman, A. (1981) 'Benn and British socialism', *International,* vol.6, no.3, September.

Geras, N. (1973) 'Proletarian self-emancipation', *Radical Philosophy,* no.6, Winter.

Geras, N. (1981) 'Marxism and pluralism', *New Left Review,* 125, January-February.

Glynn, A. (1979) 'Profits — catastrophic drop', *Militant International Review,* Autumn.

Grant, T. (1970) 'Perspectives for Britain', *Militant International,* no.2.

Grant, T. 'British perspectives and prospects', *Militant International Review,* no.6.

Grant, T. (1979) 'After the elections', *Militant International,* Autumn.

Grant, T. (1980-1) 'British captalism faces catastrophe', *Militant International,* Winter.

Grant, T. (1974) 'Decisive turn in Britain', *Militant International,* Winter.

Grant, T. (1971) 'British perspectives', *Militant International,* February.

Gouldner, A. (1955) 'Metaphysical pathos and the theory of bureaucracy', *American Political Science Review,* vol.59, part 2.

Hallas, D. (1977) 'How can we move on?', *Socialist Register.*

Hallas, D. (1982) 'Revolutionaries and the Labour Party', *International Socialism,* no.16, Spring.

Harman, C., 'The inconsistencies of Ernest Mandel', *International Socialism,* no.41.

Harris, N. (1976) 'Mao and the Chinese revolution', *International Socialism*, 92.

Higgins, J. (1963) 'Ten years for the locusts', *International Socialism*, 4, Autumn.

Hobsbawm, E. *(1979)* 'Syndicalism and the working class', *New Society*, 5 April.

Howell, J. (1976) 'Big Flame: resituating socialist strategy and organisation', *Socialist Register*.

Hyman, R. (1973) 'Industrial conflict and the political economy', *Socialist Register*.

Hyman, R. (1974) 'Workers control and revolutionary theory', *Socialist Register*.

Jeffreys, S. (1975) 'The challenge of the rank and file', *International Socialism*, March.

Jessop, R. (1970) 'Civility and traditionalism in British political culture', *British Journal of Political Science*.

Jessop, R. (1971) 'Some recent theories of the state', *Cambridge Journal of Economics*.

Johnston, M. (1975) 'Trotsky and popular fronts', *Marxism Today*, October-November.

Kidron, M. (1969) 'Maginot Marxism', *International Socialism*, 36, April.

Kidron, M., 'Two valid insights don't make a theory', *International Socialism*, no.100.

Layton-Henry, Z., 'Labour's lost youth', *Journal of Contemporary History*, vol.11.

Livingstone, K. (1981) 'Interview', *Marxism Today*, November.

Mair, P. (1979) 'The Marxist left' in H.M. Drucker (ed.) *Multi-Party Britain*, London: Macmillan.

Mandel, E. (1975) 'Liebman and Leninism', *Socialist Register*.

Mandel, E., 'Towards a revolutionary strategy for Western Europe', *New Left Review*, 100.

Mandel, E. and Ross, J. (1982) 'The need for a revolutionary International', *International Marxist Review*, Spring.

Mann, M. (1970) 'The social cohesion of liberal democracy', *American Sociological Review*, Vol. XXXV.

Mann, M. (1976) 'The new working class', *New Society*, November-December.

Meikle, S. (1981) 'Has Marxism a future?', *Critique*, 13.

Miliband, R. (1977) 'The future of socialism in England', *Socialist Register*.

Miliband, R. (1976) 'Moving on', *Socialist Register*.

Nairn, T. (1970) 'The fateful meridian', *New Left Review*, 60, March-April.

O'Brien, J. (1977-8) 'American Leninism in the 1970s', *Radical America,* Winter.

Pablo, M. (1949) 'The evolution of Yugoslav centrism', *Fourth International,* November.
Pablo, M. (1958) 'The rise and decline of Stalinism', *Fourth International,* Winter.
Pablo, M. (1974) 'Where are we Going?', *Education For Socialists,* part 4, vol. 2, New York: Pathfinder, March.
Panitch, L., 'Trade unions and the capitalist state', *New Left Review,* 125.
Purdy, D. (1973) 'The permanent arms economy', *Bulletin of Socialist Economists,* Spring.

Richards, F. (1975) 'The question of the International', *Revolutionary Communist,* No. 2 May.
Ross, J. (1977) 'Capitalism, socialism and personal life', *Socialist Woman,* vol.6, no.2, Summer.
Rowbotham, S. (1977) 'Leninism in the lurch', *Red Rag,* no.12, Spring.
Rustin, M. (1981) 'Labour's constitutional crisis', *New Left Review,* 126, March-April.

Shaw, M. (1973) 'Which way for student revolutionaries?', *International Socialism,* March.
Shaw, M. (1978) 'The making of a party?', *Socialist Register.*

Taaffe, P. (1978) 'The brutal face of Toryism', *Militant International Review,* 14, Summer.
Taaffe, P. (1978) 'The British Communist Party in crisis', *Militant International Review,* 15, Autumn.
Thompson, E.P. (1965) 'The peculiarities of the English', *Socialist Register.*

Walsh, L. (1980) '40 years since Leon Trotsky's assassination', *Miltant International Review,* 20, Summer.
Walters, J. (1969-70) 'Some notes on British Trotskyist history', *Marxist Studies,* vol.2, no.1, Winter.
Williams, R. (1973) 'Base and superstructure', *New Left Review,* 82, November-December.
Wintour, P. (1980) '*New Statesman,* 18 January.
Woods, A. (1980) 'The crisis of Thatcherism', *Militant International Review,* 19, Spring.
Woods, A. (1980) 'Britain's crisis: are import controls the answer?' *Militant International Review,* 20, Summer.

Index

Ali, Tariq 136, 159
Alternative Economic Strategy 195
Anarchist Federation 27
Anti-Internment League 139, 172
Anti-Nazi League 108, 115, 120

Banda, Michael 71
Behan, Brian 72, 77, 85, 86
Benn, Tony 161, 184, 190, 205
Bertrand Russell Peace Foundation
    128
Bevanism 68–9, 72
Bevin, Ernest 30
Bidwell, Sidney 28
Big Flame 142, 154
Birchell, Ian 97
Black Dwarf 133
Blackburn, Robin 135–6
Blanco, Hugo 137
Bonapartism 12
Building Workers Campaign
    Committee 39
Burnham, James 24, 86

Campaign Against Youth
    Unemployment 169
Campaign for Nuclear

Disarmament 101, 120, 127,
    130, 132–3, 154, 161, 172, 174,
    188
Cannon, J.P. 56, 58, 59, 61–3, 84
Castro, Fidel 125–6
Claudin, Fernando 18
Clause 4 181
Club, The 67–9
Coates, David 29
Coates, Ken 77, 83, 128, 163
Cochran-Clarke 58, 63, 65
Cominform 37
Communist Party of Great Britain
    28, 29, 34, 36–40, 109, 112, 114,
    133, 200

Daily Worker 70
Deutscher, Isaac 10, 14, 59, 64
Duncan, Pete 170

Entrism 31, 32, 34, 38, ch.3 passim,
    67, 76, 108-9, ch.7 passim (*see
    also* Labour Party)
    +*sui generis* ch.3 passim

Forester, Tom 180
Frank, Pierre 15

Fryer, Peter 71, 76, 82

Geras, Norman 25
Glyn, Andrew 195–6
Gordon, Sam 62
Grant, Ted 41, 45, 46–7, 49, ch.7
   passim

Hallas, Duncan 91, 92, 94, 102–3
Haston, Jock 29, 31, 37, 41, 68
Howell, David 27

Independent Labour Party 14, 29,
   37, 163
Institute for Workers Control 129
International Communist League 9
International Group 99, 127
International Marxist Group ch.6
   passim
International Socialism 100
International Socialism Group ch.6
   passim
Internationalist 127
Irish Solidarity Campaign 139–40

Jordan, Pat 127, 136, 138, 159

Keep Left 99, 127
Kemp, Tom 85
Kidron, Michael 95, 98–9

Labour Party 3, 27, 31–3, 34, 73–5,
   99, 128–9 (*see also* entrism)
Lawrence, John 45, 59, 69
Luxemburg, Rosa 100

MacIntyre, Alasdair 78
MacIntyre, Stuart 200
Mandel, Ernest 8, 33, 56, 123, 134,
   159
Marxist Worker Group 154
Maslow-Fischer Group 14
Michels, Roberto 16
Militant Tendency ch.7 passim
Militant Workers Federation 39
Morrow, Felix 5

National Abortion Campaign 145,
   155, 169
National Union of Students 133
Non-Conscription League 27
Northern Ireland 137–43

Pablo, Michel 41, 43, 53–66, 70, 123
Protz, Roger 105

rank-and-filism 104, 108–18
Red Mole 133
Revolution 154
Revolutionary Communist Group
   119, 142–3
Revolutionary Socialist League
   126–9
Revolutionary Socialist Students
   Federation 133, 135
Rosenberg, Arthur 203
Ross, John 145–6
Rowbotham, Sheila 146

Slaughter, Cliff 85, 86–7
Socialist Action 161
Socialist Current 127
Socialist League 161–2, 201
Socialist Review Group 68, 90–1,
   99–100, 127
Socialist Unity 120, 160–1
Socialist Worker 104, 105, 112
Spartacus League 130, 133, 157
state capitalism 12, 45–7, 68, 91–9,
   118–19

Taaffe, Peter 172, 176
Tatchell, Peter 187
Thermidor 12
Thornett, Alan 81, 83–4
Treit Group 14
Tribunites 194
Troops out movement 142

Underhill, Reg 182
united front 20–1
Urbahns, Hugo 9

Vietnamese Solidarity Campaign 128–9
Voice of the Unions 128
Voorhis Act 62

Week, The 127, 128
women's movement 143–54, 172
Womens Voice 145
Workers International League 27, 34, 81, 165-6

Workers International News 127
Workers Action 181
Workers' Fight 103, 104
Workers' League 119
Workers' Power 119

Yaffe, David 105
Young Communist League 27
Young Guard 99, 127
Young Socialists (Labour Party) 78, 101, 127, 129, 186–8